PRACTICAL CRYPTOGRAPHY

Algorithms and Implementations Using C++

PRACTICAL CRYPTOGRAPHY

Algorithms and Implementations Using C++

Edited by
Saiful Azad
Al-Sakib Khan Pathan

CRC Press
Taylor & Francis Group
Boca Raton London New York

CRC Press is an imprint of the
Taylor & Francis Group, an **informa** business

AN AUERBACH BOOK

CRC Press
Taylor & Francis Group
6000 Broken Sound Parkway NW, Suite 300
Boca Raton, FL 33487-2742

First issued in paperback 2019

ISBN-13: 978-1-4822-2889-2 (hbk)
ISBN-13: 978-0-367-37815-8 (pbk)

Visit the Taylor & Francis Web site at
http://www.taylorandfrancis.com

and the CRC Press Web site at
http://www.crcpress.com

To the Almighty Allah, who has given us the capability to share our knowledge with other knowledge seekers.

—The Editors

Contents

About the Editors

 **Saiful Azad** earned his PhD in information engineering from the University of Padova, Italy, in 2013. He completed his BSc in computer and information technology at the Islamic University of Technology (IUT) in Bangladesh, and his MSc in computer and information engineering at the International Islamic University Malaysia (IIUM). After the completion of his PhD, he joined the Department of Computer Science at the American International University–Bangladesh (AIUB) as a faculty member. His work on underwater acoustic networks began during his PhD program and remains his main research focus. Dr. Azad's interests also include the design and implementation of communication protocols for different network architectures, QoS issues, network security, and simulation software design. He is one of the developers of the DESERT underwater simulator. He is also the author of more than 30 scientific papers published in international peer-reviewed journals or conferences. Dr. Azad also serves as a reviewer for some renowned peer-reviewed journals and conferences.

Al-Sakib Khan Pathan earned his PhD degree (MS leading to PhD) in computer engineering in 2009 from Kyung Hee University in South Korea. He earned his BS degree in computer science and information technology from IUT, Bangladesh, in 2003. He is currently an assistant professor in the Computer Science Department of IIUM. Until June 2010 he served as an assistant professor in the Computer Science and Engineering Department of BRAC University, Bangladesh. Prior to holding this position, he worked as a researcher at the networking lab of Kyung Hee University, South Korea, until August 2009. Dr. Pathan's research interests include wireless sensor networks, network security, and e-services technologies. He has been a recipient of several awards/ best paper awards and has several publications in these areas. He has served as chair, an organizing committee member, and a technical program committee member in numerous international conferences/ workshops, including GLOBECOM, GreenCom, HPCS, ICA3PP, IWCMC, VTC, HPCC, and IDCS. He was awarded the IEEE Outstanding Leadership Award and Certificate of Appreciation for his role in the IEEE GreenCom 2013 conference. He is currently serving as area editor of *International Journal of Communication Networks and Information Security,* editor of *International Journal of Computational Science and Engineering, Inderscience,* associate editor of IASTED/ACTA Press *International Journal of Computer Applications,* guest editor of many special issues of top-ranked journals, and editor/ author of 12 books. One of his books has twice been included in Intel Corporation's Recommended Reading List for Developers, the second half of 2013 and the first half of 2014; three other books are included in IEEE Communications Society's (IEEE ComSoc) Best Readings in Communications and Information Systems Security, 2013; and a fifth book is in the process of being translated to simplified Chinese language from the English version. Also, two of his journal papers and one conference paper are included under different categories in IEEE Communications Society's Best Readings Topics on Communications and Information Systems Security, 2013. Dr. Pathan also serves as a referee of numerous renowned journals. He is a senior member of the Institute of Electrical and Electronics Engineers (IEEE), United States; IEEE ComSoc Bangladesh Chapter; and several other international professional organizations.

1

BASICS OF SECURITY AND CRYPTOGRAPHY

AL-SAKIB KHAN PATHAN

Contents

Keywords

Asymmetric
Cipher
Cryptography
Cryptology
Key
Plaintext
Private
Public
Security
Symmetric

To begin with, the purpose of this book is not to delve into the history of cryptography or to analyze the debate on the first occurrence of the technique in communications technologies. Instead, we aim to clarify various basic terminologies to give lucid understanding of the subject matter. Throughout the book, we will see various approaches to utilizing cryptographic techniques along with practical codes; however, the intent of this first chapter is to set the basics for the rest of the content.

The formal definition of *cryptography* could be noted in various ways; however, one is enough if that sums up all the associated meanings.

Cryptography is basically the science that employs mathematical logic to keep the information secure (a formal definition is mentioned later in this chapter for quick reference). It enables someone to securely store sensitive information or transmit information securely through insecure networks to keep it from being hacked, masqueraded, or altered. The history of cryptography starts from the ancient era when it was practiced by secret societies or by troops in battlefields. The necessity of such an approach increased with time. In the current information era, there is indeed no time at which information security is not necessary, and hence cryptography stands with strength among various essential technologies. From military to civilian or from government to individual, information security is tremendously necessary. Consequently, several algorithms are proposed, and they are implemented with various hardware. The basic idea of a cryptographic algorithm is to scramble information in such a way that illegitimate entities cannot unearth the concealed information. Cryptographic algorithms are also used to preserve the integrity of a message.

There are various terminologies/words or set of words that are often associated with the fields of cryptography. Here, let us learn the basic definitions of the major terminologies that may be frequently used in the relevant fields and within this book.

> **Plaintext:** This is the information that a sender wants to transmit to a receiver. A synonym of this is *cleartext*.
>
> **Encryption:** Encryption is the process of encoding messages (or information) in such a way that eavesdroppers or hackers cannot read it, but authorized parties can. In an encryption scheme, the message or information (i.e., plaintext) is encrypted using an encryption algorithm, turning it into an unreadable *ciphertext*.
>
> **Ciphertext:** Ciphertext (sometimes spelled *cyphertext*) is the result of encryption performed on plaintext using an algorithm, called a cipher.
>
> **Cipher:** A cipher (sometimes spelled *cypher*) is an algorithm for performing encryption or decryption—a series of well-defined steps that can be followed as a procedure. A relatively less common term is *encipherment*. A cipher is also called a *cryptoalgorithm*.
>
> **Decryption:** This is the process of decoding the encrypted text (i.e., ciphertext) and getting it back in the plaintext format.

Cryptographic key: Generally, a key or a set of keys is involved in encrypting a message. An identical key or a set of identical keys is used by the legitimate party to decrypt the message. A key is a piece of information (or a parameter) that determines the functional output of a cryptographic algorithm or cipher. Sometimes key means just some steps or rules to follow to twist the plaintext before transmitting it via a public medium (i.e., to generate ciphertext).

Stream cipher: A stream cipher is a method of encrypting text (to produce ciphertext) in which a cryptographic key and algorithm are applied to each binary digit in a data stream, one bit at a time. This method is not much used in modern cryptography. A typical operational flow diagram of stream cipher is shown in Figure 1.1.

Block cipher: A block cipher is a method of encrypting text (to produce ciphertext) in which a cryptographic key and algorithm are applied to a block of data (for example, 64 contiguous bits) at once as a group rather than one bit at a time. A sample diagram for a block cipher operation is shown in Figure 1.2. The feedback mechanism shown with a dotted line is optional but may be used to strengthen the process. A stronger mode is cipher feedback (CFB), which combines the plain block with the previous cipher block before encrypting it.

Cryptology: Cryptology is the general area of mathematics, such as number theory, and the application of formulas and algorithms, that underpin cryptography and cryptanalysis.

Cryptography: *Cryptography* and *cryptology* are often used as synonyms. However, a better understanding is that *cryptology* is the umbrella term under which comes cryptography

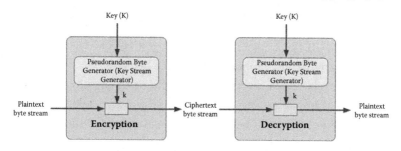

Figure 1.1 Operational diagram for a stream cipher.

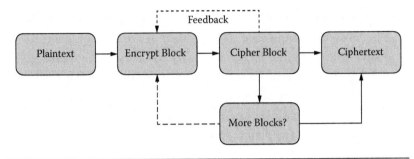

Figure 1.2   Sample operational diagram of a block cipher.

and cryptanalysis. Cryptography is the science of information security. Cryptography includes techniques such as microdots, merging words with images, and other ways of hiding information in storage or transit. In today's computer-centric world, cryptography is most of the time associated with scrambling plaintext into ciphertext, and then back again (i.e., decryption). Individuals who practice this field are known as cryptographers.

Cryptanalysis: Cryptanalysis refers to the study of ciphers, ciphertext, or cryptosystems (that is, secret code systems) with the goal of finding weaknesses in these that would permit retrieval of the plaintext from the ciphertext, without necessarily knowing the key or the algorithm used for that. This is also known as breaking the cipher, ciphertext, or cryptosystem.

Cryptosystem: This is the shortened version of *cryptographic system*. A cryptosystem is a pair of algorithms that take a key and convert plaintext to ciphertext and back.

Symmetric cryptography: Symmetric cryptography (or symmetric key encryption) is a class of algorithms for cryptography that use the same cryptographic keys for both encryption of plaintext and decryption of ciphertext. Figure 1.3 shows the overview of the steps in symmetric cryptography.

Symmetric key ciphers are valuable because

• It is relatively inexpensive to produce a strong key for these types of ciphers.
• The keys tend to be much smaller in size for the level of protection they afford.
• The algorithms are relatively inexpensive to process.

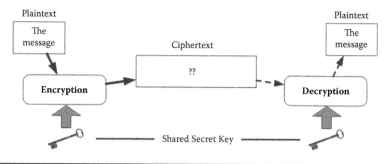

Figure 1.3 Operational model of symmetric cryptography.

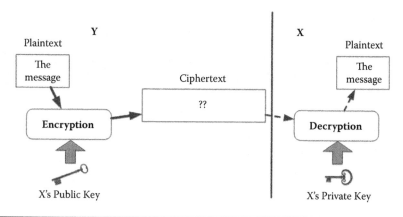

Figure 1.4 Operational model of asymmetric key cryptography or public-key cryptography. The public key and the private key of user X are mathematically linked.

Public-key cryptography or asymmetric cryptography: Public-key cryptography (PKC), also known as asymmetric cryptography, refers to a cryptographic algorithm that requires two separate keys, one of which is secret (or private) and the other public. Although different, the two parts of this key pair are mathematically linked. Figure 1.4 shows a pictorial view of PKC operations.

Public-key cryptography enables the following:

1. Encryption and decryption, which allow two communicating parties to disguise data that they send to each other. The sender encrypts, or scrambles, the data before sending them via a communication medium (or such). The receiver decrypts, or unscrambles, the data after receiving them.

While in transit, the encrypted data are not understood by an intruder (or illegitimate third party).

2. Nonrepudiation (formally defined later), which prevents:
   - The sender of the data from claiming, at a later date, that the data were never sent.
   - The data from being altered.

Digital signature: A digital signature is an electronic signature that can be used to authenticate the identity of the sender of a message or the signer of a document, and possibly to ensure that the original content of the message or document that has been sent is unchanged. Digital signatures are usually easily transportable, cannot be imitated by someone else, and can be automatically timestamped.

Digital certificate: There is a difference between digital signature and digital certificate. A digital certificate provides a means of proving someone's identity in electronic transactions. The function of it could be considered pretty much like a passport or driving license does in face-to-face interactions. For instance, a digital certificate can be an electronic "credit card" that establishes someone's credentials when doing business or other transactions via the web. It is issued by a certification authority (CA). Typically, such a card contains the user's name, a serial number, expiration dates, a copy of the certificate holder's public key (used for encrypting messages and digital signatures), and the digital signature of the certificate-issuing authority so that a recipient can verify that the certificate is real.

Certification authority (CA): As understood from the definition above, a certification authority is an authority in a network that issues and manages security credentials and public keys for message encryption.

Now, let us talk about the general aspects and issues of security. Security, with its dimensions in fact, is a vast field of research. Information security basically tries to provide five types of functionalities:

1. Authentication
2. Authorization

3. Confidentiality or privacy
4. Integrity
5. Nonrepudiation

1.1 The Perimeter of Cryptography in Practice

Most of the time, cryptography is associated with the confidentiality (or privacy) of information only. However, except authorization, it can offer other four functions of security (i.e., authentication, confidentiality, integrity, and nonrepudiation). Let us now see what these terms mean in this context to talk about the functionalities that cryptography usually has or is supposed to provide.

Authentication: Authentication means the process of verification of the identity of the entities that communicate over a network. Without authentication, any user with network access can use readily available tools to forge originating Internet Protocol (IP) addresses and impersonate others. Therefore, cryptosystems use various mechanisms to authenticate both the originators and recipients of information. An example could be that a user needs to key in his or her login name and password for email accounts that are authenticated from the server.

Authorization: Authorization is a basic function of security that cryptography cannot provide. Authorization refers to the process of granting or denying access to a network resource or service. In other words, authorization means access control to any resource used for computer networks. Most of the computer security systems that we have today are based on a two-step mechanism. The first step is authentication, and the second step is authorization or access control, which allows the user to access various resources based on the user's identity.

There is a clear difference between authentication and authorization. We see that if a user is authenticated, only then may he or she have access to any system. Again, an authenticated person may not be authorized to access everything in a system. Authentication is a relatively stronger aspect of security than authorization, as it comes before authorization.

An example case could be as follows: An employee in a company needs an authentication code to identify him- or herself to the network server. There may be several levels of employees who have different access permissions to the resources kept in the server. All of the employees here need authentication to enter the server, but not everybody is authorized to use all the resources available in the system. If someone is authorized and accesses the protected resources, that person has already authenticated him- or herself correctly to the system. Someone who is not authorized to use the system (or server's resources) but gets access illegally might have used tricks to deceive the system to authenticate him- or herself (which the server has accepted mistakenly). In any case, accessing of the protected materials needs authorization that covers authentication. Authentication, only by itself, may not have *authorization* associated with it for a particular network or system resource.

Confidentiality or privacy: It means the assurance that only authorized users can read or use confidential information. Without confidentiality, anyone with network access can use readily available tools to eavesdrop on network traffic and intercept valuable proprietary information. If privacy or confidentiality is not guaranteed, outsiders or intruders could steal the information that is stored in plaintext. Hence, cryptosystems use different techniques and mechanisms to ensure information confidentiality. When cryptographic keys are used on plaintext to create ciphertext, privacy is assigned to the information.

Integrity: Integrity is the security aspect that confirms that the original contents of information have not been altered or corrupted. If integrity is not ensured, someone might alter information or information might become corrupted, and the alteration could be sometimes undetected. This is the reason why many cryptosystems use techniques and mechanisms to verify the integrity of information. For example, an intruder might covertly alter a file, but change the unique digital thumbprint for the file, causing other users to detect the tampering by comparing the changed digital thumbprint to the digital thumbprint for the original contents.

Nonrepudiation: For information communication, assurance is needed that a party cannot falsely deny that a part of the actual communication occurred. Nonrepudiation makes sure that each party is liable for its sent message. If nonrepudiation is not ensured, someone can communicate and then later either falsely deny the communication entirely or claim that it occurred at a different time, or even deny receiving any piece of information. Hence, this aspect ensures accountability of each entity taking part in any communication event.

Now, the question is: How can we ensure nonrepudiation? To provide nonrepudiation, systems must provide evidence of communications and transactions that should involve the identities or credentials of each party so that it is impossible to refute the evidence. For instance, someone might deny sending an email message, but the messaging system adds a timestamp and digitally signs the message with the message originator's digital signature. As the message contains a timestamp and a unique signature, there is strong evidence to identify both the originator of the message and the date and time of origin. If the message originator later denies sending the message, the false claim is easily refuted. Likewise, to provide nonrepudiation for mail recipients, mail systems might generate mail receipts that are dated and signed by the recipients.

1.2 Things That Cryptographic Technologies Cannot Do

Cryptographic technologies cannot provide solutions to all security issues. We previously have learned that they cannot provide the authorization aspect of security—that process is basically the task of the system or network operating system. In general, cryptography-based security systems provide sufficient security when used properly within the capabilities and limitations of the cryptographic technology. However, such a technology only provides part of the overall security for any network and information. The overall strength of any security system depends on many factors, such as the suitability of the technology, adequate security procedures and processes, and how well people use the procedures, processes, and technology. To put it in another way, *security depends on the appropriate protection mechanism of the weakest link in the entire security system.*

A company may have all the best cryptographic technologies installed in its computers and systems; however, all these protection efforts would collapse if someone (perhaps an intruder or an employee) can easily walk into offices and obtain valuable proprietary information that has been printed out as plaintext hard copy. Hence, one must not simply rely on cryptography-based security technologies to overcome other weaknesses and flaws in the security systems.

For example, if someone transmits valuable information as ciphertext over communications networks to protect confidentiality but stores the information as plaintext on the sender or receiver computer, it's still a vulnerable situation. Those computers must be protected to make sure the information is actually protected or kept confidential, possibly keeping the information in encrypted format as well—maybe with passwords to access the computer or folders or such. Also, the entire network must have strong firewalls and maintain those in secure facilities. The latter tasks are not of cryptography or cryptographic technologies. When building a secure system, we have to take into consideration a lot of issues of security, which are often dependent on the requirements and settings of the system.

2

CLASSICAL CRYPTOGRAPHIC ALGORITHMS

SHEIKH SHAUGAT ABDULLAH AND SAIFUL AZAD

Contents

Keywords

Caesar cipher
Monoalphabetic cipher
Playfair cipher
Polyalphabetic cipher

The history of cryptography starts from the ancient era when it was practiced by the secret societies or by the troops on the battlefield.

The necessity of such an approach has increased with time. In the current information era, there is indeed no time at which information security is not necessary, and hence cryptography. From military to civilian, or from government to individual, information security is tremendously necessary. Consequently, several algorithms are proposed, and they are implemented with various hardware. In this chapter, we discuss a couple of renowned classical encryption techniques.

2.1 Caesar Cipher

Caesar cipher or Caesar's shift cipher is an extensively known and the easiest encryption technique, named after Julius Caesar, who used it in his military campaigns. Julius Caesar replaced each letter in the plaintext by the letter three positions further down the alphabet. It was the first recorded use of encryption for the sake of securing messages. Hence, it has become so important that it is still included in more advanced encryption technique at times (e.g., Vigenère cipher).

Actually, Caesar cipher is a type of substitution cipher in which each letter of the alphabet is substituted by a letter a certain distance away from that letter (Table 2.1). When the last letter, *Z*, is reached, it wraps back around to the beginning. For example, with a shift of three (i.e., key = 3) to the right, *A* would be replaced by *D*, *B* would become *E*, and so on.

2.1.1 Algorithm

Step 0: Mathematically, map the letters to numbers (i.e., *A* = 1, *B* = 2, and so on).

Step 1: Select an integer key *K* in between 1 and 25 (i.e., there are total 26 letters in the English language).

Step 2: The encryption formula is "Add *k* mod 26"; that is, the original letter *L* becomes $(L + k)\%26$.

Step 3: The deciphering is "Subtract *k* mod 26"; that is, the encrypted letter *L* becomes $(L - k)\%26$.

Table 2.1 Caesar Cipher, Plaintext–Ciphertext Conversion for Key Value 3 to the Right

A	B	C	D	E	F	G	H	I	J	K	L	M	N	O	P	Q	R	S	T	U	V	W	X	Y	Z
d	e	f	g	h	i	j	k	l	m	n	o	p	q	r	s	t	u	v	w	x	y	z	a	b	c

2.1.2 Implementation

```cpp
#include <iostream>
#include <stdlib.h>
#include <string>
using namespace std;

charcaesar(char c, int k)//'c' holds the letter to be
    encrypted or decrypted and 'k' holds the key
{
if(isalpha(c) && c ! = toupper(c))
    {
        c = toupper(c);//use upper to keep from having
            to use two separate for A..Z a..z
        c = (((c-65)+k)% 26) + 65; //Encryption, (add k
            with c) mod 26
    }
else
    {
        c = ((((c-65)-k) + 26)% 26) + 65; //Decryption,
            (subtract k from c) mod 26
        c = tolower(c);//use lower to keep from having
            to use two separate for A..Z a..z
    }
return c;
}

int main()
{
string input, output;
int choice = 0;


while (choice ! = 2) {
cout<<endl<< "Press 1: Encryption/Decryption; Press 2:
quit: " ;

try {
cin>> choice;
if (choice ! = 1 && choice ! = 2) throw "Incorrect
Choice";
    }
catch (const char* chc) {
cerr<< "INCORRECT CHOICE !!!!" <<endl;
return 1;
    }
```

```
if (choice = = 1) {
int key;
try {
cout<<endl<< "Choose key value (choose a number
    between 1 to 26): ";
cin>> key;
cin.ignore();
if (key < 1 || key > 26) throw "Incorrect key";
        }
catch (const char* k) {
cerr<< "INCORRECT KEY VALUE CHOSEN !!!" <<endl;
return 1;
        }

try {
cout<<endl<< "NOTE: Put LOWER CASE letters for
encryption and" <<endl;
cout<< "UPPER CASE letters for decryption" <<endl;
cout<<endl<< "Enter cipertext (only alphabets) and
press enter to continue: ";
getline(cin, input);

for (inti = 0; i<input.size(); i++) {
if ((!(input[i] > = 'a' && input[i] < = 'z')) &&
(!(input[i] > = 'A' && input[i] < = 'Z'))) throw
"Incorrect string";
        }
    }
catch (const char* str) {
cerr<< "YOUR STRING MAY HAVE DIGITS OR SPECIAL SYMBOLS
!!!" <<endl;
cerr<< "PLEASE PUT ONLY ALPHABETS !!! " <<endl;
return 1;
        }

for(unsigned int x = 0; x <input.length(); x++) {
output + = caesar(input[x], key); //calling the Caesar
function, where the actual encryption and decryption
takes place
        }

cout<< output <<endl;
output.clear();
    }
  }
}
```

2.1.3 Limitations

The Caesar cipher was reasonably secure in earlier days (until the ninth century) because most of the enemies of Julius Caesar were illiterate. They thought the encrypted text was written in some foreign language. However, there are several techniques to break Caesar cipher these days.

Caesar cipher is vulnerable to brute-force attack because it depends on a single key with 25 possible values if the plaintext is written in English. Therefore, by trying each option and checking which one results in a meaningful word, it is possible to find out the key. Once the key is found, the full ciphertext can be deciphered accurately.

Frequency analysis is another way to break Caesar cipher, which is smarter and faster than brute force. We will learn more about frequency analysis later in this chapter.

2.2 Monoalphabetic Cipher

Another type of substitution cipher is monoalphabetic cipher, where the same letters of the plaintext are always replaced by the same letters in the ciphertext. The word *mono* means "one," and therefore, each letter is one-to-one mapped with a single ciphertext letter. A sample plaintext–ciphertext alphabet mapping is given in Table 2.2. Here, *A* in the plaintext will be replaced by *q* in the ciphertext, and so on.

Unlike Caesar cipher, this technique uses a random key for every single letter (i.e., total of 26 keys). So breaking the code for a single letter doesn't necessarily decipher the whole encrypted text, which makes the monoalphabetic cipher secure against brute-force attack.

2.2.1 Algorithm

Step 0: Generate plaintext–ciphertext pair by mapping each plaintext letter to a different random ciphertext letter.

Step 1: To encipher, for each letter in the original text, replace the plaintext letter with a ciphertext letter.

Step 2: For deciphering, reverse the procedure in step 1.

Table 2.2 Sample Plaintext–Ciphertext Letters Mapping in Monoalphabetic Cipher

A	B	C	D	E	F	G	H	I	J	K	L	M	N	O	P	Q	R	S	T	U	V	W	X	Y	Z
q	w	E	r	t	y	u	I	o	p	a	s	d	f	g	h	j	k	L	z	x	c	v	b	n	m

2.2.2 Implementation

```cpp
#include <iostream>
#include <vector>
#include <string>
#include <stdlib.h>
using namespace std;


typedef vector <char>CharVec;
CharVec Plain;
CharVec Cipher;


voidPutCharInVec ()
{
cout<< "Plain: " <<endl;
for(inti = 0; i< 26; i++) {
Plain.push_back(i+97); //Assigning the plain
characters in Vector
   }


for(inti = 0; i< 26; i++) {
cout<< Plain[i] << "\t" ;
   }
cout<<endl;
  //Assigning the random characters in Vector to use
as key
cout<< "Cipher: " <<endl;
bool exist;
intnum;
for(inti = 0; i< 26; i++) {
  // Generating unique random numbers as keys
while (exist) {
exist = false;
num = rand()% 26 + 1;
for (vector <char> :: iterator it = Cipher.begin(); it
! = Cipher.end(); it++) {
if ((*it) = = num) {
exist = true;
break;
         }
      }
   }
Cipher.push_back(((i + num)% 26) + 65);
  }
```

```cpp
for(inti = 0; i< 26; i++) {
cout<< Cipher[i] << "\t" ;
   }
cout<<endl;
}


charMonoalphabetic (char c)
{
  //Encryption
if (c ! = toupper(c)) {
for (inti = 0; i< 26; i++) {
if (Plain[i] = = c) {
return Cipher[i];
        }
      }
   }
  //Decryption
else {
for (inti = 0; i< 26; i++) {
if (Cipher[i] = = c) {
return Plain[i];
        }
      }
   }
return 0;
}

int main ()
{
string input, output;

PutCharInVec();
int choice = 0;
while (choice ! = 2) {
cout<<endl<< "Press 1: Encryption/Decryption; Press 2:
quit: " ;

try {
cin>> choice;
cin.ignore();
if (choice ! = 1 && choice ! = 2) throw "Incorrect
Choice";
      }
catch (const char* chc) {
cerr<< "INCORRECT CHOICE !!!!" <<endl;
```

```
return 1;
    }
if (choice = = 1) {
try {
cout<<endl<< "NOTE: Put LOWER CASE letters for
encryption and" <<endl;
cout<< "UPPER CASE letters for decryption" <<endl;
cout<<endl<< "Enter cipertext (only alphabets) and
press enter to continue: ";
getline(cin, input);

for (inti = 0; i<input.size(); i++) {
if ((!(input[i] > = 'a' && input[i] < = 'z')) &&
(!(input[i] > = 'A' && input[i] < = 'Z'))) throw
"Incorrect string";
        }
    }
catch (const char* str) {
cerr<< "YOUR STRING MAY HAVE DIGITS OR SPECIAL SYMBOLS
!!!" <<endl;
cerr<< "PLEASE PUT ONLY ALPHABETS !!! " <<endl;
return 1;
        }

for(unsigned int x = 0; x <input.length(); x++) {
output + = Monoalphabetic(input[x]);
        }
cout<< output <<endl;
output.clear();
    }

  }
return 0;
}
```

2.2.3 *Limitations*

Despite its advantages, the random key for each letter in monoalphabetic substitution has some downsides too. It is very difficult to
remember the order of the letters in the key, and therefore, it takes a
lot of time and effort to encipher or decipher the text manually.

On the other hand, monoalphabetic substitution is vulnerable to frequency analysis because it does not change the relative

letter frequencies. As human language is not random, so frequencies of different letters are different in the regular text (e.g., *e* and *t* are most frequent; *the*, *and*, *a*, and *an* are very common). The frequency distribution of each letter in the ciphertext can be calculated by using the statistical analyzer. Then, the distribution result is compared to the standard letter frequency statistics to make assumptions at possible letter replacements. Sometimes backtracking is necessary to confirm the assumptions.

To improve the security of monoalphabetic cipher, multiple ciphertext letters need to be mapped with each corresponding plaintext letter. This technique is called polyalphabetic cipher, and it will be described later in the chapter.

2.3 Playfair Cipher

As seen in the previous section, not even a large number of keys in a monoalphabetic cipher provides the desired security. To improve the security, one approach is to use the digraph substitution cipher, where multiple letters are encrypted at a time. The Playfair cipher was the earliest practical digraph substitution cipher. The technique was invented by Charles Wheatstone in 1854. However, it was named after his friend Lord Playfair, who promoted the use of this cipher. Playfair was massively used by British forces in the Second Boer War and World War I. It was also used by the Australians for tactical purposes during World War II.

Playfair actually encrypts digraphs or pairs of letters rather than single letters like the plain substitution cipher (e.g., Caesar cipher). It is equivalent to a monoalphabetic cipher with a set of $25 \times 25 = 625$ characters (i.e., for each possible pair) for the English language. Therefore, security is significantly improved over the simple monoalphabetic cipher.

2.3.1 Algorithm

Step 0: Select the character key. The maximum size of the key is 25, and it can only be letters.

Step 1: Identify double letters in the key and count them as one.

Table 2.3   Sample Playfair Matrix for Key *Simple*

S	I/J	M	P	L
E	A	B	C	D
F	G	H	K	N
O	Q	R	T	U
V	W	X	Y	Z

Step 2: Set the 5 × 5 matrix by filling the first positions with the key. Fill the rest of the matrix with other letters. *I* and *J* will be placed in the same cell as shown in Table 2.3.

Step 3: Identify double letters in the plaintext and replace the duplicate letter with *x* (e.g., *killer* will become *kilxer*).

Step 4: Plaintext is encrypted in pairs, two letters at a time. If the plaintext has an odd number of characters, append an *x* to the end to make it even.

Step 5: For encryption: (1) If both letters fall in the same row, substitute each with the letter to its right in a circular pattern. (2) If both letters fall in the same column, substitute each letter with the letter below it in a circular pattern. (3) Otherwise, each letter is substituted by the letter in the same row, but in the column of the other letter of the pair.

Step 6: For deciphering, reverse the procedure in step 5, step 4, and finally, step 3, respectively.

2.3.2 Implementation

```
#include <iostream>
#include <string>
#include <vector>
using namespace std;

classPlayFair
{
public:

PlayFair ();
  ~PlayFair () {}

voidsetKey (string k) {key = k;}
stringgetKey () {return key;}
```

```cpp
stringkeyWithoutDuplicateAlphabet (string k);
string encrypt (string str);
string decrypt (string str);

voidsetMatrix ();
voidshowMatrix ();

intfindRow (char ch);
intfindCol (char ch);

charfindLetter (intx_val, inty_val);

private:

char matrix[5][5];
string key;
};

PlayFair::PlayFair ()
{
  // Initializing the playfair matrix
for (inti = 0; i< 5; i++) {
for (int j = 0; j < 5; j++) {
matrix[i][j] = 0;
      }
    }
}

stringPlayFair::keyWithoutDuplicateAlphabet (string k)
{
stringstr_wo_dup;//string without duplicate alphabets

for (string::iterator it = k.begin(); it ! = k.end();
it++) {
      boolalphabet_exist = false;
      for (string::iterator it1 = str_wo_dup.begin();
      it1 ! = str_wo_dup.end(); it1++) {
      if (*it1 = = *it) {
alphabet_exist = true;
        }
      }

if (!alphabet_exist) {
str_wo_dup.push_back(*it);
    }
  }
```

```
returnstr_wo_dup;
}


voidPlayFair::setMatrix ()
{
stringkwda = keyWithoutDuplicateAlphabet(getKey());
// Getting the key with unique characters

inti_val, j_val;

int count = 0;
  // Populating the Playfair matrix with the key and
other letters
for (inti = 0; i< 5; i++) {
for (int j = 0; j < 5; j++) {
        if (count = = kwda.length()) break;
        else {
        matrix[i][j] = toupper(kwda[(5 * i) + j]);
          ++count;
        }
    }
if (count = = kwda.length()) break;
    }

for (inti = 0; i< 26; i++) {
        charch = 65 + i;
        boolalphabet_exist = false;

        for (string::iterator it = kwda.begin();
        it ! = kwda.end(); it++) {
        if (ch = = toupper(*it)) {
                alphabet_exist = true;
            }
        }

        if (ch = = 'J') alphabet_exist = true;//since
        i and j both co-exist in the same cell, we'll
        only put i in the cell

    bool exit = false;
    if (!alphabet_exist) {
    for (inti = 0; i< 5; i++) {
            for (int j = 0; j < 5; j++) {
            if (!isalpha(matrix[i][j])) {
                    matrix[i][j] = toupper(ch);
                    exit = true;
```

```
                    }
            if (exit = = true) break;
            }
            if (exit = = true) break;
        }
    }
}
}

voidPlayFair::showMatrix()
{
for (inti = 0; i< 5; i++) {
        for (int j = 0; j < 5; j++) {
        if (matrix[i][j] ! = 'I') cout<< matrix[i][j] <<
        "\t";
        elsecout<< "I/J" << "\t";
        }
        cout<<endl;
    }
cout<<endl;
}

intPlayFair::findRow (char ch)
{
  //Finding the specific row for a character
if (ch = = 'j') ch = 'i';
for (inti = 0; i< 5; i++) {
        for (int j = 0; j < 5; j++) {
        if (matrix[i][j] = = toupper(ch)) {return i;}
        }
    }
return -1; //If not found
}

intPlayFair::findCol (char ch)
{
  //Finding the specific row for a character
if (ch = = 'j') ch = 'i';
for (inti = 0; i< 5; i++) {
        for (int j = 0; j < 5; j++) {
        if (matrix[i][j] = = toupper(ch)) {return j;}
        }
    }
return -1; //If not found
}
```

```
stringPlayFair::encrypt (string str)
{
string output;

   //replace (by x) the repeating plaintext letters
that are in the same pair for (inti = 1; i<str.
length(); i = i + 2) {
        if (str[i-1] = = str[i]) {
        string temp1, temp2;

        for (int j = 0; j <i; j++) {
                temp1.push_back(str[j]);
          }

        for (int j = i; j <str.length(); j++) {
            temp2.push_back(str[j]);
        }

        str.clear();
        str = temp1 + 'x' + temp2;
        }
}

for (inti = 0; i<str.length(); i = i + 2) {

            //for the letter pair falls in the same row if
            (findRow(str[i]) = = findRow(str[i+1])) {
            output.push_back(matrix[findRow(str[i])]
            [(findCol(str[i]) + 1)% 5]);
            output.push_back(matrix[findRow(str[i + 1])]
            [(findCol(str[i + 1]) + 1)% 5]);
            }
            //for the letter pair falls in the same
            column
            else if (findCol(str[i]) = =
            findCol(str[i+1])) {
            output.push_back(matrix[(findRow(str[i])
            + 1)% 5][findCol(str[i])]);
            output.push_back(matrix[(findRow(str[i + 1])
            + 1)% 5][findCol(str[i + 1])]);
            }

             //for other cases
            else {
            output.push_back(matrix[findRow(str[i])]
            [findCol(str[i + 1])]);
```

```
                output.push_back(matrix[findRow(str[i + 1])]
                [findCol(str[i])]);
                }
}


if ((str.length()% 2) ! = 0) {
              output[output.length() - 1] =
toupper(str[str.length() - 1]);
      }


return output;
}

stringPlayFair::decrypt (string str)
{
string output;

for (inti = 0; i<str.length(); i = i + 2) {
          //for the letter pair falls in the same row if
          (findRow(str[i]) = = findRow(str[i+1])) {
          int y;
          if ((findCol(str[i]) - 1) > = 0)
          y = (findCol(str[i]) - 1);
          else y = 4;
          output.push_back(matrix[findRow(str[i])]
          [y]);
          if ((findCol(str[i + 1]) - 1) > = 0)
          y = (findCol(str[i + 1]) - 1);
          else y = 4;
          output.push_back(matrix[findRow(str[i + 1])]
          [y]);
          }
          //for the letter pair falls in the same
          coloumn
          else if (findCol(str[i]) = =
          findCol(str[i+1])) {
          int x;
          if ((findRow(str[i]) - 1) > = 0) x =
          (findRow(str[i]) - 1);
          else x = 4;
          output.push_back(matrix[x][findCol(str[i])]);
          if ((findRow(str[i + 1]) - 1) > = 0) x =
          (findRow(str[i + 1]) - 1);
          else x = 4;
```

```
                output.push_back(matrix[x][findCol(str[i
                + 1])]);
                }

                //for other cases
                else {
                output.push_back(matrix[findRow(str[i])]
                [findCol(str[i + 1])]);
                output.push_back(matrix[findRow(str[i + 1])]
                [findCol(str[i])]);
                }
        }

    //remove x from the string
for (inti = 0; i<output.length(); i++) {
            if (output[i] = = 'X') {
            output.erase(output.begin() + i);
            }
        }

return output;
}
int main () {
PlayFair pf;
string key, input;
    // Input the key to generate Playfair matrix
cout<< "Put key value (put alphabets/words): " <<endl;
getline(cin,key);
cout<< key <<endl;
    // Generating the Playfair matrix
pf.setKey(key);
pf.setMatrix();
pf.showMatrix();
    // Input the data to encrypt or decrypt
cout<< "Put your text " <<endl;
getline(cin,input);

cout<< "Press 1: Encrypt | 2: Decrypt" <<endl;
int choice;
cin>> choice;

if (choice = = 1) cout<<pf.encrypt(input) <<endl;
elsecout<<pf.decrypt(input) <<endl;
return 0;
}
```

2.3.3 Limitations

Even though Playfair is considerably complicated to break, it is still vulnerable to frequency analysis because it leaves some formation of plaintext intact. However, in the case of Playfair, frequency analysis will be applied on the 25*25 = 625 possible digraphs rather than the 25 possible monographs (i.e., in the case of monoalphabetic). Frequency analysis thus needs a lot of ciphertext in order to work. Therefore, assuming some of the words from the plaintext using the knowledge of area, time, or context of the message can be helpful for retrieving the key, and so far this is the simplest way to crack this cipher.

2.4 Polyalphabetic Cipher

A polyalphabetic substitution cipher is a series of simple substitution ciphers. It is used to change each character of the plaintext with a variable length. The Vigenère cipher is a special example of the polyalphabetic cipher.

In 1467, the Alberti cipher introduced by Leon Battista Alberti was the first polyalphabetic cipher. Typically, Alberti used a mixed set of alphabet for encryption, but that set was not fixed. Based on the requirement, he occasionally switched to a different alphabet set, including uppercase letters or numbers.

To reduce the effectiveness of frequency analysis on the ciphertext, the polyalphabetic cipher uses a collection of standard Caesar ciphers. Usually, the polyalphabetic cipher defines a text string (i.e., a word) as a key. In the case of encryption/decryption, this key is repeated until it reaches the length of the plaintext/ciphertext. An example is depicted in Table 2.4.

As can be observed from the table, the key *run* is repeated until it reaches the length of the plaintext. Now, the Vigenère table is utilized to find out the ciphertext that is illustrated in Table 2.5.

Table 2.4 Sample Polyalphabetic Encryption for Key *Run*

Plaintext	t	o	b	e	o	r	n	o	t	t	o	b	e	t	h	a	t	i	s	t	h	e
Key	r	u	n	r	u	n	r	u	n	r	u	n	r	u	n	r	u	n	r	u	n	r
Cipher	K	I	O	V	I	E	E	I	G	K	I	O	V	N	U	R	N	V	J	N	U	V

Table 2.5 Vigenère Table (Also Known as Tabula Recta)

A	B	C	D	E	F	G	H	I	J	K	L	M	N	O	P	Q	R	S	T	U	V	W	X	Y	Z
B	C	D	E	F	G	H	I	J	K	L	M	N	O	P	Q	R	S	T	U	V	W	X	Y	Z	A
C	D	E	F	G	H	I	J	K	L	M	N	O	P	Q	R	S	T	U	V	W	X	Y	Z	A	B
D	E	F	G	H	I	J	K	L	M	N	O	P	Q	R	S	T	U	V	W	X	Y	Z	A	B	C
E	F	G	H	I	J	K	L	M	N	O	P	Q	R	S	T	U	V	W	X	Y	Z	A	B	C	D
F	G	H	I	J	K	L	M	N	O	P	Q	R	S	T	U	V	W	X	Y	Z	A	B	C	D	E
G	H	I	J	K	L	M	N	O	P	Q	R	S	T	U	V	W	X	Y	Z	A	B	C	D	E	F
H	I	J	K	L	M	N	O	P	Q	R	S	T	U	V	W	X	Y	Z	A	B	C	D	E	F	G
I	J	K	L	M	N	O	P	Q	R	S	T	U	V	W	X	Y	Z	A	B	C	D	E	F	G	H
J	K	L	M	N	O	P	Q	R	S	T	U	V	W	X	Y	Z	A	B	C	D	E	F	G	H	I
K	L	M	N	O	P	Q	R	S	T	U	V	W	X	Y	Z	A	B	C	D	E	F	G	H	I	J
L	M	N	O	P	Q	R	S	T	U	V	W	X	Y	Z	A	B	C	D	E	F	G	H	I	J	K
M	N	O	P	Q	R	S	T	U	V	W	X	Y	Z	A	B	C	D	E	F	G	H	I	J	K	L
N	O	P	Q	R	S	T	U	V	W	X	Y	Z	A	B	C	D	E	F	G	H	I	J	K	L	M
O	P	Q	R	S	T	U	V	W	X	Y	Z	A	B	C	D	E	F	G	H	I	J	K	L	M	N
P	Q	R	S	T	U	V	W	X	Y	Z	A	B	C	D	E	F	G	H	I	J	K	L	M	N	O
Q	R	S	T	U	V	W	X	Y	Z	A	B	C	D	E	F	G	H	I	J	K	L	M	N	O	P
R	S	T	U	V	W	X	Y	Z	A	B	C	D	E	F	G	H	I	J	K	L	M	N	O	P	Q
S	T	U	V	W	X	Y	Z	A	B	C	D	E	F	G	H	I	J	K	L	M	N	O	P	Q	R
T	U	V	W	X	Y	Z	A	B	C	D	E	F	G	H	I	J	K	L	M	N	O	P	Q	R	S
U	V	W	X	Y	Z	A	B	C	D	E	F	G	H	I	J	K	L	M	N	O	P	Q	R	S	T
V	W	X	Y	Z	A	B	C	D	E	F	G	H	I	J	K	L	M	N	O	P	Q	R	S	T	U
W	X	Y	Z	A	B	C	D	E	F	G	H	I	J	K	L	M	N	O	P	Q	R	S	T	U	V
X	Y	Z	A	B	C	D	E	F	G	H	I	J	K	L	M	N	O	P	Q	R	S	T	U	V	W
Y	Z	A	B	C	D	E	F	G	H	I	J	K	L	M	N	O	P	Q	R	S	T	U	V	W	X
Z	A	B	C	D	E	F	G	H	I	J	K	L	M	N	O	P	Q	R	S	T	U	V	W	X	Y

Every plaintext letter tells the position of the row, and every keyword letter tells the position of the column. For instance, *t* is 20th in the alphabet and *r* is 18th in the English alphabet table. Therefore, *t* is substituted by the alphabet that is in row 20 and column 18 in the Vigenère table, i.e., *K*. In this way, all the plaintext letters are substituted. As can be observed from the table, the letter *t* is sometimes enciphered as a *K* and sometimes as a *G* since the relative key letter is once *r* and another time *n*.

In case of decryption, a similar table is utilized, but in a different way. First, the keyword letter needs to be found in the first row. After that, we have to trace down until the ciphertext letter is found. Once discovered, the plaintext letter is then found at the first column of that row.

2.4.1 Algorithm

Step 0: Select a multiple-letter key.

Step 1: To encrypt, the first letter of the key encrypts the first letter of the plaintext, the second letter of the key encrypts the second letter of the plaintext, and so on.

Step 2: When all letters of the key are used, start over with the first letter of the key.

Step 3: The decryption process is the reverse of step 1. The number of letters in the key determines the period of the cipher.

2.4.2 Implementation

```cpp
#include <iostream>
#include <string>
#include <cmath>
using namespace std;
charvigenere_table[26][26] = {
'A', 'B', 'C', 'D', 'E', 'F', 'G', 'H', 'I', 'J', 'K',
'L', 'M', 'N', 'O', 'P', 'Q', 'R', 'S', 'T', 'U', 'V',
'W', 'X', 'Y', 'Z',
'B', 'C', 'D', 'E', 'F', 'G', 'H', 'I', 'J', 'K', 'L',
'M', 'N', 'O', 'P', 'Q', 'R', 'S', 'T', 'U', 'V', 'W',
'X', 'Y', 'Z', 'A',
'C', 'D', 'E', 'F', 'G', 'H', 'I', 'J', 'K', 'L', 'M',
'N', 'O', 'P', 'Q', 'R', 'S', 'T', 'U', 'V', 'W', 'X',
'Y', 'Z', 'A', 'B',
'D', 'E', 'F', 'G', 'H', 'I', 'J', 'K', 'L', 'M', 'N',
'O', 'P', 'Q', 'R', 'S', 'T', 'U', 'V', 'W', 'X', 'Y',
'Z', 'A', 'B', 'C',
'E', 'F', 'G', 'H', 'I', 'J', 'K', 'L', 'M', 'N', 'O',
'P', 'Q', 'R', 'S', 'T', 'U', 'V', 'W', 'X', 'Y', 'Z',
'A', 'B', 'C', 'D',
'F', 'G', 'H', 'I', 'J', 'K', 'L', 'M', 'N', 'O', 'P',
'Q', 'R', 'S', 'T', 'U', 'V', 'W', 'X', 'Y', 'Z', 'A',
'B', 'C', 'D', 'E',
'G', 'H', 'I', 'J', 'K', 'L', 'M', 'N', 'O', 'P', 'Q',
'R', 'S', 'T', 'U', 'V', 'W', 'X', 'Y', 'Z', 'A', 'B',
'C', 'D', 'E', 'F',
'H', 'I', 'J', 'K', 'L', 'M', 'N', 'O', 'P', 'Q', 'R',
'S', 'T', 'U', 'V', 'W', 'X', 'Y', 'Z', 'A', 'B', 'C',
'D', 'E', 'F', 'G',
```

`'I'`, `'J'`, `'K'`, `'L'`, `'M'`, `'N'`, `'O'`, `'P'`, `'Q'`, `'R'`, `'S'`,
`'T'`, `'U'`, `'V'`, `'W'`, `'X'`, `'Y'`, `'Z'`, `'A'`, `'B'`, `'C'`, `'D'`,
`'E'`, `'F'`, `'G'`, `'H'`,
`'J'`, `'K'`, `'L'`, `'M'`, `'N'`, `'O'`, `'P'`, `'Q'`, `'R'`, `'S'`, `'T'`,
`'U'`, `'V'`, `'W'`, `'X'`, `'Y'`, `'Z'`, `'A'`, `'B'`, `'C'`, `'D'`, `'E'`,
`'F'`, `'G'`, `'H'`, `'I'`,
`'K'`, `'L'`, `'M'`, `'N'`, `'O'`, `'P'`, `'Q'`, `'R'`, `'S'`, `'T'`, `'U'`,
`'V'`, `'W'`, `'X'`, `'Y'`, `'Z'`, `'A'`, `'B'`, `'C'`, `'D'`, `'E'`, `'F'`,
`'G'`, `'H'`, `'I'`, `'J'`,
`'L'`, `'M'`, `'N'`, `'O'`, `'P'`, `'Q'`, `'R'`, `'S'`, `'T'`, `'U'`, `'V'`,
`'W'`, `'X'`, `'Y'`, `'Z'`, `'A'`, `'B'`, `'C'`, `'D'`, `'E'`, `'F'`, `'G'`,
`'H'`, `'I'`, `'J'`, `'K'`,
`'M'`, `'N'`, `'O'`, `'P'`, `'Q'`, `'R'`, `'S'`, `'T'`, `'U'`, `'V'`, `'W'`,
`'X'`, `'Y'`, `'Z'`, `'A'`, `'B'`, `'C'`, `'D'`, `'E'`, `'F'`, `'G'`, `'H'`,
`'I'`, `'J'`, `'K'`, `'L'`,
`'N'`, `'O'`, `'P'`, `'Q'`, `'R'`, `'S'`, `'T'`, `'U'`, `'V'`, `'W'`, `'X'`,
`'Y'`, `'Z'`, `'A'`, `'B'`, `'C'`, `'D'`, `'E'`, `'F'`, `'G'`, `'H'`, `'I'`,
`'J'`, `'K'`, `'L'`, `'M'`,
`'O'`, `'P'`, `'Q'`, `'R'`, `'S'`, `'T'`, `'U'`, `'V'`, `'W'`, `'X'`, `'Y'`,
`'Z'`, `'A'`, `'B'`, `'C'`, `'D'`, `'E'`, `'F'`, `'G'`, `'H'`, `'I'`, `'J'`,
`'K'`, `'L'`, `'M'`, `'N'`,
`'P'`, `'Q'`, `'R'`, `'S'`, `'T'`, `'U'`, `'V'`, `'W'`, `'X'`, `'Y'`, `'Z'`,
`'A'`, `'B'`, `'C'`, `'D'`, `'E'`, `'F'`, `'G'`, `'H'`, `'I'`, `'J'`, `'K'`,
`'L'`, `'M'`, `'N'`, `'O'`,
`'Q'`, `'R'`, `'S'`, `'T'`, `'U'`, `'V'`, `'W'`, `'X'`, `'Y'`, `'Z'`, `'A'`,
`'B'`, `'C'`, `'D'`, `'E'`, `'F'`, `'G'`, `'H'`, `'I'`, `'J'`, `'K'`, `'L'`,
`'M'`, `'N'`, `'O'`, `'P'`,
`'R'`, `'S'`, `'T'`, `'U'`, `'V'`, `'W'`, `'X'`, `'Y'`, `'Z'`, `'A'`, `'B'`,
`'C'`, `'D'`, `'E'`, `'F'`, `'G'`, `'H'`, `'I'`, `'J'`, `'K'`, `'L'`, `'M'`,
`'N'`, `'O'`, `'P'`, `'Q'`,
`'S'`, `'T'`, `'U'`, `'V'`, `'W'`, `'X'`, `'Y'`, `'Z'`, `'A'`, `'B'`, `'C'`,
`'D'`, `'E'`, `'F'`, `'G'`, `'H'`, `'I'`, `'J'`, `'K'`, `'L'`, `'M'`, `'N'`,
`'O'`, `'P'`, `'Q'`, `'R'`,
`'T'`, `'U'`, `'V'`, `'W'`, `'X'`, `'Y'`, `'Z'`, `'A'`, `'B'`, `'C'`, `'D'`,
`'E'`, `'F'`, `'G'`, `'H'`, `'I'`, `'J'`, `'K'`, `'L'`, `'M'`, `'N'`, `'O'`,
`'P'`, `'Q'`, `'R'`, `'S'`,
`'U'`, `'V'`, `'W'`, `'X'`, `'Y'`, `'Z'`, `'A'`, `'B'`, `'C'`, `'D'`, `'E'`,
`'F'`, `'G'`, `'H'`, `'I'`, `'J'`, `'K'`, `'L'`, `'M'`, `'N'`, `'O'`, `'P'`,
`'Q'`, `'R'`, `'S'`, `'T'`,
`'V'`, `'W'`, `'X'`, `'Y'`, `'Z'`, `'A'`, `'B'`, `'C'`, `'D'`, `'E'`, `'F'`,
`'G'`, `'H'`, `'I'`, `'J'`, `'K'`, `'L'`, `'M'`, `'N'`, `'O'`, `'P'`, `'Q'`,
`'R'`, `'S'`, `'T'`, `'U'`,
`'W'`, `'X'`, `'Y'`, `'Z'`, `'A'`, `'B'`, `'C'`, `'D'`, `'E'`, `'F'`, `'G'`,
`'H'`, `'I'`, `'J'`, `'K'`, `'L'`, `'M'`, `'N'`, `'O'`, `'P'`, `'Q'`, `'R'`,
`'S'`, `'T'`, `'U'`, `'V'`,

```
'X', 'Y', 'Z', 'A', 'B', 'C', 'D', 'E', 'F', 'G', 'H',
'I', 'J', 'K', 'L', 'M', 'N', 'O', 'P', 'Q', 'R', 'S',
'T', 'U', 'V', 'W',
'Y', 'Z', 'A', 'B', 'C', 'D', 'E', 'F', 'G', 'H', 'I',
'J', 'K', 'L', 'M', 'N', 'O', 'P', 'Q', 'R', 'S', 'T',
'U', 'V', 'W', 'X',
'Z', 'A', 'B', 'C', 'D', 'E', 'F', 'G', 'H', 'I', 'J',
'K', 'L', 'M', 'N', 'O', 'P', 'Q', 'R', 'S', 'T', 'U',
'V', 'W', 'X', 'Y'
};

void Encrypt (string in, string &out, string k) {
inti = 0;
for (string :: iterator it = in.begin(); it ! =
in.end(); it++) {
if (*it ! = ' ') {
int row = toupper(*it) - 'A';
int column = toupper(k[i% k.length()]) - 'A';
out + = vigenere_table[row][column];
       }
else {
out + = ' ';
       }

i++;
   }

}

void Decrypt (string in, string &out, string k) {
inti = 0;
for (string :: iterator it = in.begin(); it ! =
in.end(); it++) {
if (*it ! = ' ') {
int column = toupper(k[i% k.length()]) - 'A';
int row;
for (row = 0; row < 26; row++) {
if (vigenere_table[row][column] = = *it) break;
         }
out + = 'A' + row;
      }
else {
out + = ' ';
      }
i++;
```

```cpp
    }
}

int main ()
{
string input, output, key;
        cout<< "Put key value (put alphabets/words): ";
getline(cin,key);
int choice = 0;

while (choice ! = 3) {
cout<<endl<< "Press 1: Encryption, 2: Decryption; 3:
quit: " ;

try {
cin>> choice;
cin.ignore();
if (choice ! = 1 && choice ! = 2 && choice ! = 3)
throw "Incorrect Choice";
        }
catch (const char* chc) {
cerr<< "INCORRECT CHOICE !!!!" <<endl;
return 1;
        }
if (choice = = 1 || choice = = 2) {
try {
cout<<endl<< "Enter cipertext (only alphabets) and
press enter to continue: ";
getline(cin, input);

for (inti = 0; i<input.size(); i++) {
if ((!(input[i] > = 'a' && input[i] < = 'z')) &&
(!(input[i] > = 'A' && input[i] < = 'Z')) &&
(!(input[i] = = ' ')))
throw "Incorrect string";
            }
        }
catch (const char* str) {
cerr<< "YOUR STRING MAY HAVE DIGITS OR SPECIAL SYMBOLS
!!!" <<endl;
cerr<< "PLEASE PUT ONLY ALPHABETS !!! " <<endl;
return 1;
        }
```

```
if (choice = = 1) {
Encrypt(input, output, key);
cout<<endl<< "Cipher text: " << output <<endl;
      }
else if (choice = = 2) {
input = output;
output.clear();
Decrypt(input, output, key);
cout<<endl<< "Plain text: " << output <<endl;
      }
   }

  }
return 0;
}
```

2.4.3 Limitations

Even though polyalphabetic is more secure than simple substitution cipher, it can still be broken by analyzing the period. In the above example, KOIV is repeated after nine letters, and NU is repeated after six letters. So the period being 3 is a good assumption here, as 3 is a common divisor of 6 and 9. Frequency analysis is applicable here again by knowing which letters were encoded with the same key.

3

ROTOR MACHINE

SHEIKH SHAUGAT ABDULLAH AND SAIFUL AZAD

Contents

Keywords

Enigma
Polyalphabetic cipher
Rotor machine
Streamline cipher

The first mechanical encryption device was introduced in 1920 and named the rotor machine. The most famous example of a rotor machine is the Enigma, invented by the Germans; it was extensively used during World War II.

The concept of the rotor machine was developed independently by a number of inventors at a similar time. Four inventors had been credited with inventing it: Edward Hebern, Arvid Damm, Hugo Koch, and Arthur Scherbius. However, in later discovery, it was found that the first inventors of the rotor machine were two Dutch naval officers, Theo A. van Hengel and R.P.C. Spengler, in 1915 [1].

3.1 Background

In classical cryptographic algorithms, which are discussed in Chapter 2, a simple technique of substitution is utilized where a plaintext is replaced systematically using a secret scheme. For instance, monoalphabetic ciphers replace one character/letter with another character. This technique is vulnerable, since a simple frequency analysis could find out the plaintext easily. Therefore, polyalphabetic ciphers are proposed where a single character may be replaced by multiple alphabets. However, since ciphertext is calculated by hand, only a handful of different alphabets can be utilized. Anything more complex using polyalphabetic would be impractical. The invention of rotor machines resolved that limitation, which provides a realistic way of using a huge number of alphabets.

3.2 Basic Concept

A rotor machine has a keyboard and a series of rotors, where the output pins of one rotor are connected to the input of another. Moreover, a rotor is a mechanical wheel wired to perform a general substitution. So, the number of general substitution for each letter in the plaintext actually depends on the number of rotors. Figure 3.1 depicts a simple rotor machine.

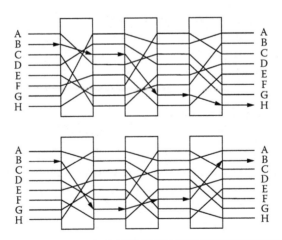

Figure 3.1 A three-rotor machine for an eight-letter alphabet before and after the first rotor has rotated one place.

For example, in a three-rotor machine, the first rotor might substitute *A » E*, the second rotor might substitute *E » K*, and the third rotor might substitute *K » Y*. Therefore, after encryption, *A* will become *Y*. To protect data frequency analysis, some of the rotors shift after each output. In rotor machine encryption, a combination of several rotors and shifting of *n* number of rotors leads to a 26^n. A large number of combinations makes it harder to break the code.

3.3 Systematization

It is relatively straightforward to create a machine to perform simple substitution in monoalphabetic algorithms. However, it is challenging to create a machine that can perform polyalphabetic substitutions. In the case of the rotor machine, the idea is to change the wiring of the machine with each keystroke. The wiring is placed inside a rotor. After a keystroke, the rotor is rotated with a gear. Therefore, a keystroke that outputs an *S* might generate an *A* the next time. Hence, for every keystroke a new substitution takes place.

3.4 Algorithm

Step 0: Select how many rotors will be used and make the rotors ready by placing 26 unique random character pairs.

Step 1: To encrypt, for each character in the alphabet set, for each rotor, find the match from the rotor pair sequentially. After each encryption, rotate the rotors accordingly.

Step 2: To decrypt, apply the same procedure of step 1, with reverse sequential order of the rotors.

3.5 Implementation

```
#include <iostream>
#include <queue>
#include <vector>
#include <cstdlib>
#include <string>
using namespace std;

typedef pair<int,int>Rotor_Pair;
class Enigma {
```

```
public:
voidcreate_rotor(vector <Rotor_Pair>&rtq);
voidshow_rotor(vector <Rotor_Pair>&rtq);
voidmanage_rotors ();
void encrypt();
void decrypt();
chartranspos_en (char ch);
chartranspos_de (char ch);
        voiddisplay_rotors ();
private:
vector<Rotor_Pair>first_rotor;
vector<Rotor_Pair>second_rotor;
vector<Rotor_Pair>third_rotor;
vector< vector <Rotor_Pair>>all_rotors;
int count;
};

void Enigma::create_rotor(vector <Rotor_Pair>&rtq)
{
vector<int>temp_q;

int current = rand()% 26 + 1;
intnum = rand()% 26 + 1;

rtq.push_back(make_pair(current,num));
temp_q.push_back(num);

for (inti = 0; i< 25; i++) {
current = current% 26 + 1;
bool exist = true;

    //Selecting unique random pairs for each of the
rotors

while (exist) {
exist = false;
num = rand()% 26 + 1;
for (vector <int> :: iterator it = temp_q.begin(); it
    ! = temp_q.end(); it++) {
if ((*it) = = num) {
exist = true;
break;
            }
        }
    }
```

```
temp_q.push_back(num);
Rotor_Pairrp = make_pair(current,num);
rtq.push_back(rp);
    }
}

void Enigma :: show_rotor (vector <Rotor_Pair>&rtq)
{
vector<Rotor_Pair>temp_q;
temp_q = rtq;
cout<<endl;

for (unsigned inti = 0; i<26; i++) {
Rotor_Pairrp = rtq[i];
cout<<rp.first<< "\t" <<rp.second<<endl;
    }
}

void Enigma :: manage_rotors ()
{
count = 0;
srand (5);
create_rotor(first_rotor); //Creating the first rotor
all_rotors.push_back(first_rotor);//Assign the first
rotor
create_rotor(second_rotor); //Creating the second rotor
all_rotors.push_back(second_rotor); //Assign the
second rotor
create_rotor(third_rotor); //Creating the third rotor
all_rotors.push_back(third_rotor); //Assign the third
rotor
}

void Enigma :: display_rotors ()
{
for (vector < vector <Rotor_Pair>> :: iterator it =
all_rotors.begin(); it ! = all_rotors.end(); it++) {
      show_rotor(*it);
    }
}

char Enigma :: transpos_en (char ch)
{
count++;
ch = toupper (ch);
intpos = ch - 65 + 1; //Converting ASCII to decimal
```

```
int index = 0;
   // Finding the specific position for each of the
character
for (vector <Rotor_Pair> :: iterator it = first_rotor.
begin(); it ! = first_rotor.end(); it++) {
if ((*it).second = = pos) break;
else index++;
   }
   // Rotating the first rotor
Rotor_Pairtrp = first_rotor.front();
first_rotor.erase(first_rotor.begin());
first_rotor.push_back(trp);

pos = (second_rotor[index]).first;
index = 0;
   // Finding the specific position for each of the
character
for (vector <Rotor_Pair> :: iterator it = second_
rotor.begin(); it ! = second_rotor.end(); it++) {
if ((*it).second = = pos) break;
else index++;
   }
   // Rotating the second rotor
if (count% 26 = = 0) {
Rotor_Pairtrp = second_rotor.front();
second_rotor.erase(second_rotor.begin());
second_rotor.push_back(trp);
   }

pos = (third_rotor[index]).first;
index = 0;
   // Finding the specific position for each of the
character
for (vector <Rotor_Pair> :: iterator it = third_rotor.
begin(); it ! = second_rotor.end(); it++) {
if ((*it).second = = pos) break;
   }
   // Rotating the third rotor
if (count% 676 = = 0) {
Rotor_Pairtrp = third_rotor.front();
third_rotor.erase(third_rotor.begin());
third_rotor.push_back(trp);
   }
ch = pos - 1 + 65; //Converting Decimal to ASCII
returntolower(ch);
}
```

```cpp
void Enigma :: encrypt ()
{
   // Input the data to encrypt
cout<< "Put a text to encrypt" <<endl;
string input, output;
getline(cin, input);
   // For each input character, call "transpos_en"
function if found in alphabet set
for (string :: iterator it = input.begin(); it ! =
input.end(); it++) {
if (isalpha(*it))
output + = transpos_en(*it);
else output + = 32;
   }
cout<< output <<endl;
}

char Enigma :: transpos_de (char ch)
{
count++;
ch = toupper (ch);
intpos = ch - 65 + 1; //Converting ASCII to Deciaml
int index = 0;
   // Finding the specific position for each of the
character
for (vector <Rotor_Pair> :: iterator it = third_rotor.
begin(); it ! = third_rotor.end(); it++) {
if ((*it).first = = pos) break;
else index++;
   }
   // Rotating the third rotor
if (count% 676 = = 0) {
Rotor_Pairtrp = third_rotor.front();
third_rotor.erase(third_rotor.begin());
third_rotor.push_back(trp);
   }

pos = (second_rotor[index]).second;
index = 0;
   // Finding the specific position for each of the
character
for (vector <Rotor_Pair> :: iterator it = second_
rotor.begin(); it ! = second_rotor.end(); it++) {
if ((*it).first = = pos) break;
else index++;
   }
```

```
    // Rotating the second rotor
if (count% 26 = = 0) {
Rotor_Pairtrp = second_rotor.front();
second_rotor.erase(second_rotor.begin());
second_rotor.push_back(trp);
    }

pos = (first_rotor[index]).second;
index = 0;
    // Finding the specific position for each of the
character
for (vector <Rotor_Pair> :: iterator it = first_rotor.
begin(); it ! = first_rotor.end(); it++) {
if ((*it).first = = pos) break;
else index++;
    }
    // Rotating the first rotor
Rotor_Pairtrp = first_rotor.front();
first_rotor.erase(first_rotor.begin());
first_rotor.push_back(trp);

ch = pos - 1 + 65;//Converting Decimal to ASCII
returntolower(ch);
}

void Enigma :: decrypt ()
{
    // Input the data to decrypt
cout<< "Put a text to decrypt" <<endl;
string input, output;
getline(cin, input);
    // initializing the rotor settings
int count = 0;
for (vector < vector <Rotor_Pair>> :: iterator p =
all_rotors.begin(); p ! = all_rotors.end(); p++) {
        if (count = = 0) first_rotor = *p;
        else if (count = = 1) second_rotor = *p;
        elsethird_rotor = *p;
        count++;
}

display_rotors(); //Showing the rotor pairs
    //For each input character, call "transpos_de"
function if found in alphabet set
for (string :: iterator it = input.begin(); it ! =
input.end(); it++) {
```

```
if (isalpha(*it))
output + = transpos_de(*it);
else output + = 32;
    }


cout<< output <<endl;
}


int main()
{
   Enigma enigma;
enigma.manage_rotors();//Creating the rotors and
populate them with character pairs
enigma.display_rotors(); //Show the rotor pairs
enigma.encrypt();//Encryption
enigma.decrypt(); //Decryption
return 0;
}
```

3.6 Limitations

The technique used in the rotor machine was very strong if used correctly and securely. However, the German messages encrypted with the rotor machine Enigma were deciphered by the Allies during World War II. It has been claimed that as a result of this cryptanalysis, World War II was shortened by 2 years. Using a reasonably small range of probable initial permutations, Polish mathematician and cryptologist Marian Rejewski was able to find the possible message keys. What he assumed, and later on discovered to be true, was that most of the time the German operators would choose very simple message keys, like *AAA* or *XYZ* or *ABC*. So, he expected that if he made lists of all the possible message keys, many simple keys would appear. Then that list could be used to find the key. His technique was proven to be correct when he managed to break a lot of ciphertext within a very short time.

Reference

1. Karl de Leeuw. The Dutch invention of the rotor machine, 1915–1923. *Cryptologia*, 27(1), 73–94, 2003.

4

BLOCK CIPHER

TANVEER AHMED, MOHAMMAD ABUL KASHEM, AND SAIFUL AZAD

Contents

Keywords

Block cipher
Cipher block chaining
Cipher feedback
Counter
Electronic code block
Feistel cipher
Output feedback

A stream cipher is one that encrypts/decrypts a data stream character by character, i.e., one character at a time. All the ciphers discussed in Chapter 3 are stream ciphers. On the other hand, a block cipher encrypts/decrypts a block of n characters and produces an output of similar length. The Data Encryption Standard (DES), Advanced Encryption Standard (AES), etc., are examples of block ciphers. Most of the symmetric key-based block cipher algorithms currently in use are based on a structure known as Feistel block cipher [1]. It is worth mentioning that although this structure was proposed several years ago, it is still utilized by many significant symmetric block ciphers currently in operation. In general, block cipher algorithms ensure higher security over stream cipher algorithms. In this chapter, we discuss the basic principles behind block cipher algorithms and Feistel block cipher in detail.

4.1 Block Cipher Principles

To enhance the security of symmetric key algorithms, Calude Shannon introduced two principles: confusion and diffusion [2]. He argued that these principles should be followed to design any secure cryptographic system. They are detailed below:

- **Confusion:** Shannon said confusion makes the relation between the key and the ciphertext as complex as possible. Actually, every character in the key influences every other character of the ciphertext block. This relationship needs to be loosened in such a way that even though the attacker gets some grip on the statistics of the ciphertext, he or she may not be able to deduce the key. A good confusion could be achieved if each character of the ciphertext depends on several parts of the key. For any attacker, it must appear that this dependence is random. This could be achieved by utilizing complex substitution techniques in the algorithm.

- **Diffusion:** This refers to the property that the statistical structure of the plaintext is dissipated into long-range statistics of the ciphertext [3]. In contrast to confusion, diffusion spreads the influence of a single plaintext character over many ciphertext characters, or in other words, each ciphertext character is affected by many ciphertext characters. In binary block cipher, an algorithm must be designed with a combination of permutation and should be followed by a function. The binary block is permuted repeatedly, followed by applying a function to that permuted block.

4.2 The Feistel Block Structure

In Figure 4.1, the Feistel block structure is depicted. As can be observed from the figure, a plaintext of length n bits and a key K are

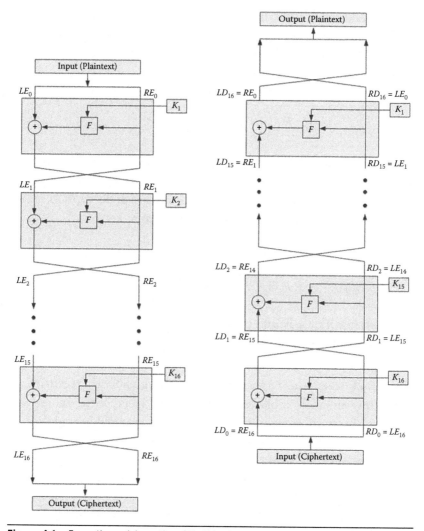

Figure 4.1 Encryption and decryption of the Feistel network.

passed as input to the structure. This n-bit plaintext block is then divided into two halves, LE_0 and RE_0, i.e., $LE_0 = RE_0 = n/2$. These two halves of data blocks are passed through r rounds. In each round, a separate key K_i is utilized that is generally derived from K. All the subkeys that are derived from K are different from each other, i.e., $K \neq K_i \neq K_j$. A round i receives two inputs, LE_{i-1} and RE_{i-1}, from the previous round $i - 1$. Each round comprises both substitution and permutation operations. A substitution is performed on the left half of the block by XORing it with the output of a round function F.

Each F takes the right half block and a subkey K_i as input and produces an output of the same size. These activities can be expressed using the following expressions:

$$LE_i = RE_{i-1}$$

$$RE_i = LE_{i-1} \otimes F(RE_{i-1}, K_i)$$

Following the substitution, the two halves are interchanged to achieve permutation. After the last round, the two halves are combined to produce the ciphertext block. In the case of decryption, similar procedures are followed, but in opposite order, i.e.,

$$RE_{i-1} = LE_i$$

$$LE_{i-1} = RE_i \otimes F(RE_{i-1}, K_i) = RE_i \otimes F(LE_i, K_i)$$

The strength of a Feistel network depends on the selection of the following parameters:

- **Block size:** The larger the block, the greater the security. However, a larger block size reduces the speed of the encryption/decryption technique. Therefore, a reasonable trade-off is considered in terms of choosing the size of a block.
- **Key size:** Like the block size, larger is better. Again, a larger key may increase the processing time, and hence reduce the encryption/decryption speed.
- **Number of rounds:** In general, a single round is inadequate to assure a required level of security. But, multiple rounds offer increasing security.
- **Subkey generation algorithm:** For greater security, a subkey generation algorithm also plays an important role. A complex algorithm makes the cryptanalysis difficult. All the subkeys must be generated in such a way that they have greater resistance to brute-force attacks and greater confusion.
- **Round function:** Again, a greater complex round function makes the cryptanalysis difficult, and hence increases the security.

4.3 Block Cipher Modes

What if the size of a message is longer than the considered block size? To resolve this issue, there are five block cipher modes that have been defined by the National Institute of Standards and Technology (NIST). All these modes of operation are briefly described below.

4.3.1 Electronic Codebook (ECB) Mode

This is the simplest mode of operation. In this mode, a plaintext is divided into blocks of n bits and every block is encrypted/decrypted separately using a similar secret key. This is depicted in Figure 4.2. A plaintext is divided into m different blocks, i.e., $P_1, P_2, P_3, ..., P_m$. After encryption, it produces m blocks of ciphertext, namely, $C_1, C_2, C_3, ..., C_m$. The ECB encryption and decryption can be defined as follows:

Encryption:

$$C_1 = E_K(P_1)$$

Decryption:

$$P_1 = D_K(C_1) = E_K^{-1}(E_K(P_1))$$

In this scheme, since all the blocks are independent of each other, it does not suffer any propagation error. There are a couple of problems with this approach, which is absent in the single-block case. If a plaintext block contains two identical n-bit blocks, the corresponding

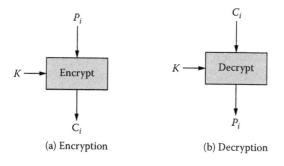

(a) Encryption   (b) Decryption

Figure 4.2 Electronic codebook (ECB) mode.

ciphertext blocks will be also identical. These regularities provide sufficient hints to a cryptoanalyst to decipher the message.

4.3.2 Cipher Block Chaining (CBC)

To overcome the deficiencies of the ECB, IBM invented the CBC mode in 1976. In this mode, every block of the plaintext is XORed with the previous ciphertext block. Therefore, identical blocks in the plaintext would not produce identical ciphertext blocks. Since the decryption is dependent on the previous block, a single bit error in a block will cause the failure. Since there is no previous ciphertext block for the first plaintext block, a fixed initialization vector (IV) is XORed with this block. The IV is not secret and must be known to the receiver. To make every message unique, a different IV could be utilized for every plaintext, which must be generated in such a way that a malicious user has no influence on it. The encryption/decryption of CBC can be expressed as follows:

Encryption:

$$C_1 = E_K(P_1 \oplus IV)$$

$$C_i = E_K(P_i \oplus C_{i-1}), \text{ where } i \geq 2$$

Decryption:

$$P_1 = E_K^{-1}(C_1 \oplus IV)$$

$$P_i = E_K^{-1}(C_i \oplus C_{i-1}), \text{ where } i \geq 2$$

Figure 4.3 illustrates the CBC scheme. The CBC also suffers from a couple of problems. For instance, if someone predictably changes bits in IV intentionally, the corresponding bits of the received value of P_1 can be changed.

4.3.3 Cipher Feedback (CFB) Mode

All the modes discussed previously require a fixed data block. If there are not enough bits to fill up a block, the padding bits are affixed to make it of a desirable size. Unlike the ECB and CBC, the CFB

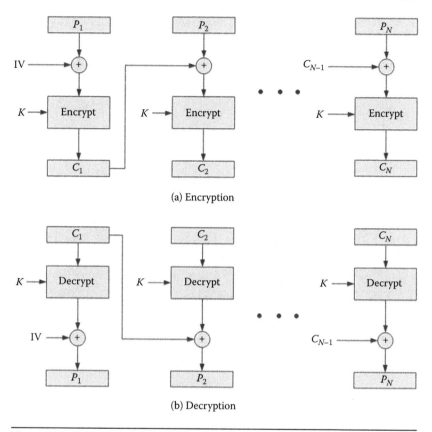

(a) Encryption

(b) Decryption

Figure 4.3 Cipher block chaining (CBC) mode.

mode is a stream cipher. One desirable property of a stream cipher is that it produces the ciphertext of the same length as the plaintext. Like the CBC, the CFB requires an IV for the initial input block that is n bits long. It also requires an integer value, denoted by s, that is assumed to be the unit of transmission. Figure 4.4 illustrates the CFB scheme. As can be observed from the figure, the first input block is the IV, and the forward cipher operation is performed over it to produce the first output block. Keeping the s most significant bits, the remaining $n - s$ bits are discarded. Then, s bits are XORed with the first plaintext segment of s bits to produce a first ciphertext segment of s bits. To produce the second input block, the IV is circularly shifted s bits to the left and the recently produced ciphertext segment is placed in the least significant s bits. This process continues until all the plaintext segments produce the relative ciphertext segment.

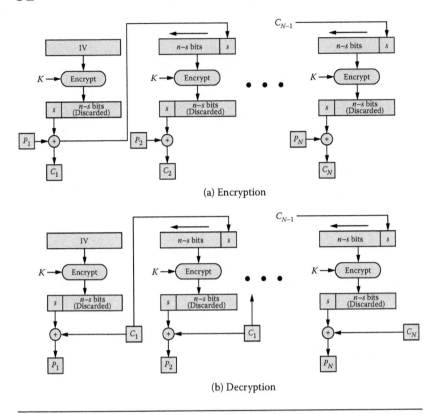

(a) Encryption

(b) Decryption

Figure 4.4 Cipher feedback (CFB) mode.

The decryption utilizes a scheme similar to that for encryption, except that the received ciphertext segment is XORed with the output block of the encryption function. Note that there is no decryption function utilized to decrypt a ciphertext, but an encryption function is used. All the operations can be expressed as below:

Encryption:

$$C_1 = E_K(IV) \oplus P_1$$

$$C_i = E_K(C_{i-1}) \oplus P_1, \text{ where } i \geq 2$$

Decryption:

$$P_1 = E_K(IV) \oplus C_1$$

$$P_i = E_K(C_{i-1}) \oplus C_1, \text{ where } i \geq 2$$

The CFB suffers from error propagation since all the ciphertext segments are related to each other.

4.3.4 Output Feedback (OFB) Mode

The OFB mode is similar in terms of structure to that of the CFB. Like the CFB, the first input block requires the IV, which is then encrypted with a secret key to produce an output block of n bits. Unlike the CFB, the ciphertext segment is not fed back to the next input block. Instead, the output of the encryption function is fed back to the next input block. In the first input block, the IV and a secret key are required by an encryption function that produces an output block. All the bits except the most significant s bits are discarded. These bits are fed back to the next input block. These s bits are also XORed with the plaintext to produce a ciphertext segment of s bits. To produce the second input block, the IV is circularly left shifted to s number of bits, and the least significant s bits are replaced by the s bits received from the previous output block. The OFB mode is illustrated in Figure 4.5. In case of decryption, no ciphertext segment is required, unlike CFB. The encryption/decryption operations can be expressed as follows:

Encryption:

$$s_1 = E_K(IV) \quad \text{and} \quad C_1 = (s_1 \oplus P_1)$$

$$s_i = E_K(s_{i-1}) \quad \text{and} \quad C_i = (s_i \oplus P_i), \text{ where } i \geq 2$$

Decryption:

$$s_1 = E_K(IV) \quad \text{and} \quad C_1 = (s_1 \oplus C_1)$$

$$s_i = E_K(s_{i-1}) \quad \text{and} \quad C_i = (s_i \oplus C_i), \text{ where } i \geq 2$$

Since all the ciphertext segments are independent of each other, this mode is more vulnerable to a message stream modification attack than CFB.

4.3.5 Counter (CTR) Mode

In this mode, a counter equal to the plaintext block is used to produce an output block. If there is a sequence of plaintext blocks, in that case,

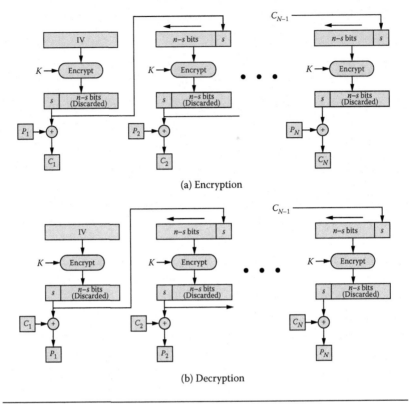

Figure 4.5 Output feedback (OFB) mode.

a sequence of counters is utilized. Each counter is distinct from the other. In general, the counter is initialized to some value that is then incremented by 1 for every subsequent block. Every block receives a counter and a key, and produces an output block. The resultant output block is XORed with the corresponding plaintext block to produce the ciphertext block. The encryption/decryption scheme can be expressed as below:

Encryption:

$$C_i = E_K(CTR_i) \oplus P_i$$

Decryption:

$$P_i = E_K(CTR_i) \oplus C_i$$

One notable advantage of this technique is that unlike the CFB and OFB modes, both the CTR encryption and the CTR decryption

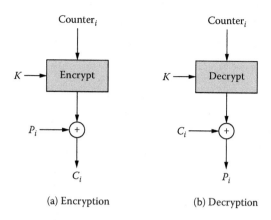

(a) Encryption (b) Decryption

Figure 4.6 Counter (CTR) mode.

can be parallelized since the second encryption can begin before the first one has finished. Moreover, if necessary, any particular ciphertext block/plaintext block can be recovered independently if the corresponding counter block can be determined. Figure 4.6 illustrates the CTR mode.

References

1. H. Feistel. Cryptography and computer privacy. *Scientific American*, May 1973.
2. C. Shannon. Communication theory of secrecy systems. *Bell Systems Technical Journal*, No. 4, 1949.
3. W. Stallings. *Cryptography and network security*, 4th ed. Pearson, India, 2006.

5

DATA ENCRYPTION STANDARD

EZAZUL ISLAM AND SAIFUL AZAD

Contents

Keywords

Block cipher
Data Encryption Algorithm
Data Encryption Standard

The Data Encryption Standard (DES) was developed in the early 1970s at IBM, and later, in 1977, the algorithm was submitted to the National Bureau of Standards (NBS) to be approved as Federal Information Processing Standard 46 (FIPS 46). With the consultation of the National Security Agency (NSA), the NBS accepted a slightly changed version of DES as FIPS 46 in the same year to provide security for the unclassified electronic data of the U.S. government. The data are encrypted using DES in 64-bit blocks, which are encrypted using a 56-bit symmetric key to provide confidentiality and privacy.

Some experts refer to DES as an encryption standard and Data Encryption Algorithm (DEA) as the basic algorithm. In recent times, DEA and DES are used interchangeably. On the other hand, there is another extension of DEA that is named Triple DEA (TDEA). The Triple DEA and DEA are typically referred to as Triple DES and DES, respectively. For our readers' convenience, we use DES and 3DES in this chapter to refer to these algorithms.

Like most of the symmetric block algorithms, DES is also based on a structure referred to as a Feistel cipher, which was already introduced to the reader in Chapter 4. The DES is comprised of 16 rounds, where a separate key is utilized in each round. All 16 keys are generated from a 56-bit key. Before introducing DES to the reader in detail, it is necessary to know the primitive operations that DES utilizes. Consequently, in the following section, we discuss various primitive operations related to DES with relevant examples.

5.1 Primitive Operations

All the primitive operations utilized in DES can be separated into two groups: (1) operations for encryption/decryption and (2) operations for key generation. All these operations are discussed below.

5.1.1 Operations for Encryption/Decryption

DES encryption/decryption is based on the following primitive operations:

1. **Exclusive disjunction/exclusive or (XOR).** *Exclusive disjunction* or *exclusive or* is a logical operation that outputs true whenever both inputs differ from each other (e.g., one is true and the other is false) (Table 5.1). It is symbolized by the prefix operator *J* and by the infix operators XOR, EOR, EXOR, $\underline{\vee}$, $\oplus$, $\leftrightarrow$, and $\neq$.
2. **Initial permutation (IP).** In initial permutation, the 64 bits of the data are rearranged to another 64 bits of data according to a given table (Table 5.2 in this example). Each entry in the table shows the new arrangement of a bit from its initial position. For instance, the 58th bit of data becomes the first bit of the output data after the permutation, and the 1st bit of data becomes the 40th bit of the output data after permutation. An example is given below to demonstrate the rearrangements of the bits after permutation.

Table 5.1   XOR Truth Table

INPUT		OUTPUT
0	0	0
0	1	1
1	0	1
1	1	1

Table 5.2   Table Utilized for Initial Permutation (IP)

INITIAL PERMUTATION (IP)							
58	50	42	34	26	18	10	2
60	52	44	36	28	20	12	4
62	54	46	38	30	22	14	6
64	56	48	40	32	24	16	8
57	49	41	33	25	17	9	1
59	51	43	35	27	19	11	3
61	53	45	37	29	21	13	5
63	55	47	39	31	23	15	7

Example

Actual bit sequence:

11001000001111111010100100100110101011101101101110100
11111100100

After initial permutation:

10100001001000101101101001100110111101011101111000110
11101111010

3. **Inverse permutation (IP^{-1}).** Like initial permutation, a block of code again needs to be rearranged (according to Table 5.3). This is known as inverse permutation (IP^{-1}). Using IP^{-1}, the original ordering of the bits is rearranged.

Example

Actual bit sequence:

10100001001000101101101001100110111101011101111000110
11101111010

After inverse permutation:

11001000001111111010100100100110101011101101101110100
11111100100

From this example, we can observe that if no other operation is performed, we can get the actual bit sequence returns if we do inverse permutation immediately after initial permutation.

Table 5.3   Table Utilized for Inverse Permutation (IP^{-1})

INVERSE PERMUTATION (IP^{-1})							
40	8	48	16	56	24	64	32
39	7	47	15	55	23	63	31
38	6	46	14	54	22	62	30
37	5	45	13	53	21	61	29
36	4	44	12	52	20	60	28
35	3	43	11	51	19	59	27
34	2	42	10	50	18	58	26
33	1	41	9	49	17	57	25

4. **Expansion permutation.** In every round of DES, a 64-bit block is divided into two halves of 32 bits each, namely, left and right blocks. Again, since each round utilizes a key of 48 bits, it is necessary to enlarge a block to be equivalent to the round key size. Generally, a right-side block has expanded to a 48-bit block, which is then XORed with the selected round key. A 32-bit block is expanded utilizing Table 5.4.

Example

Bits sequence in right block:

1100100000111111101010100100100110

After expansion permutation:

011001010000000111111111110101010010100100001101

5. **Substitution.** The expanded 48-bit block is required to shrink into a 32-bit block again. For this purpose, a 48-bit block is broken into a 6-bit chunk that is then fed into a substitution box (also known as S-box), which produces a 4-bit output for each 6-bit output. There are eight S-boxes utilized in the substitution procedure, which are given in Table 5.5. Since there are 64 possible input values (6 bits) and only 16 possible output values (4 bits), the S-box could map several input values to a single output value. The leftmost 6-bit chunk is substituted by S_1-box, the next 6-bit chunk is substituted by S_2-box, and so on. Consequently, the rightmost chunk is substituted by S_8-box. Again, among the 6 bits, the first and last bit form a 2-bit binary number that indicates the row number,

Table 5.4 Table Utilized in Expansion Permutation

EXPANSION PERMUTATION					
32	1	2	3	4	5
4	5	6	7	8	9
8	9	10	11	12	13
12	13	14	15	16	17
16	17	18	19	20	21
20	21	22	23	24	25
24	25	26	27	28	29
28	29	30	31	32	1

Table 5.5   All the S-Boxes Are Defined

S_1

	0000	0001	0010	0011	0100	0101	0110	0111	1000	1001	1010	1011	1100	1101	1110	1111
00	14	4	13	1	2	15	11	8	3	10	6	12	5	9	0	7
01	0	15	7	4	14	2	13	1	10	6	12	11	9	5	3	8
10	4	1	14	8	13	6	2	11	15	12	9	7	3	10	5	0
11	15	12	8	2	4	9	1	7	5	11	3	14	10	0	6	13

S_2

	0000	0001	0010	0011	0100	0101	0110	0111	1000	1001	1010	1011	1100	1101	1110	1111
00	15	1	8	14	6	11	3	4	9	7	2	13	12	0	5	10
01	3	13	4	7	15	2	8	14	12	0	1	10	6	9	11	5
10	0	14	7	11	10	4	13	1	5	8	12	6	9	3	2	15
11	13	8	10	1	3	15	4	2	11	6	7	12	0	5	14	9

S_3

	0000	0001	0010	0011	0100	0101	0110	0111	1000	1001	1010	1011	1100	1101	1110	1111
00	10	0	9	14	6	3	15	5	1	13	12	7	11	4	2	8
01	13	7	0	9	3	4	6	10	2	8	5	14	12	11	15	1
10	13	6	4	9	8	15	3	0	11	1	2	12	5	10	14	7
11	1	10	13	0	6	9	8	7	4	15	14	3	11	5	2	12

S_4

	0000	0001	0010	0011	0100	0101	0110	0111	1000	1001	1010	1011	1100	1101	1110	1111
00	7	13	14	3	0	6	9	10	1	2	8	5	11	12	4	15
01	13	8	11	5	6	15	0	3	4	7	2	12	1	10	14	9
10	10	6	9	0	12	11	7	13	15	1	3	14	5	2	8	4
11	3	15	0	6	10	1	13	8	9	4	5	11	12	7	2	14

S_5

	0000	0001	0010	0011	0100	0101	0110	0111	1000	1001	1010	1011	1100	1101	1110	1111
00	2	12	4	1	7	10	11	6	8	5	3	15	13	0	14	9
01	14	11	2	12	4	7	13	1	5	0	15	10	3	9	8	6
10	4	2	1	11	10	13	7	8	15	9	12	5	6	3	0	14
11	11	8	12	7	1	14	2	13	6	15	0	9	10	4	5	3

S_6

	0000	0001	0010	0011	0100	0101	0110	0111	1000	1001	1010	1011	1100	1101	1110	1111
00	12	1	10	15	9	2	6	8	0	13	3	4	14	7	5	11
01	10	15	4	2	7	12	9	5	6	1	13	14	0	11	3	8
10	9	14	15	5	2	8	12	3	7	0	4	10	1	13	11	6
11	4	3	2	12	9	5	15	10	11	14	1	7	6	0	8	13

S_7

	0000	0001	0010	0011	0100	0101	0110	0111	1000	1001	1010	1011	1100	1101	1110	1111
00	4	11	2	14	15	0	8	13	3	12	9	7	5	10	6	1
01	13	0	11	7	4	9	1	10	14	3	5	12	2	15	8	6
10	1	4	11	13	12	3	7	14	10	15	6	8	0	5	9	2
11	6	11	13	8	1	4	10	7	9	5	0	15	14	2	3	12

S_8

	0000	0001	0010	0011	0100	0101	0110	0111	1000	1001	1010	1011	1100	1101	1110	1111
00	13	2	8	4	6	15	11	1	10	9	3	14	5	0	12	7
01	1	15	13	8	10	3	7	4	12	5	6	11	0	14	9	2
10	7	11	4	1	9	12	14	2	0	6	10	13	15	3	5	8
11	2	1	14	7	4	10	8	13	15	12	9	0	3	5	6	11

Table 5.6   Permutation Table

			PERMUTATION				
16	7	20	21	29	12	28	17
1	15	23	26	5	18	31	10
2	8	24	14	32	27	3	9
19	13	30	6	22	11	4	25

and the middle four bits select one among the 16 columns. For instance, in S_5, a 6-bit chunk 011101 is substituted with a 4-bit chunk 1000. Here, the first bit and last bit form 01, which means row number 1 is selected. Then, the middle four bits 1110 indicate the column number, i.e., 14. If we look at row 2 and column 14, the value is 8, whose binary equivalent is 1000.

6. **Permutation.** The 32-bit block generated after substitution is rearranged using a permutation operation where a 32-bit output comes from a 32-bit input by permuting the bits of the input block. The table that is utilized in this operation is shown in Table 5.6.

Example

Before permutation:

11001000001111111010100100100110

After permutation:

10010101110010101011010011100100

5.1.2 Operations for Subkey Generation

DES subkey generation is based on the following primitive operations:

1. **Permuted choice 1 (PC-1).** DES takes a 64-bit symmetric key from the user, which is then permuted according to Table 5.7. It could be observed from the table that the first entry is 57; this means that the 57th bit of the original key K becomes the first bit of the permuted key K_P. Again, the 49th bit of the original key becomes the second bit of the permuted key.

Table 5.7 Table for Permuted Choice 1

		PERMUTED CHOICE 1				
57	49	41	33	25	17	9
1	58	50	42	34	26	18
10	2	59	51	43	35	27
19	11	3	60	52	44	36
63	55	47	39	31	23	15
7	62	54	46	38	30	22
14	6	61	53	45	37	29
21	13	5	28	20	12	4

Example

Before permutation:

K = 110010000011111110101001001001101010111011011011110
10011111100100

After permutated choice 1:

K_p = 1111010110100001101111000100111101011011011000110
1110010

2. **Left shifting.** A permuted key is then separated into two blocks, left and right, where each of them is 28 bits long. After that, each block is shifted to the left to a fixed number of bits, which again depends on the round. For a different round, the bits to be left shifted are different, which are shown in Table 5.8. For instance, in the eighth round, 2-bit left shifting takes place, whereas, in the ninth round, it is only 1 bit. When a block is shifted to the left, each bit moves one place to the left, except for the first bit, which is cycled to the end of the block.

Example

Let us assume that the shifting operation is for generating a key of round 8. First, we can find out how many bits are to be shifted from Table 5.8, which is 2 bits in this example.
Before left shifting:

1111010110100001110111100010

After left shifting:

1101011010000111011110001011

Table 5.8   Schedule of Left Shifting

ROUND NUMBER	BITS ROTATED
1	1
2	1
3	2
4	2
5	2
6	2
7	2
8	2
9	1
10	2
11	2
12	2
13	2
14	2
15	2
16	1

Table 5.9   Table for Permuted Choice 2

PERMUTED CHOICE 2							
14	17	11	24	1	5	3	28
15	6	21	10	23	19	12	4
26	8	16	7	27	20	13	2
41	52	31	37	47	55	30	40
51	45	33	48	44	49	39	56
34	53	46	42	50	36	29	32

3. **Permuted choice 2 (PC-2).** After the left shifting operation, both separated blocks are combined together, which form a block of 56 bits. Then, they are rearranged and shrunk to produce a round key of 48 bits. This permuted choice 2 is performed utilizing Table 5.9.

Example

Before permuted choice 2:

110010000011111110101001001001101010111011011011101110100111

After permutated choice 2:

111111001010011000101011101111101111111100010000

5.2 Basic Structure

A basic structure of DES is portrayed in Figure 5.1. DES supports a 64-bit block that is subjected to go through an initial permutation. This permuted block is then passed through 16 rounds, where every round is comprised of various operations, depicted in Figure 5.2. The operations of 48-bit key generations for every round from a 64-bit key are also portrayed in both figures. After visiting the last round, a 32-bit swapping is performed on the 64-bit block. Finally, the ciphertext is generated after the inverse permutation operation.

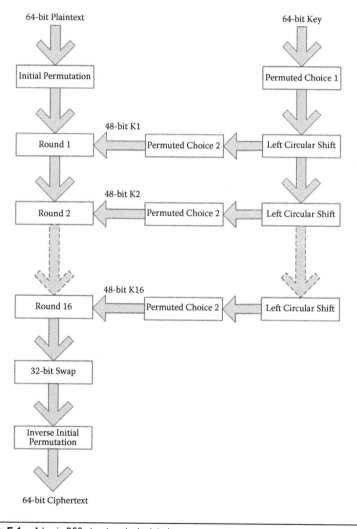

Figure 5.1   A basic DES structure is depicted.

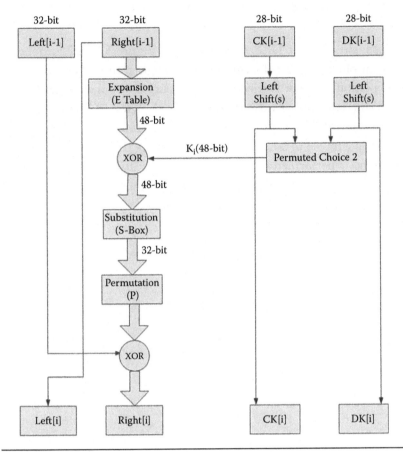

Figure 5.2   Single-round operations in DES.

5.3 DES Encryption Algorithm

Following is the pseudocode for DES encryption in which the function named *Encrypt* takes the plaintext message as a parameter and performs the essential operations to produce the ciphertext.

Algorithm 5.1: Encrypt (M)

```
Begin
        C ← IP(M)
        for round ← 1 to 16
                KEYi ← SubKey (K, round)
                L(i-1) ← LEFT (C)
                R(i-1) ← RIGHT (C)
                Li ← R(i-1)
```

```
        Ri ← L(i-1) xor (Permutation (Substitution
(KEYi xor Expansion(R(i-1)))))
        end for
        C ← swap(C)
        C ← IP-1(C)
        return C
End
```

5.4 DES Decryption Algorithm

For decryption, the steps are the same as for encryption, but the difference is in the order of using the keys for each of the rounds.

Algorithm 5.2: Decrypt (C)

```
Begin
        M ← IP(C)
        for round ← 16 to 1
                KEYi ← SubKey (K, round)
                Li ← LEFT (M)
                Ri ← RIGHT (M)
                R(i-1) ← Li
                L(i-1) ← Ri xor (Permutation (Substitution
(KEYi xor Expansion(R(i-1)))))
        end for
        M← swap(M)
        M← IP-1(M)
        return M
End
```

5.5 Implementation

DES implementation using C++ is described below.

5.5.1 C++ Library Headers

The following built-in headers are utilized in the program:

cstring: Used for the purpose of string manipulation, string length measurement, and moving the contents of the message to work with and the ciphertext. When working with message encryption and decryption, there is a need for string handling. During the process of encryption and decryption, the functionalities are like string length calculation, string copy from one place to another, and the input-output of a string message or ciphertext.

iostream: The basic header file of the C++ library. It is the header that consists of the core library of C++. The core library is mostly focused on the input-output stream-related functions. I and O refer to input and output, respectively. On the other hand, stream refers to the flow of bits in the input and output buffers of the computer system.

cstdlib: Defines multiple general purpose functions, such as the functions related to random number generation, communication with the system, and arithmetic operations.

5.5.2 The DES Class

```
class DES{
public:
    int keyi[16][48],
        total[64],
        left[32],
        right[32],
        ck[28],
        dk[28],
        expansion[48],
        z[48],
        xor1[48],
        sub[32],
        p[32],
        xor2[32],
        temp[64],
        pc1[56],
        ip[64],
        inv[8][8];

        char final[1000];
    void keygen();
        void PermChoice1();
        void split_key();
//left circular shifts take place
        void PermChoice2();
```

```
//16 keys of 56 bits keys are created
    void IP();
//L0 and R0 are created using IP : 64 bit total
//32 bit R(n-1) is expanded into 48 bit
    void Expansion();
        //Expansion applied on the right half, R(n-1)
        //32 bit R(n-1) becomes 48 bit R(n-1) now
    void xor_oneE(int);
        //xor the 48 bit key(n) with 48 bit R(n-1)
    void substitution();
        //48 bit resultant becomes 32 bit now using 16 S
          boxes
    void permutation();
        //permutation operation takes place on 32 bit
          message bit
    void xor_two();
        //now the resultant of 32 bit is xored with
          L(n-1)
        //xored resultant becomes R(n)
    void inverse();
        //inver permutation of R(n)L(n)
    void xor_oneD(int);
        //xor of 48 bit key and expanded message for
          decryption
    char *Encrypt(char *);
    char *Decrypt(char *);
};
```

All the member variables and functions of the DES class are publicly accessible. For this reason, the members are declared in the public scope. No private or public differentiation is needed due to our basic target of this presentation being to provide a technical knowledge of how DES works, but not to provide the concept of object orientation.

5.5.3 Introducing the Member Variables of DES Class

Here, in the above class declaration, int keyi[16][48] is a two-dimensional array that holds all 16 keys that are made after applying permutation choice 2. Permutation choice 2 is applied with the help of the C++ function *void PermChoice2()*, defined in class DES.

5.5.4 Introducing the Member Functions of DES Class

The member function *IP()* is responsible for the initial permutation operation on the message text that is to be encrypted.

5.5.5 The Keygen() Function

```
1.      void DES::keygen(){
2.             PermChoice1();
3.             split_key();
4.             int noshift = 0,round;
5.             for(round = 1; round< = 16; round++){
6.                    if(round = =1||round = =2||round =
                      =9||round = =16)
7.                           noshift = 1;
8.                    else
9.                           noshift = 2;
10.
11.                   while(noshift>0){
12.                          int t;
13.                          t = ck[0];
14.                          for(int i = 0; i<28; i++)
15.                                  ck[i] = ck[i+1];
16.                          ck[27] = t;
17.                          t = dk[0];
18.                          for(int i = 0; i<28; i++)
19.                                  dk[i] = dk[i+1];
20.                          dk[27] = t;
21.                          noshift— ;
22.                   }
23.                   cout << endl << "round " << round
                      << endl;
24.                   PermChoice2();
25.                   for(int i = 0; i<48; i++) //stores
                      each of the subkeys
26.                   keyi[round-1][i] = z[i];
27.            }
28.      }
```

A key is utilized to create the 16 different subkeys. To make those subkeys, various operations have to be conducted so that the subkeys show proper variations that will help make those keys as strong as possible. Basic functionalities of the function *keygen()* are selecting a secret key, operating permutation choice 1 on that key, splitting that single key into two parts, conducting a left circular shift to produce 16 subkeys, and finally, generating 16 secret keys by applying permutation choice 2 on them.

PermChoice1() converts the actual 64-bit secret key into a 56-bit secret key. The details of the *PermChoice1()* function are described in the next section of this chapter. Another function, named *split_key()*, splits the 56-bit permuted key into two parts so that each of the parts becomes 28 bits in length. In the fourth line of the above code, the variables to track the number of shift and round are declared. There are 16 rounds of processing steps, as the subkeys are 16 in number.

The sixth line shows the number of left circular shifts, which varies according to the round. All the rounds do not have the same number of left circular shifts. From lines 11 to 22 left circular shift operations take place. The shifting operations are applied on the arrays named ck and dk, as the split subkeys are stored in these arrays. Line 23 outputs the current round number. The scope of the for loop is from lines 5 to 27; the code inside this scope is repeated for each of the 16 rounds. Shifted bits are stored into ck and dk arrays in lines 15 and 19 respectively. Then in the 24th line, permutation choice 2 comes into action, actually permuting each of the 56-bit subkeys to convert all of them into 48-bit subkeys. After the execution of the *PermChoice2()* function, the array named z[] holds the permuted bits of the 48-bit subkey, and in line 26 the 48-bit subkey is stored in the keyi[][] array. Thus, each of the 16 subkeys of 48 bits is created and stored into the keyi[][] array.

5.5.6 The PermChoice1() Function

```
1. void DES::PermChoice1(){//Permutation Choice-1
2.      cout << "key: " << endl;
3.      for (int i = 0; i < 64; i++) {
4.                 cout << key[i] << "\t";
5.             if (((i + 1)% 8) == 0) cout << endl;
6.      }
7.      int k = 57,i;
8.      for(i = 0; i<28; i++){
9.          pc1[i] = key[k-1];
10.         if(k-8>0) k = k-8;
11.         else k = k+57;
12.     }
13.     k = 63;
```

```
14.    for(i = 28; i<52; i++){
15.           pc1[i] = key[k-1];
16.           if(k-8>0) k = k-8;
17.           else   k = k+55;
18.    }
19.    k = 28;
20.    for(i = 52; i<56; i++){
21.           pc1[i] = key[k-1];
22.           k = k-8;
23.    }
24.    cout << endl << "After permutation choice 1:"
       << endl;
25.    for (i = 0; i < 56; i++){
26.           cout << pc1[i] << "\t";
27.           if (((i + 1)% 7) = = 0) cout << endl;
28.    }
29.    }
```

In the above function definition, at first the *PermChoice1()* function was called to make the first permutation operation on the single secret key. After conducting the first permutation operations on the 64-bit secret key, the resultant key holds 56 bits. The rest of the bits are removed from the actual key. The final product of the above function is the 56-bit secret key. All of the cout keywords in the source code are to provide a proper output so that the user can get a proper idea of how the program is running and whether all the statements are giving the correct output or not.

For each of the blocks in a 64-bit key, the last bit of every octet is removed. There are eight blocks in a 64-bit key. If each of them loses 1 bit, the total number of bits becomes 56 bits. Thus, 56-bit key is produced and is stored in the array named pc1[].

5.5.7 The Split_Key() Function

```
1.     void DES::split_key(){
2.            int i,k = 0;
3.            for(i = 0; i<28; i++){ //creates 56
              bits key with Permutation by PC-1
4.                   ck[i] = pc1[i];
5.            }
6.            for(i = 28; i<56; i++){
7.                   dk[k] = pc1[i];
```

```
8.                          k++;
9.                      }
10.                     cout << endl << "Print C0 " << endl;
11.                     for(i = 0; i<28; i++){ //left 28
                        bits of permuted 56 bit key
12.                         cout << ck[i] << "\t";
13.                         if (((i + 1)% 7) = = 0) cout
                            << endl;
14.                     }
15.                     cout << endl << "Print D0 " << endl;
16.                     for(i = 28; i<56; i++){ //right 28
                        bits of permuted 56 bit key
17.                         cout << dk[i] << "\t";
18.                         if (((i + 1)% 7) = = 0) cout
                            << endl;
19.                     }
20.     }
```

After executing the function *split_key()*, the 56-bit key stored in pc1[64] is divided into two parts. One is stored in ck[28] and another in dk[28]. Both of the arrays can hold 28 bits of values, so that lines 3 to 9 are executed to split the 56-bit key into two parts and store them in the ck[28] and dk[28] arrays. The rest of the lines, 10 to 19, are outputting the split key for test purposes, whether the split has taken place perfectly or not.

5.5.8 *The PermChoice2() Function*

```
1.      void DES::PermChoice2(){
2.                  int per[56],i,k;
3.                  for(i = 0; i<28; i++) per[i] =
                    ck[i];
4.                  for(k = 0,i = 28; i<56; i++) per[i]
                    = dk[k++];
5.                  z[0] = per[13];
6.                  z[1] = per[16];
7.                  z[2] = per[10];
8.                  z[3] = per[23];
9.                  z[4] = per[0];
10.                 z[5] = per[4];
11.                 z[6] = per[2];
12.                 z[7] = per[27];
13.                 z[8] = per[14];
```

```
14.              z[9]  = per[5];
15.              z[10] = per[20];
16.              z[11] = per[9];
17.              z[12] = per[22];
18.              z[13] = per[18];
19.              z[14] = per[11];
20.              z[15] = per[3];
21.              z[16] = per[25];
22.              z[17] = per[7];
23.              z[18] = per[15];
24.              z[19] = per[6];
25.              z[20] = per[26];
26.              z[21] = per[19];
27.              z[22] = per[12];
28.              z[23] = per[1];
29.              z[24] = per[40];
30.              z[25] = per[51];
31.              z[26] = per[30];
32.              z[27] = per[36];
33.              z[28] = per[46];
34.              z[29] = per[54];
35.              z[30] = per[29];
36.              z[31] = per[39];
37.              z[32] = per[50];
38.              z[33] = per[46];
39.              z[34] = per[32];
40.              z[35] = per[47];
41.              z[36] = per[43];
42.              z[37] = per[48];
43.              z[38] = per[38];
44.              z[39] = per[55];
45.              z[40] = per[33];
46.              z[41] = per[52];
47.              z[42] = per[45];
48.              z[43] = per[41];
49.              z[44] = per[49];
50.              z[45] = per[35];
51.              z[46] = per[28];
52.              z[47] = per[31];
53.              cout << endl << "After permutation
                 choice 2 " << endl;
54.              for(int i = 0; i<48; i++){
                 //creates the 48 bits permutation
                 table(PC-2)
55.                  cout << z[i] << "\t";
```

```
56.                        if (((i + 1)% 6) = = 0) cout
                           << endl;
57.                        }//for ends here
58.                    } //PermChoice2 function ends here
```

The above function, *PermChoice2()*, is called separately for each of the 16 rounds. Hence, the function is called 16 times. The basic target of the function is to reduce the 56-bit key of the current round to a 48-bit key. After permuting the secret key into 48 bits, the result is stored in the array named z[48], which holds the 48-bit key. When the permuting operation is finished, the next step starts automatically to store the 48-bit permuted key into another array, declared keyi[16][48]. That holds all 16 keys, which are 48 bits in size individually.

5.5.9 The Encrypt(char *) Function

Here comes the part to do something with the plaintext that is the actual message to be encrypted. For this situation, the plaintext also has 64 bits; the whole message/plaintext is divided into blocks of 64 bits.

```
1.      char* DES::Encrypt(char *Text1){
2.                      int i,a1,j,nB,m,iB,k,K,B[8],n,
                        t,d,round, mc = 0;
3.                      char *Text = new char[1000];
4.                      strcpy(Text,Text1);
5.                      i = strlen(Text);
6.                      a1 = i%8;
7.
8.                      if(a1 ! = 0)
9.                          for(j = 0; j<8-a1;
                            j++,i++) Text[i] = ' ';
                            //add padding bits with
                            space
10.                     Text[i] = '\0';
11.                     for(iB = 0,nB = 0,m = 0;
                        m<(strlen(Text)/8); m++){
12.                     //Repeat for TextLength/8
                        times.
13.                     for(iB = 0,i = 0; i<8;
                        i++,nB++){
14.                         n = (int)Text[nB];
```

```
15.                    cout << " n is " << n
                       << endl;
16.                    for(K = 7; n> = 1; K— )
                       {
17.                            B[K] = n%2;
                               //Converting
                               8-Bytes to
                               64-bit Binary
                               Format
18.                            cout << "B[" <<
                               K << "] is " <<
                               B[K] << endl;
19.                            n/= 2;
20.                    }
21.                    for(; K> = 0; K— ) B[K]
                       = 0;
22.                    for(K = 0; K<8;
                       K++,iB++) total[iB] =
                       B[K];
23.                    //Now 'total' contains
                       the 64-Bit binary
                       format of Bytes
24.            }
25.            IP();
26.            for(i = 0; i<64; i++)
               total[i] = ip[i];
               //Store values of ip[64] into
               total[64]
27.            for(i = 0; i<32; i++) left[i]
               = total[i];
28.            for(; i<64; i++) right[i-32]
               = total[i];
29.            for(round = 1; round< = 16;
               round++){
30.                    Expansion(); //E bit
                       selection
31.                    //Performing expansion
                       on 'right[32]' to get
                       'expansion[48]'
32.                    xor_oneE(round);
33.                    //Performing XOR
                       operation on
                       expansion[48],z[48] to
                       get xor1[48]
34.                    substitution();
```

```
35.                          //Perform substitution
                             on xor1[48] to get
                             sub[32]
36.                          permutation();
37.                          //Performing
                             Permutation on sub[32]
                             to get p[32]
38.                          xor_two();   //xor with
                             32 bit L0 and f value
39.                          //Performing XOR
                             operation on
                             left[32],p[32] to get
                             xor2[32]
40.                          for(i = 0; i<32; i++)
                             left[i] = right[i];
41.                          //Dumping right[32]
                             into left[32]
42.                          for(i = 0; i<32; i++)
                             right[i] = xor2[i];
43.                          //Dumping xor2[32] into
                             right[32]
44.                      }
45.                      for(i = 0; i<32; i++) temp[i]
                         = right[i];//Dumping–
                         >[swap32bit]
46.                      for(; i<64; i++) temp[i] =
                         left[i-32];//
                         left[32],right[32] into
                         temp[64]
47.                      inverse();
48.                      //Inversing the bits of
                         temp[64] to get inv[8][8]
49.                      /* Obtaining the Cypher-Text
                         into final[1000]*/
50.                      k = 128;
51.                      d = 0;
52.                      for(i = 0; i<8; i++){
53.                          for(j = 0; j<8; j++){
54.                              d = d+inv[i]
                                 [j]*k;
55.                              k = k/2;
56.                          }
57.                          final[mc++] = (char)d;
58.                          k = 128;
59.                          d = 0;
```

```
60.                              }
61.                    }//for loop ends here
62.                    final[mc] = '\0';
63.                    return(final);
64.     }
```

Before executing the encryption process, the plaintext is padded with some space characters to make the plaintext string length divisible by 8; thus, the number of bits in the plaintext is always a multiple of 64. A character size is 1 byte, and 1 byte represents 8 bits. After padding the plaintext with an empty space character, the for loop in the 11th line rotates for each of the eight characters in the plaintext, because eight characters consist of 64 bits. In lines 13 to 23, each of the 8 bytes is converted into 64 bits and stored in the total[64] array. Thus, the for loop continues for each of the 64 bits in the plaintext bit stream.

The function *Encrypt(char *)* takes a parameter that will receive the plaintext message and continue its next steps. In lines 8 and 9, extra bits are added to make the size of the plaintext string a multiple of 8. In this way, it is ensured that each of the blocks has 8 bits. After the execution of lines 10 to 24, the array total[64] contains the 64-bit format of the plaintext message.

In line 25, the initial permutation operation is done over the 64-bit block of plaintext message. It actually reorganizes the bit stream into some predefined sequences. The operations of the function *IP()* will be discussed in the latter sections of this chapter. In lines 26, 27, and 28, three operations are done. In line 26, initial permuted bits are copied into total[64]. In line 27, half of the 64 bits of the total bit stream are copied into the left[32] array, and the second half of the same array is copied into right[32] array. Thus, the 64-bit plaintext message is divided into two parts and stored into two arrays, left[32] and right[32].

From lines 29 to 44, several rounds of the same operations have been conducted to continue the whole encryption process—16 rounds in the process. Now, before starting the for loop, assuming that the left[32] array holds the 32 bits of the plaintext message and the right[32] array contains the right bits of the plaintext message, the operations are briefly mentioned below.

```
17.    };
18.    int a[8][6],k = 0,i,j,p,q,count = 0,g = 0,v;
19.    for(i = 0; i<8; i++){
20.    for(j = 0; j<6; j++){
21.    a[i][j] = xor1[k++];
22.    }
23.    }
24.    for(i = 0; i<8; i++){
25.    p = 1;
26.    q = 0;
27.    k = (a[i][0]*2)+(a[i][5]*1);
28.    j = 4;

29.    while(j>0){
30.    q = q+(a[i][j]*p);
31.    p = p*2;
32.    j- ;
33.    }

34.    count = i+1;
35.    switch(count){
36.    case 1:
37.    v = s1[k][q];
38.    break;
39.    case 2:
40.    v = s2[k][q];
41.    break;
42.    case 3:
43.    v = s3[k][q];
44.    break;
45.    case 4:
46.    v = s4[k][q];
47.    break;
48.    case 5:
49.    v = s5[k][q];
50.    break;
51.    case 6:
52.    v = s6[k][q];
53.    break;
54.    case 7:
55.    v = s7[k][q];
56.    break;
57.    case 8:
58.    v = s8[k][q];
59.    break;
60.    }
```

```
61.     int d,i = 3,a[4];
62.     while(v>0){
63.     d = v%2;
64.     a[i- ] = d;
65.     v = v/2;
66.     }
67.     while(i> = 0){
68.     a[i- ] = 0;
69.     }
70.     for(i = 0; i<4; i++)
71.     sub[g++] = a[i];
72.     }
73.     }
```

The function substitution has eight *S*-boxes that are used for substituting the extra bits from the 48-bit XORed result. Now, the basic target of this function is to reduce the bit size of the 48-bit content that was XORed with the 48-bit key; the new size of that XORed content will be 32 after the execution of the function. For the 48-bit content there are eight blocks of bits in which each of the blocks has six bits. The first and the last bit together indicate the row number of the *S*-box, and the other four bits indicate the column number in the *S*-box array. Out of eight blocks, each of them indicates the respective *S*-boxes; for example, the first block of 6 bits refers to s1[4][16], the second block refers to s2[4][16], and so on up to s8[4][16]. After finishing the function call, the 48-bit content is converted into 32-bit content and stored in the sub[32] array. With this bit value the next function, *permutation()*, continues.

5.5.14 The Permutation() Function

```
void DES::permutation(){
        p[0]  = sub[15];
        p[1]  = sub[6];
        p[2]  = sub[19];
        p[3]  = sub[20];
        p[4]  = sub[28];
        p[5]  = sub[11];
        p[6]  = sub[27];
        p[7]  = sub[16];
        p[8]  = sub[0];
        p[9]  = sub[14];
```

```
    p[10]  =  sub[22];
    p[11]  =  sub[25];
    p[12]  =  sub[4];
    p[13]  =  sub[17];
    p[14]  =  sub[30];
    p[15]  =  sub[9];
    p[16]  =  sub[1];
    p[17]  =  sub[7];
    p[18]  =  sub[23];
    p[19]  =  sub[13];
    p[20]  =  sub[31];
    p[21]  =  sub[26];
    p[22]  =  sub[2];
    p[23]  =  sub[8];
    p[24]  =  sub[18];
    p[25]  =  sub[12];
    p[26]  =  sub[29];
    p[27]  =  sub[5];
    p[28]  =  sub[21];
    p[29]  =  sub[10];
    p[30]  =  sub[3];
    p[31]  =  sub[24];
}
```

The above function is utilized to permute the content of the sub[32] and stores all 32 bits in another array named p[32]. Finishing the function execution, the p[32] array holds the 32 permuted bits.

5.5.15 *The xor_two() Function*

```
1.      void DES::xor_two(){
2.      int i;
3.      for(i = 0; i<32; i++){
4.              xor2[i] = left[i]^p[i];
5.      }
6.      }
```

The above function actually makes an XOR operation between the content of the left[32] array and the immediately permuted 32 bits of p[32]. The result of 32 bits is saved in xor2[32]. After the function execution, the next operations continue from line 40 in the function named *Encrypt(char *)*. Readers are requested to jump into that specific line of code to have a look at the next steps.

*5.5.16 The Decrypt(char *) Function*

```
1.      char * DES::Decrypt(char *Text1){
2.              int i,a1,j,nB,m,iB,k,K,B[8],n,t,d,round;
3.              char *Text = new char[1000];
4.              unsigned char ch;
5.              strcpy(Text,Text1);
6.              i = strlen(Text);
7.              //keygen();
8.              int mc = 0;
9.              for(iB = 0,nB = 0,m = 0;
                m<(strlen(Text)/8); m++){
10.                     /*Repeat for TextLength/8 times*/
11.                     for(iB = 0,i = 0; i<8; i++,nB++){
12.                             ch = Text[nB];
13.                             n = (int)ch;//(int)Text[nB];
14.                             for(K = 7; n> = 1; K- ){
15.                                     B[K] = n%2; //
                                        Converting 8-Bytes to
                                        64-bit Binary Format
16.                                     n/= 2;
17.                             }
18.                             for(; K> = 0; K- ) B[K] = 0;
19.                             for(K = 0; K<8; K++,iB++)
                                total[iB] = B[K];
20.                             /*Now 'total' contains the
                                64-Bit binary format of
                                8-Bytes*/
21.                     }
22.                     IP();
23.                     for(i = 0; i<64; i++) total[i] =
                        ip[i];
24.                     for(i = 0; i<32; i++) left[i] =
                        total[i];
25.                     for(; i<64; i++) right[i-32] =
                        total[i];
26.                     for(round = 1; round< = 16;
                                round++){
27.                             Expansion();
28.                             xor_oneD(round);
29.                             substitution();
30.                             permutation();
```

```
31.                         xor_two();
32.                         for(i = 0; i<32; i++) left[i]
                            = right[i];
33.                         for(i = 0; i<32; i++)
                            right[i] = xor2[i];
34.               }//16 rounds end here
35.               for(i = 0; i<32; i++) temp[i] =
                  right[i];
36.               for(; i<64; i++) temp[i] =
                  left[i-32];
37.               inverse();
38.               /* Obtaining the Cypher-Text into
                  final[1000]*/
39.               k = 128;
40.               d = 0;
41.               for(i = 0; i<8; i++){
42.                         for(j = 0; j<8; j++){
43.                                 d = d+inv[i][j]*k;
44.                                 k = k/2;
45.                         }
46.                         final[mc++] = (char)d;
47.                         k = 128;
48.                         d = 0;
49.                   }
50.         }       //for loop ends here
51.         final[mc] = '\0';
52.         char *final1 = new char[1000];
53.         for(i = 0,j = strlen(Text);
            i<strlen(Text); i++,j++)
54.         final1[i] = final[j];
55.         final1[i] = '\0';
56.         return(final);
57.   }
```

The function prototype of the function *Decrypt(char *)* indicates that it takes a character pointer as a parameter and returns another memory address so that the type is also a pointer. This is a function responsible for decrypting or deciphering the encrypted message. For the decryption process, all the steps are the same, but the way of choosing the keys is different. During decryption, the order of the key is reversed. That means when decrypting the ciphertext, the last key will be used first, then the second last, and so on. Both of the functions *Encrypt(char *)* and *Decrypt(char *)* are the same, but in the *Decrypt(char *)* function *xor_oneD(round)* is called instead of *xor_oneE(round)*. Among the previously selected 16 keys, *xor_oneD(round)* chooses the key in reverse order. That is the main difference between the encryption and decryption.

5.5.17 The Main() Function

```
1.      int main(){
2.             DES d1;
3.             d1.keygen();
4.             char *str = new char[1000];
5.             cout<<"\nEnter a string : ";
6.             cin >> str;
7.             char *str1 = new char[1000];
8.             str1 = d1.Encrypt(str);
9.             cout<<"\nEncrypted Text: "<<str1<<endl;
10.            cout<<"\no/p Text: "<<d1.
               Decrypt(str1)<<endl;
11.     }
```

The *main()* function is the supreme controller in most of the programming languages. In this chapter, C++ language is used to demonstrate the DES encryption-decryption, and there is also a *main()* function in this program, as usual. The function *main()* at first creates an object of the DES class; in this program DES is a user-defined class for demonstration purposes. The details of the DES class have been discussed in the prior sections of this chapter.

Now for creating an object of DES class, the function *keygen()* is called in the third line using the object created so far. Then, a string variable is declared to store the input string, which can store 1000 characters. After declaring the string variable, the string gets the input in the sixth line. In the eighth line, the function *Encrypt(char *)* is called to encrypt the plaintext and return the decrypted message into the string variable str1. A statement in line 9 shows the encrypted text that is already stored in str1. After all, the 10th line of the code calls the *Decrypt(char *)* function, and that function returns the decrypted plaintext so that users can see the decrypted text on the screen. Finally, a plaintext string is inputted through the keyboard, which is then encrypted and also decrypted to demonstrate that the program is working fine.

6

ADVANCED ENCRYPTION STANDARD

ASIF UR RAHMAN, SAEF ULLAH MIAH, AND SAIFUL AZAD

Contents

Keywords

Advanced Encryption Standard
Block cipher

6.1 Overview

The Advanced Encryption Standard (AES) is a renowned symmetric key algorithm that utilizes a same secret key to encrypt and decrypt a message. It overcomes the limitation of the smaller key size of the Data Encryption Standard (DES) by utilizing a bigger and variable-length key that may take 149 trillion years to crack (assuming a machine could try 255 keys per second— National Institute of Standards and Technology [NIST]). Moreover, it also resolves the slow processing speed of Triple DES (3DES) and utilizes lower resources than that. Therefore, it is preferred as the encryption and decryption standard by the U.S. government. This standard is described in Federal Information Processing Standard (FIPS). AES is now being used worldwide for encrypting digital information, including financial, telecommunications, and government data.

AES supports secret keys of length 128, 192, or 256 bits to encrypt and decrypt a data block of 128 bits. Like other block cipher techniques, it is based on permutations and substitutions. Its design supports implementation in both hardware and software. Moreover, it is royalty-free to use, unlike some commercial encryption algorithms.

6.2 History

Because of the limitations of the previous encryption standard (i.e., DES), the NIST was searching for a new symmetric block cipher technique that could be considered a more robust replacement. In the new proposed technique, it was looking for a cipher that could support multiple key sizes (i.e., key lengths), capable of running efficiently in both hardware and software, and also have a good defense mechanism against various attacking techniques. Thus, a process was initiated on January 2, 1997, where it published a Request for Comments (RFC) for the "Development of a Federal Information Processing Standard for Advanced Encryption Standard." The entire selection process was fully made open to public scrutiny and comments, because full visibility of any process would ensure the best possible analysis of the designs.

In this flow of the process, NIST publicly called for nominees for the new algorithm on September 12, 1997. The first AES conference was held from August 20–23, 1998. At that conference NIST selected 15 candidates for the AES, which were then subjected to preliminary analysis by the world cryptographic community, including the National Security Agency (NSA). All the selected algorithms were presented, analyzed, and tested at the second AES conference, which was held on March 22–23, 1999. On August 9, 1999, NIST selected five algorithms for extensive analysis:

1. MARS, submitted by a team from IBM
2. RC6, submitted by RSA Security
3. Rijndael, submitted by two Belgian cryptographers, Joan Daemen and Vincent Rijmen
4. Serpent, submitted by Ross Anderson, Eli Biham, and Lars Knudsen
5. Twofish, submitted by a team of researchers, including Bruce Schneier

Finally, on October 2, 2000, Rijndael, by Joan Daemen and Vincent Rijmen, was chosen as the Advanced Encryption Standard. On February 28, 2001, the algorithm was included in the publication of a draft by FIPS. Then it was open for public review for 90 days. After that, it was finally included in the Federal Register on December 6, 2001.

6.3 Design Consideration

One of the principal design goals of AES was to keep it simpler to implement in both hardware and software. Therefore, unlike DES, instead of operating on bits, it operates on bytes, which makes it easier to implement and explain. It works by repeating the same defined steps multiple times, which are called rounds. Each round consists of several processing steps, including one that utilizes an encryption/decryption subkey that is generated from the shared key. Since AES is an iterative symmetric block cipher, it shares a single secret key among the two communicating parties involved in encryption and decryption operations. The allowable key lengths in AES are 128, 192, and 256 bits. Every key is expanded so that a separate subkey ($w[i, j]$, where i and j provide the byte range) could be utilized for every round. Number of rounds of AES generally depends on the key length. A relationship between key length, number of columns in a state, and number of rounds is mentioned in Table 6.1. For instance, if the key length (N_k) is 128 bits or 16 bytes or 4 words, the number of columns (N_b) would be 4 and only 10 rounds (N_r) are performed, where Nb = key length/32.

Table 6.1 Relationship between Key Lengths, Number of Columns in a State, and Total Number of Rounds in AES

KEY LENGTH (N_k) (1 WORD = 32 BITS/4 BYTES)	NUMBER OF COLUMNS IN STATE (N_b)	ROUNDS (N_r)
4	4	10
6	6	12
8	8	14

$$
\begin{array}{|cccc|}
\hline
S_{0,0} & S_{0,1} & S_{0,2} & S_{0,3} \\
S_{1,0} & S_{1,1} & S_{1,2} & S_{1,3} \\
S_{2,0} & S_{2,1} & S_{2,2} & S_{2,3} \\
S_{3,0} & S_{3,1} & S_{3,2} & S_{3,3} \\
\hline
\end{array}
$$

Figure 6.1 A state of 128-bit key AES, where $S_{r,c}$ denotes a byte of the rth row and the cth column.

AES, as well as most of the encryption algorithms, is reversible, which means that for the steps performed to complete an encryption, similar steps could be followed to complete a decryption, but in reverse order. In the following section, a detailed description of the operations of AES is explained with examples.

6.4 Primitive Operations of AES

Internally, all the AES operations are performed on a two-dimensional array of bytes called the *state*. A state constitutes four rows and N_b (Table 6.1) number of columns. Hence, for a 128-bit key, a state consists of four rows and four columns, as depicted in Figure 6.1.

AES is based on five primitive operations:

1. **Exclusive disjunction/exclusive OR (XOR):** *Exclusive disjunction* or *exclusive or* is a logical operation that outputs true whenever both inputs differ from each other (e.g., one is true and the other is false) (Table 6.2). It is symbolized by the prefix operator J and by the infix operators XOR, EOR, EXOR, $\veebar$, $\oplus$, $\leftrightarrow$, and $\neq$.

2. **Substitution (SubByte):** A byte is substituted by another byte. AES utilizes a lookup table, also known as S-box, to perform substitutions of encryption, and another S-box, also known as inverse S-box, for decryption. Both S-boxes are

Table 6.2   XOR Truth Table

INPUT		OUTPUT
0	0	0
0	1	1
1	0	1
1	1	1

Table 6.3   S-Box Lookup Table

							S-BOX VALUES									
SN	0	1	2	3	4	5	6	7	8	9	A	B	C	D	E	F
0	63	7C	77	7B	F2	6B	6F	C5	30	01	67	2B	FE	D7	AB	76
1	CA	82	C9	7D	FA	59	47	F0	AD	D4	A2	AF	9C	A4	72	C0
2	B7	FD	93	26	36	3F	F7	CC	34	A5	E5	F1	71	D8	31	15
3	04	C7	23	C3	18	96	05	9A	07	12	80	E2	EB	27	B2	75
4	09	83	2C	1A	1B	6E	5A	A0	52	3B	D6	B3	29	E3	2F	84
5	53	D1	00	ED	20	FC	B1	5B	6A	CB	BE	39	4A	4C	58	CF
6	D0	EF	AA	FB	43	4D	33	85	45	F9	02	7F	50	3C	9F	A8
7	51	A3	40	8F	92	9D	38	F5	BC	B6	DA	21	10	FF	F3	D2
8	CD	0C	13	EC	5F	97	44	17	C4	A7	7E	3D	64	5D	19	73
9	60	81	4F	DC	22	2A	90	88	46	EE	B8	14	DE	5E	0B	DB
A	E0	32	3A	0A	49	06	24	5C	C2	D3	AC	62	91	95	E4	79
B	E7	C8	37	6D	8D	D5	4E	A9	6C	56	F4	EA	65	7A	AE	08
C	BA	78	25	2E	1C	A6	B4	C6	E8	DD	74	1F	4B	BD	8B	8A
D	70	3E	B5	66	48	03	F6	0E	61	35	57	B9	86	C1	1D	9E
E	E1	F8	98	11	69	D9	8E	94	9B	1E	87	E9	CE	55	28	DF
F	8C	A1	89	0D	BF	E6	42	68	41	99	2D	0F	B0	54	BB	16

given in Tables 6.3 and 6.4, respectively. Each individual byte can be represented by two hex digits where the first (from right) digit represents row and the second digit represents column of the S-box lookup table in the case of encryption, and of the inverse S-box in the case of decryption. For instance, let us assume that {42} is a hexadecimal value that represents a byte. Here, 4 refers to row number and 2 refers to column number; the value over that location would substitute this value, i.e., {2C}.

3. **Rotation (ShiftRows):** A simple permutation is performed by rearranging of bytes through rotating a row by a fixed number of cells. It provides a diffusion by the cyclic left shift of the last three rows of the state by different offsets. Row 0 of the

Table 6.4 Inverse S-Box Lookup Table

INVERSE S-BOX VALUES															
SN	0	1	2	3	4	5	6	7	8	9	A	B	C	D	E	F
0	52	09	6A	D5	30	36	A5	38	BF	40	A3	9E	81	F3	D7	FB
1	7C	E3	39	82	9B	2F	FF	87	34	8E	43	44	C4	DE	E9	CB
2	54	7B	94	32	A6	C2	23	3D	EE	4C	95	0B	42	FA	C3	4E
3	08	2E	A1	66	28	D9	24	B2	76	5B	A2	49	6D	8B	D1	25
4	72	F8	F6	64	86	68	98	16	D4	A4	5C	CC	5D	65	B6	92
5	6C	70	48	50	FD	ED	B9	DA	5E	15	46	57	A7	8D	9D	84
6	90	D8	AB	00	8C	BC	D3	0A	F7	E4	58	05	B8	B3	45	06
7	D0	2C	1E	8F	CA	3F	0F	02	C1	AF	BD	03	01	13	8A	6B
8	3A	91	11	41	4F	67	DC	EA	97	F2	CF	CE	F0	B4	E6	73
9	96	AC	74	22	E7	AD	35	85	E2	F9	37	E8	1C	75	DF	6E
A	47	F1	1A	71	1D	29	C5	89	6F	B7	62	0E	AA	18	BE	1B
B	FC	56	3E	4B	C6	D2	79	20	9A	DB	C0	FE	78	CD	5A	F4
C	1F	DD	A8	33	88	07	C7	31	B1	12	10	59	27	80	EC	5F
D	60	51	7F	A9	19	B5	4A	0D	2D	E5	7A	9F	93	C9	9C	EF
E	A0	E0	3B	4D	AE	2A	F5	B0	C8	EB	BB	3C	83	53	99	61
F	17	2B	04	7E	BA	77	D6	26	E1	69	14	63	55	21	0C	7D

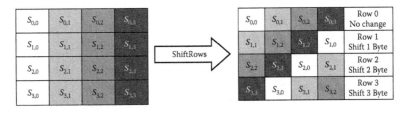

Figure 6.2 Shift row operation of AES.

state is not shifted, row 1 is shifted 1 byte, row 2 is shifted 2 bytes, and row 3 is shifted 3 bytes. This operation is illustrated in Figure 6.2.

In case of decryption, inverse shift rows (InvShiftRows) are performed, which follows a process similar to that of ShiftRows, only the shifting is done to the right.

4. **MixColumn:** It operates on each column individually where a single byte of a column is mapped into a new value that is a function of all four bytes in that column. Each column of the state is replaced by multiplying with a $4 \times N_b$ matrix in

the Galois field 2^8, also denoted as $GF(2^8)$. The mathematics behind this is beyond the scope of this book. An example matrix is given for 128-bit key in Figure 6.3.

The first result byte is calculated by multiplying four values of the state column against four values of the first row of the matrix. The result of each multiplication is then XORed to produce 1 byte like below:

$$S_{0,0} = (S_{0,0}*2) \text{ XOR } (S_{1,0}*3) \text{ XOR } (S_{2,0}*1) \text{ XOR } (S_{3,0}*1)$$

This procedure is repeated again with each byte of all columns of the state, until there is no more state column. As a result of this multiplication, the four bytes in the first column are replaced by the following:

$$S_{0,0} = (S_{0,0}*2) \text{ XOR } (S_{1,0}*3) \text{ XOR } (S_{2,0}*1) \text{ XOR } (S_{3,0}*1)$$

$$S_{1,0} = (S_{0,0}*1) \text{ XOR } (S_{1,0}*2) \text{ XOR } (S_{2,0}*3) \text{ XOR } (S_{3,0}*1)$$

$$S_{2,0} = (S_{0,0}*1) \text{ XOR } (S_{1,0}*1) \text{ XOR } (S_{2,0}*2) \text{ XOR } (S_{3,0}*3)$$

$$S_{3,0} = (S_{0,0}*3) \text{ XOR } (S_{1,0}*1) \text{ XOR } (S_{2,0}*1) \text{ XOR } (S_{3,0}*2)$$

This multiplication value also could be achieved using a two-table lookup represented in hexadecimal numbers and indexed with a hexadecimal digit. They are called the L-Table and E-Table and are given in Tables 6.5 and 6.6, respectively.

The result of the multiplication could be found from the L lookup table, followed by the addition of the results (+, not a bitwise AND), followed by a lookup to the E-table. The numbers being multiplied are 1 byte each and are represented in

$S_{0,0}$	$S_{0,1}$	$S_{0,2}$	$S_{0,3}$
$S_{1,0}$	$S_{1,1}$	$S_{1,2}$	$S_{1,3}$
$S_{2,0}$	$S_{2,1}$	$S_{2,2}$	$S_{2,3}$
$S_{3,0}$	$S_{3,1}$	$S_{3,2}$	$S_{3,3}$

02	03	01	01
01	02	03	01
01	01	02	03
03	01	01	01

Figure 6.3   128-bit key state and its multiplication matrix.

Table 6.5 L-Table

L-TABLE

SN	0	1	2	3	4	5	6	7	8	9	A	B	C	D	E	F
0		00	19	01	32	02	1A	C6	4B	C7	1B	68	33	E	DF	03
1	64	04	E0	0E	34	8D	81	EF	4C	71	08	C8	F8	69	1C	C1
2	7D	C2	1D	B5	F9	B9	27	6A	4D	E4	A6	72	9A	C9	09	78
3	65	2F	8A	05	21	0F	E1	24	12	F0	82	45	35	93	DA	8E
4	96	8F	DB	BD	36	D0	CE	94	13	5C	D2	F1	40	46	83	38
5	66	DD	FD	30	BF	06	8B	62	B3	25	E2	98	22	88	91	10
6	7E	6E	48	C3	A3	B6	1E	42	3A	6B	28	54	FA	85	3D	BA
7	2B	79	0A	15	9B	9F	5E	CA	4E	D4	AC	E5	F3	73	A7	57
8	AF	58	A8	50	F4	EA	D6	74	4F	AE	E9	D5	E7	E6	AD	E8
9	2C	D7	75	7A	EB	16	0B	F5	59	CB	5F	B0	9C	A9	51	A0
A	7F	0C	F6	6F	17	C4	49	EC	D8	43	1F	2D	A4	76	7B	B7
B	CC	BB	3E	5A	FB	60	B1	86	3B	52	A1	6C	AA	55	29	9D
C	97	B2	87	90	61	BE	DC	FC	BC	95	CF	CD	37	3F	5B	D1
D	53	39	84	3C	41	A2	6D	47	14	2A	9E	5D	56	F2	D3	AB
E	44	11	92	D9	23	20	2E	89	B4	7C	B8	26	77	99	E3	A5
F	67	4A	ED	DE	C5	31	FE	18	0D	63	8C	80	C0	F7	70	07

Table 6.6 E-Table

E-TABLE

SN	0	1	2	3	4	5	6	7	8	9	A	B	C	D	E	F
0	01	03	05	0F	11	33	55	FF	1A	2E	72	96	A1	F8	13	35
1	5F	E1	38	48	D8	73	95	A4	F7	02	06	0A	1E	22	66	AA
2	E5	34	5C	E4	37	59	EB	26	6A	BE	D9	70	90	AB	E6	31
3	53	F5	04	0C	14	3C	44	CC	4F	D1	68	B8	D3	6E	B2	CD
4	4C	D4	67	A9	E0	3B	4D	D7	62	A6	F1	08	18	28	78	88
5	83	9E	B9	D0	6B	BD	DC	7F	81	98	B3	CE	49	DB	76	9A
6	B5	C4	57	F9	10	30	50	F0	0B	1D	27	69	BB	D6	61	A3
7	FE	19	2B	7D	87	92	AD	EC	2F	71	93	AE	E9	20	60	A0
8	FB	16	3A	4E	D2	6D	B7	C2	5D	E7	32	56	FA	15	3F	41
9	C3	5E	E2	3D	47	C9	40	C0	5B	ED	2C	74	9C	BF	DA	75
A	9F	BA	D5	64	AC	EF	2A	7E	82	9D	BC	DF	7A	8E	89	80
B	9B	B6	C1	58	E8	23	65	AF	EA	25	6F	B1	C8	43	C5	54
C	FC	1F	21	63	A5	F4	07	09	1B	2D	77	99	B0	CB	46	CA
D	45	CF	4A	DE	79	8B	86	91	A8	E3	3E	42	C6	51	F3	0E
E	12	36	5A	EE	29	7B	8D	8C	8F	8A	85	94	A7	F2	0D	17
F	39	4B	DD	7C	84	97	A2	FD	1C	24	6C	B4	C7	52	F6	01

two hexadecimal digits. The first digit is used as row index and the last digit as column index of the L-table. Then, two values acquired from the L-table are added, which results in another byte. The resultant byte is used to look up from E-table, following a procedure similar to that of the L-table. For instance, let us assume that the two hex values being multiplied are 87*02. First, we have to look up the L-table to find out the substitution values, i.e., 74 and 19. Then, add the two acquired values together, which is 8D in this example. If the added value is greater than FF, then FF needs to be subtracted from the added value. The final step is to look up the addition result on the E-table. Note that any number multiplied by 1 is equal to itself and does not need to go through the above-mentioned procedure, e.g., 87*1 = 87.

An example of MixColumn during encryption is given below:

Input = 87 6E 46 A6

$S_{0,0}$ = (87*2) XOR (6E*3) XOR (46*1) XOR (A6*1)

= E(L(87) + L(02)) XOR E(L(6E) + L(03)) XOR 46 XOR A6

= E(8D) XOR E(3E) XOR 46 XOR A6

= 15 XOR B2 XOR 46 XOR A6

= 47

Similarly, one can calculate the other values of the state. In the case of decryption, the inverse mix column (InvMixColumn) technique is utilized, which follows the same process as MixColumn, but multiplications are performed on a different multiplication matrix. InvMixColumn utilizes the multiplication matrix shown in Table 6.7.

Table 6.7 Inverse Multiplication Matrix

0E	0B	0D	09
09	0E	0B	0D
0D	09	0E	0B
0B	0D	09	0E

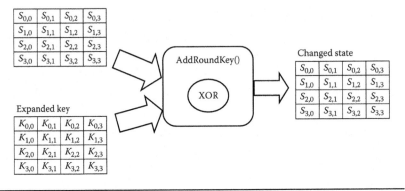

Figure 6.4   Add round key function.

> 5. **AddRoundKey:** This is a simple operation where each byte of
>   the state is XORed with each byte of the round key, which is
>   a portion of the expanded key. In the next section, a detailed
>   description of the key expansion technique of AES is elabo-
>   rated. Figure 6.4 illustrates the technique of AddRoundKey
>   transformation.

6.5 Structure of AES

The basic encryption and decryption structure of AES is illustrated in
Figure 6.5. Here, a 128-bit key length is considered. Therefore, both
encryption and decryption must go through 10 rounds before producing the desired output. There are 12 rounds for a 192-bit key and
14 rounds for a 256-bit key. It can be observed from the figure that every
round generally performs four operations: (1) SubBytes/InvSubBytes,
(2) ShiftRows/InvShiftRows, (3) MixColumns/InvMixColumns, and
(4) AddRoundKey. One of them is permutation and the other three
are substitutions. However, the final round comprises only three operations, excluding MixColumns/InvMixColumns. The expanded key
is only utilized by the AddRoundKey operations. Each operation is
easily reversible, thus making it easy to implement in both hardware
and software. Similar to most of the block ciphers, the decryption
algorithm utilizes the key in reverse order.

6.6 Overview of Key Expansion

As mentioned earlier, since AES supports symmetric key, a secret
key must be shared between the two parties. AES provides flexibility

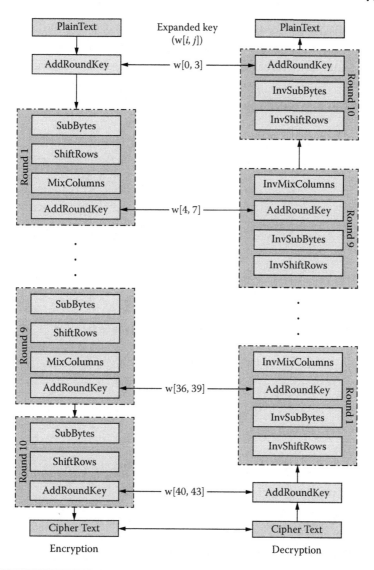

Figure 6.5 AES encryption and decryption techniques.

regarding selecting a key length. A key could be 128, 192, or 256 bits long. Since every round utilizes a new subkey, prior to encryption or decryption, the key must be expanded according to the number of rounds. This process is called *key expansion*.

The key expansion routine takes an input key of size N_k and produces a linear array of size, $N_b \times (N_r + 1)$, where a number of columns in states is (N_b) and the number of rounds (N_r) depends on key length (N_k).

For instance, N_r is 10 when N_k is 4, which is illustrated in Table 6.1. Let us denote a word in the expanded key as $w[i]$, where i is the ith word of that key. Algorithm 6.1 shows a key expansion algorithm.

Algorithm 6.1: KeyExpansion(key)

```
Begin
        word temp;
        for i ← 0 to (Nₖ - 1)
                w[i] ← (unsigned char) key[4*i] << 24) |
                        ((unsigned char) key[4*i+1] << 16) |
                        ((unsigned char) key[4*i+2]<<8) |
                        ((unsigned char) key[4*i+3]);
        end for

        for i ←(Nₖ - 1) to Nᵦ × Nᵣ
                temp = w[i-1];
                if (imodNₖ = = 0)
                        temp = SubWord(RotWord(temp)) ⊕
                        (Rcon[i/Nₖ] << 24);
                else if(Nₖ> 6 and(i mod Nₖ) = = 4)
                        temp = SubWord(temp);
                end if
                w[i] = w[i-Nₖ] ⊕ temp;
        end for
End
```

From Algorithm 6.1, we can easily identify the functions necessary for the expanding key:

1. **RotWord:** This function does a circular shift on 4 bytes, similar to the shift row function, e.g., 0, 1, 2, 3 to 1, 2, 3, 0.
2. **SubWord:** It does a similar transformation, which is described in the SubByte operation. It utilizes the S-box table to substitute a byte.
3. **XOR with round constant (Rcon):** For every round in key expansion, the result acquired from function 1 and function 2 is XORed with a round constant value Rcon[i]. These values are shown in Table 6.8.

Table 6.8 Rounds and Their Respective Constants

Round[j]	1	2	3	4	5	6	7	8	9	10
Rcon[j]	01	02	04	08	10	20	40	80	1B	36

6.7 Key Expansion Example

Let us assume that the secret key shared between two parties is *aes 128 pass key*, which is 128 bits long. Therefore, N_k is 4, N_b is 4, and N_r is 10 for this key length. A hexadecimal representation of the key is shown in Figure 6.6.

This key is utilized to expand the key to $N_b \times (N_r + 1)$ bytes, which is 44 bytes in this example. A detailed description of the steps is presented in previous sections. In this section, we demonstrate how the round key for the first round, i.e., w[4, 7], can be calculated while w[0, 3] is given. From Figure 6.6, we get

$$w[0] = 1A91F720$$

$$w[1] = 5E456706$$

$$w[2] = A25B66DE$$

$$w[3] = 5F145988$$

W[*I*]	W[*I* − 1] OR TEMP	AFTER ROTWORD	AFTER SUBWORD	RCON[*I*]	AFTER XOR WITH RCON[*I*]	W[*I* − 4]	W[*I*] = TEMP XOR W[*I* − 4]
4	5F145988	1459885F	FACBC4CF	1000000	EACBC4CF	1A91F720	E15A33EF
5	E15A33EF	5A33EFE1	BEC3DFF8	1000000	AEC3DFF8	5E456706	BF1F54E9
6	BF1F54E9	1F54E9BF	C0201E08	1000000	D0201E08	A25B66DE	1D443237
7	1D443237	4432371D	1B2394A4	1000000	0B2394A4	5F145988	42506BBF

By repeating the similar procedures, the remaining words of the expanded key are generated.

6.8 Encryption

In AES, a plaintext has to travel through N_r number of rounds before producing the cipher. Again, each round comprises four different operations. One operation is permutation and the other three are substitutions. They are (1) SubBytes, (2) ShiftRows, (3) MixColumns,

1A	5E	A2	5F
91	45	5B	14
F7	67	66	59
20	06	DE	88

Figure 6.6 Hex value representations of the secret key.

and (4) AddRoundKey. All these operations are detailed previously. Algorithm 6.2 gives a high-level description of the encryption algorithm.

Algorithm 6.2: Encryption (PlainText)

```
Begin
      State = plainText
      1. KeyExpansion
      2. AddRoundKey (State, ExpandedKey[0])
      3. for r ← 1 to (Nr - 1)
            a. SubBytes (State, S-box)
            b. ShiftRows (State)
            c. MixColumns (State)
            d. AddRoundKey (State, ExpandedKey[r])
      end for
      4. SubBytes (State, S-box)
      5. ShiftRows (State)
      6. AddRoundKey (State, ExpandedKey[Nr])
      Out = CipherText
End
```

6.9 An Encryption Example

Let us assume that the plaintext we are going to encrypt is *string 2 encrypt* using the key stated in Section 6.7. To encrypt, this string is copied to the state, and hexadecimal representations are given in Figure 6.7.

The steps of various rounds with their corresponding values are portrayed in tabular format in Table 6.9.

6.10 Decryption

The decryption routine takes the encrypted string/state as input or output of the encryption routine and performs a reverse operation.

73	6e	20	72
74	67	65	79
72	20	6e	70
69	32	63	74

Figure 6.7 Hex value representations of plaintext.

Table 6.9 Steps of the AES Encryption

ROUND NUMBER	START OF A ROUND	AFTER SUBBYTES	AFTER SHIFTROWS	AFTER MIXCOLUMNS	ROUND KEY VALUE	ROUND OUTPUT
INP	736E2072				1A5EA25F	6930822D
	74676579				91455B14	E5223E6D
	72206E70				F7676659	85470829
	69326374				2006DE88	4934BDFC
1	6930822D	F90413D8	F90413D8	C75BED01	E1BF1D42	26E4F043
	E5223E6D	D993B23C	93B23CD9	24B4D1F0	5A1F4450	7EAB95A0
	85470829	97A03095	30A597A0	C1AA32D4	3354326B	F2FE00BF
	4934BDFC	3B187AB0	B03B187A	C86DAEFE	EFE937BF	27849941
2	26E4F043	F7698C1A	F7698C1A	B368EE6F	B00F1250	0367FC3F
	7EAB95A0	F3622AE0	622AE0F3	15E988DF	253A7E2E	30D3F6F1
	F2FE00BF	89BB6308	630889BB	CD1C84AD	3B6F5D36	F673D99B
	27849941	CC5FEE83	83CC5FEE	1E1A58A1	C32A1DA2	DD304503
3	0367FC3F	7B85B075	7B85B075	1202C507	858A98C8	97885DCF
	30D3F6F1	046642A1	6642A104	93FC2B99	201A644A	B3E64FD3
	F673D99B	428F3514	3514428F	FAB799C6	016E3305	FBD9AAC3
	DD304503	C1046E7B	7BC1046E	285B20C8	90BAA705	B8E187CD
4	97885DCF	88C44C8A	88C44C8A	9346C59A	5BD14981	C8978C1B
	B3E64FD3	6D8E8466	8E84666D	DDC96918	4B51357F	96985C67
	FBD9AAC3	0F35AC2E	AC2E0F35	99A827B4	6A043732	F3AC1086
	B8E187CD	6CF817BD	BD6CF817	C02556F3	78C26560	B8E73393
5	C8978C1B	E88864AF	E88864AF	17FDC5BC	99480180	8EB5C43C
	96985C67	90464A85	464A8590	FDBCF6FF	68390C73	9585FA8C
	F3AC1086	0D91CA44	CA440D91	5EFE5C58	BABE89BB	E440D5E3
	B8E73393	6C94C3DC	DC6C94C3	0C551776	74B6D3B3	78E3C4C5
6	8EB5C43C	19D51CEB	19D51CEB	356BECA6	367E7FFF	03159359
	9585FA8C	2A972D64	972D642A	8F007EB8	82BBB7C4	0DBBC97C
	E440D5E3	69090311	03116909	790599F7	D769E05B	AE6C79AC
	78E3C4C5	BC111CA6	A6BC111C	E83B0B3D	B90FDC6F	5134D752
7	03159359	7B59DCCB	7B59DCCB	658E6FB1	6A146B94	0F9A0425
	0DBBC97C	D7EADD10	EADD10D7	7581D380	BB00B773	CE8164F3
	AE6C79AC	E450B691	B691E450	E6D537AE	7F16F6AD	99C3C103
	5134D752	D1180E00	00D1180E	D11EBBDD	AFA07C13	7EBEC7CE
8	0F9A0425	76B8F23F	76B8F23F	0B26A810	65711A8E	6E57B29E
	CE8164F3	8B0C430D	0C430D8B	6D406F86	2E2E99EA	436EF66C
	99C3C103	EE2E787B	787BEE2E	0C03D1B9	0214E24F	0E1733F6
	7EBEC7CE	F3AEC68B	8BF3AEC6	E316A973	8D2D5142	6E3BF831
9	6E57B29E	9F5B370B	9F5B370B	9BADD789	F988921C	62254595
	436EF66C	1A9F4250	9F42501A	23869375	AA841DF7	89028E82
	0E1733F6	ABF0C342	C342ABF0	CF271729	2E3AD897	E11DCFBE
	6E3BF831	9FE241C7	C79FE241	73C87D75	94B9E8AA	E77195DF
10	62254595	AA3F6E2A	AA3F6E2A		A72FBDA1	0D10D38B
	89028E82	A7771913	771913A7		22A6BB4C	55BFA8EB
	E11DCFBE	F8A48AAE	8AAEF8A4		82B860F7	08169853
	E77195DF	94A32A9E	9E94A32A		08B159F3	9625FAD9

Ciphertext: 0D 10 D3 8B 55 BF A8 EB 08 16 98 53 96 25 FA D9.

The state value of each step will be the opposite of the encryption state value. Again, a higher-level description of the decryption algorithm is given in Algorithm 6.3.

Algorithm 6.3: Decryption (CipherText)

```
Begin
        State = CipherText
        1. KeyExpansion
        2. AddRoundKey (State, ExpandedKey[0])
        3. for r ← (Nr - 1) to 1
                a. InverseShiftRows (State)
                b. InverseSubBytes (State, S-box)
                c. AddRoundKey (State, ExpandedKey[r])
                d. InverseMixColumns (State)
        end for
        4. InverseSubBytes (State, S-box)
        5. InverseShiftRows (State)
        6. AddRoundKey (State, ExpandedKey[Nr])
        out = PlainText
End
```

6.11 Limitations

In our implementation, there is no restriction on key selection; no weak or semiweak key has been identified for this AES implementation. The implementation here covers only electronic code block (ECB) encryption mode.

6.12 Pros and Cons of AES

Actually, AES has many pros rather than noticeable cons. As AES was developed after DES, all known attacks on DES have been tested on AES, and all the test results were satisfactory. AES is more secure to brute-force attack than DES because of its larger key size. AES is not prone to statistical attacks, and it has been demonstrated that it is not possible with common techniques to do statistical analysis of ciphertext in AES. As yet, there are no differential and linear attacks on AES. The best part of AES is that the algorithms used in it are so simple that they can be easily implemented using cheap processors and a minimum amount of memory.

On the other hand, AES needs more processing and more rounds of communication than DES, and we can hardly tell this is AES's disadvantage.

6.13 Implementation

```cpp
#include<iostream>
#include<vector>
#include<fstream>
#include<string>
#include<sstream>
using namespace std;

#define word unsigned int
#define byte unsigned char

class AES
{
    vector<word> ExpandedKey;
    int Nk,//width of key block
        Nr,//number of round
        Nb;//block size
    static const byte S_Box 256];
    static const byte Si_Box 256];
    static const byte Rcon[30];
    static const byte ColMixMatrix[4][4];
    static const byte InvColMixMatrix[4][4];
    static const byte AlogTable[256];
    static const byte LogTable[256];
    string cipherText;
    byte state[4][4];

#ifdef _KEY_TEST_
    fstream in;

#endif

#ifdef _TEST_STATE_
    fstream stest_fin;
#endif

    byte Mul(byte a, byte b);
```

```
    void MixColumns();
    void ShiftRows();
    void SubBytes();
    byte SubByte(byte oneByte);
    word SubWord(word val);
    word RotWord(word val);

    void InvMixColumns();
    void InvShiftRows();
    byte InvSubByte(byte oneByte);
    void InvSubBytes();

    void AddRoundKey(int roundNo);
    void KeyExpansion(string key);
    string ToString();

public:
    static enum KeySize {AES128 = 128, AES192 = 192,
    AES256 = 256};

    AES(string key, int bitSize);
    ~AES();
    void Encrypt(string plainText);
    string GetCipherText();
    void Decrypt(string cipherText);
};

#include"AES.h"

    byte AES::Mul(byte a, byte b)
    {
        if(a && b)
                    return AlogTable[((unsigned char)
                    LogTable[a] + (unsigned char)
                    LogTable[b])%255];
        return 0;
    }

    void AES::InvMixColumns()
    {
      byte temp[4];
      for(int c = 0; c < Nb; c ++)
      {
          //4 rows and Nb columns to store temp mix
            col value
```

```cpp
        for(int r = 0; r < 4; r ++)
        {
            temp[r] = Mul(InvColMixMatrix[r][0],
                          (state[0][c]) )
                        ^ Mul(InvColMixMatrix[r]
                          [1],(state[1][c]))
                        ^ Mul(InvColMixMatrix[r]
                          [2],(state[2][c]))
                        ^ Mul(InvColMixMatrix[r]
                          [3],(state[3][c]));
        }

        state[0][c] = temp[0];
        state[1][c] = temp[1];
        state[2][c] = temp[2];
        state[3][c] = temp[3];
    }
}

void AES::MixColumns()
{
    byte temp[4];
    for(int c = 0; c < Nb; c ++)
    {
        //4 rows and Nb columns to store temp mix
        //col value
        for(int r = 0; r < 4; r ++)
        {
            temp[r] = Mul(ColMixMatrix[r][0],
                          (state[0][c]) )
                        ^ Mul(ColMixMatrix[r]
                          [1],(state[1][c]))
                        ^ Mul(ColMixMatrix[r]
                          [2],(state[2][c]))
                        ^ Mul(ColMixMatrix[r]
                          [3],(state[3][c]));
        }

        state[0][c] = temp[0];
        state[1][c] = temp[1];
        state[2][c] = temp[2];
        state[3][c] = temp[3];
    }
}
void AES::InvShiftRows()
```

```
{
    //row is always 4
    for(int r = 0; r < 4; r ++)
    {
        byte temp[4];

        temp[0]  =  state[r][0];
        temp[1]  =  state[r][1];
        temp[2]  =  state[r][2];
        temp[3]  =  state[r][3];

        for(int c = 0; c < Nb; c ++)
        {
            state[r][(r+c)% Nb] = temp[c];
        }

    }

}

void AES::ShiftRows()
{
    //row is always 4
    for(int r = 0; r < 4; r ++)
    {
        byte temp[4];
        for(int c = 0; c < Nb; c ++)
        {
            temp[c]  =  state[r][(r+c)% Nb];
        }
        //temp[0]  =  state[r][(r+0)% Nb];
        //temp[1]  =  state[r][(r+1) % Nb];
        //temp[2]  =  state[r][(r+2) % Nb];
        //temp[3]  =  state[r][(r+3) % Nb];

        state[r][0]  =  temp[0];
        state[r][1]  =  temp[1];
        state[r][2]  =  temp[2];
        state[r][3]  =  temp[3];
    }

}

byte AES::InvSubByte(byte oneByte)
{
```

```cpp
    //one byte represent in hex (xy) x is row
    //index and y is column index
    return Si_Box[oneByte];
}

void AES::InvSubBytes()
{
    for(int i = 0; i < 4; i ++)
    {
        for(int j = 0; j < Nb; j ++)
        {
            state[i][j] = InvSubByte(state[i][j]);
        }
    }
}

void AES::SubBytes()
{
    for(int i = 0; i < 4; i ++)
    {
        for(int j = 0; j < Nb; j ++)
        {
            state[i][j] = SubByte(state[i][j]);
        }
    }
}

byte AES::SubByte(byte oneByte)
{
    //one byte represent in hex (xy) x is row
    //index and y is column index
        return S_Box[oneByte];
}

word AES::SubWord(word val)
{
    byte oneByte;
    word res = 0;
    for(int i = 0; i< 4; i ++)
    {
        res = res << 8;
        oneByte = (val >> 24) & 0xFF;
        res = res | SubByte(oneByte);
        val = val << 8;
    }
```

```
        return res;
    }


word AES::RotWord(word val)
{
    word res = val << 8;
    res = res | (val >> 24);
    return res;
}


void AES::AddRoundKey(int roundNo)
{

    for(int col = 0; col < Nb; col++)
    {

        word roundKeyVal = ExpandedKey
        [(roundNo*Nb)+col];
        for(int row = 3; row > = 0; row- )
        {

            state[row][col] ^ = (roundKeyVal &0xFF);
            roundKeyVal = roundKeyVal >> 8;
        }
    }
}
AES::~AES()
{
    #ifdef _KEY_TEST_
        if(in)
        {
            in.close();
        }
    #endif
    #ifdef _TEST_STATE_
        if(stest_fin)
            stest_fin.close();
    #endif
}


AES::AES(string key, int bitSize)
{
    Nr = bitSize/32 + 6;
    Nk = bitSize/32;
    Nb = 4;//always 4
```

```cpp
    ExpandedKey.resize(Nk*(Nr+1));

    #ifdef _TEST_STATE_
        stest_fin.open("128_enc_test.txt",ios::in);
        if(!stest_fin )
        {
            cout << "Cannot not open" << endl;
            exit(1);
        }
    #endif//_Debug_
    #ifdef _KEY_TEST_
        in.open("128_key_test.txt",ios::in);
        if(!in )
        {
            cout << "Cannot not open" << endl;
            exit(1);
        }
    #endif//_Debug_
    KeyExpansion(key);

}
void AES::KeyExpansion(string key)
{
    word temp;
    for(int i = 0; i < Nk; i ++)
    {
        ExpandedKey [i] = ((unsigned char) key[4*i]
        << 24) |
                                ((unsigned char)
                                key[4*i+1] << 16) |
                                ((unsigned char)
                                key[4*i+2]<<8) |
                                ((unsigned char)
                                key[4*i+3]);
            cout << hex << ExpandedKey[i] << endl;
    }
    for(int i = Nk; i < Nb*(Nr+1); i++)
    {
        temp = ExpandedKey[i-1];
        if(i% Nk = = 0)
        {
            temp = SubWord(RotWord(temp)) ^
            (Rcon[i/Nk] << 24);
        }
        else if(Nk >6 && i%Nk = = 4)
```

```
{
    temp = SubWord(temp);
}
ExpandedKey[i] = ExpandedKey[i-Nk] ^ temp;

#ifdef _KEY_TEST_
        int x;
        string inpHexVal;
        std::stringstream exKeyHexVal;
        in >> x >> inpHexVal;
        exKeyHexVal << hex <<
        ExpandedKey[i];
        if(x == i && inpHexVal ==
        exKeyHexVal.str() && 0)
            cout << i << " : ok " << endl;
        else
        {
            temp = ExpandedKey[i-1];
            if(i% Nk = = 0)
            {
                    ofstream out ("keyval.
                    txt", ios::app);
                    out << dec <<i << ":not
                    ok:" << endl;
                    out << "temp:" <<hex <<
                    temp << endl;
                    out << "rot:" <<hex <<
                    RotWord(temp) << endl;
                    out << "sub:" <<hex <<
                    SubWord(RotWord(temp))
                    << endl;
                    out << "After xor
                    Rcon:" <<hex <<
                    (SubWord(RotWord
                    (temp))^ (Rcon[i/Nk] <<
                    24)) << endl;
                    out << "Rcon :" <<hex
                    << (Rcon[i/Nk] <<24) <<
                    endl;
                    out << "W[i-nk] :"
                    <<hex <<
                    ExpandedKey[i-Nk] <<
                    endl;
                    out << "final :" <<hex
                    << ExpandedKey[i]
```

```
                        << " and " << inpHexVal
                        <<", "<<exKeyHexVal.
                        str() << endl <<endl <<
                        endl;
                        out.close();
                }
                else if(Nk >6 && i%Nk == 4)
                {
                        ofstream out ("keyval.
                        txt", ios::app);
                        out << i << ": not ok:"
                        << endl;
                        out << "temp : " <<hex
                        << temp << endl;
                        out << "sub : " <<hex
                        << SubWord(temp) <<
                        endl;
                        out << "final :" <<hex
                        << ExpandedKey[i] <<
                        endl <<endl << endl;
                        out.close();
                }
                else
                {
                        ofstream out ("keyval.
                        txt", ios::app);
                        out << dec <<i <<
                        " : not ok : " << endl;
                        out << "temp : " <<hex
                        << temp << endl;
                        out << "W[i-nk] : "
                        <<hex <<
                        ExpandedKey[i-Nk] <<
                        endl;
                        out << "final :" <<hex
                        << ExpandedKey[i] <<
                        " and " << inpHexVal
                        <<", "<<exKeyHexVal.
                        str() << endl <<endl <<
                        endl;
                }
        }
    #endif//_DEBUG_
}
}
```

```cpp
#ifdef _DEBUG_
    void printState()
    {
        ofstream out("enc_step.txt",ios::app);
        for(int i = 0; i< 4; i ++)
        {
            for(int j = 0; j < Nb; j++)
            {
                    out << hex << (int)
                    state[i][j] <<" ";
            }
            out << endl;
        }
        out << endl << endl;
    }
#endif// _DEBUG_

#ifdef _TEST_STATE_
    void testState(int round)
    {
        cout << round << endl;
        for(int i = 0; i< 4; i ++)
        {
            int x;
            stest_fin >> x;
            for(int j = 0; j < Nb; j++)
            {
                    string inpHexVal;
                    std::stringstream exKeyHexVal;
                    stest_fin >> inpHexVal;
                    exKeyHexVal << hex << (int)
                    state[i][j];

                    if(x = = round && inpHexVal = =
                    exKeyHexVal.str())
                        cout << " ok ";
                    else
                    {
                        cout << " not ok " <<
                        inpHexVal << " " <<
                        exKeyHexVal.str() << endl;
                    }
            }
            cout << endl;
        }
        cout << endl << endl;
```

```cpp
    }
#endif//_TEST_STATE_

void AES::Encrypt(string plainText)
{
    if((plainText.length()% (4*Nb)) ! = 0)
        plainText.append((4*Nb) - (plainText.
        length()%(4*Nb)),'\0');
    int count = 0;
    while (count < (plainText.length()))
    {
        //copy one block into state
        for(int c = 0; c <Nb; c++)
        {
            for(int r = 0; r< 4; r ++)
                    state[r][c] =
                    plainText[count+(c*Nb)+r];
        }
        AddRoundKey(0);

        #ifdef _DEBUG_
            cout << "After Add round Key 0" << endl;
            printState();
        #endif//_DEBUG_
            int i;
        for(i = 1; i < Nr; i ++)
        {

            #ifdef _TEST_STATE_
                    cout << i << endl;
                    testState(i);
            #endif//_TEST_STATE_
            SubBytes();
            #ifdef _DEBUG_
                cout << "After Subbytes "<< dec<<
                i << endl;
                printState();
            #endif//_DEBUG_

            ShiftRows();
            #ifdef _DEBUG_
                cout << "After ShifRows "<< dec<<
                i << endl;
                printState();
            #endif//_DEBUG_
```

```cpp
        MixColumns();
        #ifdef _DEBUG_
                cout << "After MixColumns "<<
                dec<< i << endl;
                printState();
        #endif//_DEBUG_

        AddRoundKey(i);
        #ifdef _DEBUG_
                cout << "Add round Key " << i <<
                endl;
                printState();
        #endif//_DEBUG_
                //exit (1);
    }

        SubBytes();
        #ifdef _DEBUG_
                cout << "Round Subbytes"<< dec<<
                i << endl;
                printState();
        #endif//_DEBUG_

        ShiftRows();
        #ifdef _DEBUG_
                cout << "Round ShiftRows"<< dec<<
                i << endl;
                printState();
        #endif//_DEBUG_
        AddRoundKey(Nr);
        #ifdef _DEBUG_
                cout << "Add round Key " << i <<
                endl;
                printState();
        #endif//_DEBUG_
        #ifdef _TEST_STATE_
                //testState(i);
                printState();
        #endif//_TEST_STATE_
        cipherText = cipherText + ToString();
        count+ = 4*Nb;
    }
}
string AES::GetCipherText()
{
```

```
        return cipherText;
}
string AES::ToString()
{
    string str;
    for(int c = 0;c<Nb; c ++)
    {
        for(int r = 0; r< Nb; r++)
        {
            str.push_back(state[r][c]);
        }
    }
    return str;
}


void AES::Decrypt(string cipherText)
{
    if((cipherText.length()% (4*Nb)) ! = 0)
        cipherText.append((4*Nb) - (cipherText.
        length()%(4*Nb)),'\0');
    int count = 0;
    while (count < (cipherText.length()))
    {
        //copy one block into state
        for(int c = 0; c <Nb; c++)
        {
            for(int r = 0; r< 4; r ++)
                    state[r][c] =
                    cipherText[count+(c*Nb)+r];
        }
        AddRoundKey(Nr);
        #ifdef _DEBUG_D_
            cout << "After Add round Key 0" << endl;
            printState();
        #endif//_DEBUG_
            int i;
        for(i = Nr-1; i>0; i— )
        {
            #ifdef _TEST_STATE_
                    cout << i << endl;
                    testState(i);
            #endif//_TEST_STATE_
            InvShiftRows();
            #ifdef _DEBUG_D_
```

```
            cout << "After ShiftRows "<< dec<<
            i << endl;
            printState();
#endif//_DEBUG_
    InvSubBytes();
#ifdef _DEBUG_D_
            cout << "After Subbytes "<< dec<<
            i << endl;
            printState();
#endif//_DEBUG_
    AddRoundKey(i);
#ifdef _DEBUG_D_
            cout << "Add round Key " << i <<
            endl;
            printState();
#endif//_DEBUG_
    InvMixColumns();
#ifdef _DEBUG_D_
            cout << "After MixColumns "<<
            dec<< i << endl;
            printState();
#endif//_DEBUG_
    }
    InvSubBytes();
#ifdef _DEBUG_D_
            cout << "Round Subbytes"<< dec<<
            i << endl;
            printState();
#endif//_DEBUG_
    InvShiftRows();
#ifdef _DEBUG_D_
            cout << "Round ShiftRows"<< dec<<
            i << endl;
            printState();
#endif//_DEBUG_
    AddRoundKey(0);
#ifdef _DEBUG_D_
            cout << "Add round Key " << i <<
            endl;
            printState();
#endif//_DEBUG_
#ifdef _TEST_STATE_
            //testState(i);
            printState();
#endif//_TEST_STATE_
```

```
            count+ = 4*Nb;
    }
}

const byte AES::LogTable[256] = {
    0, 0, 25, 1, 50, 2, 26, 198, 75, 199, 27, 104, 51,
    238, 223, 3,
    100, 4, 224, 14, 52, 141, 129, 239, 76, 113, 8,
    200, 248, 105, 28, 193,
    125, 194, 29, 181, 249, 185, 39, 106, 77, 228, 166,
    114, 154, 201, 9, 120,
    101, 47, 138, 5, 33, 15, 225, 36, 18, 240, 130, 69,
    53, 147, 218, 142,
    150, 143, 219, 189, 54, 208, 206, 148, 19, 92, 210,
    241, 64, 70, 131, 56,
    102, 221, 253, 48, 191, 6, 139, 98, 179, 37, 226,
    152, 34, 136, 145, 16,
    126, 110, 72, 195, 163, 182, 30, 66, 58, 107, 40,
    84, 250, 133, 61, 186,
    43, 121, 10, 21, 155, 159, 94, 202, 78, 212, 172,
    229, 243, 115, 167, 87,
    175, 88, 168, 80, 244, 234, 214, 116, 79, 174, 233,
    213, 231, 230, 173, 232,
    44, 215, 117, 122, 235, 22, 11, 245, 89, 203, 95,
    176, 156, 169, 81, 160,
    127, 12, 246, 111, 23, 196, 73, 236, 216, 67, 31,
    45, 164, 118, 123, 183,
    204, 187, 62, 90, 251, 96, 177, 134, 59, 82, 161,
    108, 170, 85, 41, 157,
    151, 178, 135, 144, 97, 190, 220, 252, 188, 149,
    207, 205, 55, 63, 91, 209,
    83, 57, 132, 60, 65, 162, 109, 71, 20, 42, 158, 93,
    86, 242, 211, 171,
    68, 17, 146, 217, 35, 32, 46, 137, 180, 124, 184,
    38, 119, 153, 227, 165,
    103, 74, 237, 222, 197, 49, 254, 24, 13, 99, 140,
    128, 192, 247, 112, 7
};

const byte AES::AlogTable[256] =
{
    1, 3, 5, 15, 17, 51, 85, 255, 26, 46, 114, 150,
    161, 248, 19, 53,
    95, 225, 56, 72, 216, 115, 149, 164, 247, 2, 6, 10,
    30, 34, 102, 170,
```

```
    229, 52, 92, 228, 55, 89, 235, 38, 106, 190, 217,
    112, 144, 171, 230, 49,
    83, 245, 4, 12, 20, 60, 68, 204, 79, 209, 104, 184,
    211, 110, 178, 205,
    76, 212, 103, 169, 224, 59, 77, 215, 98, 166, 241,
    8, 24, 40, 120, 136,
    131, 158, 185, 208, 107, 189, 220, 127, 129, 152,
    179, 206, 73, 219, 118, 154,
    181, 196, 87, 249, 16, 48, 80, 240, 11, 29, 39,
    105, 187, 214, 97, 163,
    254, 25, 43, 125, 135, 146, 173, 236, 47, 113, 147,
    174, 233, 32, 96, 160,
    251, 22, 58, 78, 210, 109, 183, 194, 93, 231, 50,
    86, 250, 21, 63, 65,
    195, 94, 226, 61, 71, 201, 64, 192, 91, 237, 44,
    116, 156, 191, 218, 117,
    159, 186, 213, 100, 172, 239, 42, 126, 130, 157,
    188, 223, 122, 142, 137, 128,
    155, 182, 193, 88, 232, 35, 101, 175, 234, 37, 111,
    177, 200, 67, 197, 84,
    252, 31, 33, 99, 165, 244, 7, 9, 27, 45, 119, 153,
    176, 203, 70, 202,
    69, 207, 74, 222, 121, 139, 134, 145, 168, 227, 62,
    66, 198, 81, 243, 14,
    18, 54, 90, 238, 41, 123, 141, 140, 143, 138, 133,
    148, 167, 242, 13, 23,
    57, 75, 221, 124, 132, 151, 162, 253, 28, 36, 108,
    180, 199, 82, 246, 1
};

const byte AES::Si_Box 256] =
{
    82, 9, 106, -43, 48, 54, -91, 56, -65, 64, -93,
    -98, -127, -13, -41, -5,
    124, -29, 57, -126, -101, 47, -1, -121, 52, -114,
    67, 68, -60, -34, -23, -53,
    84, 123, -108, 50, -90, -62, 35, 61, -18, 76, -107,
    11, 66, -6, -61, 78,
    8, 46, -95, 102, 40, -39, 36, -78, 118, 91, -94,
    73, 109, -117, -47, 37,
    114, -8, -10, 100, -122, 104, -104, 22, -44, -92,
    92, -52, 93, 101, -74, -110,
    108, 112, 72, 80, -3, -19, -71, -38, 94, 21, 70,
    87, -89, -115, -99, -124,
```

```
    -112, -40, -85, 0, -116, -68, -45, 10, -9, -28, 88,
    5, -72, -77, 69, 6,
    -48, 44, 30, -113, -54, 63, 15, 2, -63, -81, -67,
    3, 1, 19, -118, 107,
    58, -111, 17, 65, 79, 103, -36, -22, -105, -14,
    -49, -50, -16, -76, -26, 115,
    -106, -84, 116, 34, -25, -83, 53, -123, -30, -7,
    55, -24, 28, 117, -33, 110,
    71, -15, 26, 113, 29, 41, -59, -119, 111, -73, 98,
    14, -86, 24, -66, 27,
    -4, 86, 62, 75, -58, -46, 121, 32, -102, -37, -64,
    -2, 120, -51, 90, -12,
    31, -35, -88, 51, -120, 7, -57, 49, -79, 18, 16,
    89, 39, -128, -20, 95,
    96, 81, 127, -87, 25, -75, 74, 13, 45, -27, 122,
    -97, -109, -55, -100, -17,
    -96, -32, 59, 77, -82, 42, -11, -80, -56, -21, -69,
    60, -125, 83, -103, 97,
    23, 43, 4, 126, -70, 119, -42, 38, -31, 105, 20,
    99, 85, 33, 12, 125
};

const byte AES::S_Box 256] =
{
    99, 124, 119, 123, -14, 107, 111, -59, 48, 1, 103,
    43, -2, -41, -85, 118,
    -54, -126, -55, 125, -6, 89, 71, -16, -83, -44,
    -94, -81, -100, -92, 114, -64,
    -73, -3, -109, 38, 54, 63, -9, -52, 52, -91, -27,
    -15, 113, -40, 49, 21,
    4, -57, 35, -61, 24, -106, 5, -102, 7, 18, -128,
    -30, -21, 39, -78, 117,
    9, -125, 44, 26, 27, 110, 90, -96, 82, 59, -42,
    -77, 41, -29, 47, -124,
    83, -47, 0, -19, 32, -4, -79, 91, 106, -53, -66,
    57, 74, 76, 88, -49,
    -48, -17, -86, -5, 67, 77, 51, -123, 69, -7, 2,
    127, 80, 60, -97, -88,
    81, -93, 64, -113, -110, -99, 56, -11, -68, -74,
    -38, 33, 16, -1, -13, -46,
    -51, 12, 19, -20, 95, -105, 68, 23, -60, -89, 126,
    61, 100, 93, 25, 115,
    96, -127, 79, -36, 34, 42, -112, -120, 70, -18,
    -72, 20, -34, 94, 11, -37,
```

```
    -32, 50, 58, 10, 73, 6, 36, 92, -62, -45, -84, 98,
    -111, -107, -28, 121,
    -25, -56, 55, 109, -115, -43, 78, -87, 108, 86,
    -12, -22, 101, 122, -82, 8,
    -70, 120, 37, 46, 28, -90, -76, -58, -24, -35, 116,
    31, 75, -67, -117, -118,
    112, 62, -75, 102, 72, 3, -10, 14, 97, 53, 87, -71,
    -122, -63, 29, -98,
    -31, -8, -104, 17, 105, -39, -114, -108, -101, 30,
    -121, -23, -50, 85, 40, -33,
    -116, -95, -119, 13, -65, -26, 66, 104, 65, -103,
    45, 15, -80, 84, -69, 22
};

const byte AES::Rcon[30] =
{
    0,1, 2, 4, 8, 16, 32,
    64, -128, 27, 54, 108, -40,
    -85, 77, -102, 47, 94, -68,
    99, -58, -105, 53, 106, -44,
    -77, 125, -6, -17, -59
};

const byte AES::ColMixMatrix[4][4] =
               {
                        2, 3,1, 1,
                        1, 2, 3, 1,
                        1, 1, 2, 3,
                        3, 1, 1, 2
                };

const byte AES::InvColMixMatrix[4][4] =
               {
                        0x0E, 0x0B,0x0D, 0x09,
                        0x09, 0x0E, 0x0B, 0x0D,
                        0x0D, 0x09, 0x0E, 0x0B,
                        0x0b, 0x0D, 0x09, 0x0E
                };

#include "AES.h"

int main(void)
{
    ///////////////////////
    ///Keys test vector
    ///////////////////////
```

```
//128
//char a[] = {0x2b,0x7e,0x15,0x16,0x28,0xae,0xd2,0
  xa6,0xab,0xf7,0x15,0x88,0x09,0xcf,0x4f,0
  x3c,'\0'};
  char a[] = {0x1a,0x91,0xf7,0x20,0x5e,0x45,0x67,0
  x06,0xa2,0x5b,0x66,0xde,0x5f,0x14,0x59
  ,0x88,'\0'};
//192
//char a[] = {0x8e,0x73,0xb0,0xf7,0xda,0x0e,0x64,0
  x52,0xc8,0x10,0xf3,0x2b,0x80,0x90,0x79,0xe5,0x62
  ,0xf8,0xea,0xd2,0x52,0x2c,0x6b,0x7b,'\0'};
//256
//char a[] = {0x60,0x3d,0xeb,0x10,0x15,0xca,0x71,0
  xbe,0x2b,0x73,0xae,0xf0,0x85,0x7d,0x77,0x81,0x1f
  ,0x35,0x2c,0x07,0x3b,0x61,0x08,0xd7,0x2d,0x98,0x
  10,0xa3,0x09,0x14,0xdf,0xf4,'\0'};
/////////////////////
//Plain Text test vector
/////////////////////
//char b[] = {0x32,0x43,0xf6,0xa8,0x88,0x5a,0x30,0
  x8d,0x31,0x31,0x98,0xa2,0xe0,0x37,0x07
  ,0x34,'\0'};
//73, 74, 72. 69, 6e, 67, 20. 32, 20, 65,
  6e,6372797074
  char b[] = {0x73, 0x74, 0x72,0x69, 0x6e, 0x67,
  0x20, 0x32, 0x20, 0x65, 0x6e, 0x63, 0x72, 0x79,
  0x70, 0x74};

  string key;
  string text;

  for(int i = 0; i < 16;i++)
  {
      key.push_back(a[i]);
      text.push_back(b[i]);
  }
  AES obj (key, AES::KeySize::AES128);

  //obj.KeyExpansion(key);
  obj.Encrypt(text);
  obj.Decrypt(obj.GetCipherText());
return 0;
}
```

6.14 Conclusion

AES was chosen as the new standard for several reasons. The purpose was to create a new algorithm that is resistant to known attacks and more reliable, as well as faster and simpler, than the existing ones, while also being implemented easily with hardware and software, including restricted environments. It is very clear that AES has satisfied all the conditions with its simple and easy implementation without compromising the security aspect. AES is more versatile, with its variable key size and block size. It was originally designed for nonclassified U.S. government information, but due to its success, AES-256 is usable for top secret government information. As of today, no successful attack on AES has been detected. This reflects how successful AES is in its categories.

7

ASYMMETRIC KEY ALGORITHMS

NASRIN SULTANA AND SAIFUL AZAD

Contents

Keywords

Asymmetric key algorithm
Digital signature
Private key
Public key

In the very early era of cryptography, multiple parties involved in secret message exchange had to depend on a secret key that they interchanged among themselves through a trusted, but noncryptographic method. Generally, simple methods like one-to-one communication through a reliable carrier were exercised to exchange any secret key. They kept this key absolutely secret among themselves. Later, this secret key would be utilized to encrypt their desired messages. Since only the parties involved in the communication had the secret key, they could only decrypt any message exchanged between them. One of the major limitations of this technique was the methods exercised to exchange a secret key. Commonly, some impractical and unsafe methods, like face-to-face meeting or trusted courier service, were employed before the modern era. Although currently the key is exchanged through an existing encryption channel, the security depends on the confidentiality of the previous key exchange. Asymmetric key, also known as public-key cryptography, resolves this issue by not disclosing the secret key to anyone. The users can now communicate and exchange messages securely over a public channel without having to agree upon any shared key beforehand.

For the last 20 years, Whitfield Diffie, Martin Hellman, and Ralph Merkle have been given credit as the cryptographers who discovered the technique of public-key cryptography, while Ron Rivest, Adi Shamir, and Leonard Adleman have been honored for developing RSA, the most integrated implementation of public-key cryptography. However, a recent announcement indicates that the history of cryptography has to be rewritten. According to the British government, public-key cryptography was originally invented at the Government Communications Headquarters (GCHQ) in Cheltenham. It was in the late 1960s that a senior member of the military did some work in the field of *nonsecret encryption*, which is related to public-key cryptography without the inclusion of the concept of digital signature. There are some evidentiary artifacts available that could support these claims.

In 1969, James Ellis, one of Britain's foremost government cryptographers, started searching for a way to resolve the key distribution problem. Later, the method explored by Ellis was unlike those of Diffie, Hellman, and Merkle in that it was extremely advanced. However, the discovery of Ellis was sworn to secrecy as he was a recruit of the British government. He conceptualized and developed the theme of separate public-key and private-key use. Meanwhile, he realized that he had to look for a special one-way function that could be reversed if the receiver end had access to some pieces of special information. Unfortunately, he failed to draw any conclusion to the work. In 1973, Clifford Cocks discovered the first workable mathematical formula for nonsecret encryption, and he recorded it in a secret British Communications-Electronics Security Group (CESG) report titled *A Note on Non-Secret Encryption*. Afterward, in 1974, a few months after Clifford's discovery, Malcolm Williamson discovered a key exchange method similar to the one discovered by Diffie, Hellman, and Merkle. However, the work of James Ellis, Clifford Cocks, and Malcolm Williamson was not patented for two reasons: (1) patenting would mean forcing GCHQ to reveal the details of their work, which would have been incompatible with GCHQ's aims as an organization, and (2) in the early 1970s, it was far from the imagination that mathematical algorithms could be patented.

In 1976, it was evident that Diffie and Hellman patented their work on public-key cryptography. At that time, Williamson was eager to go public and stop Diffie and Hellman's application for patent. He was stopped from doing so by his superiors, who did not have much foresight regarding the digital revolution and the future potential scope of public-key cryptography. In the beginning of the 1980s, Williamson's superiors realized that their decision was wrong. Development in computing and Internet technology made it clear that RSA and Diffie–Hellman–Merkle key exchanges would both be successful commercial products. Therefore, in 1996, RSA Data Security, Inc. (the company responsible for RSA products) was sold for $200 million. Finally, in 1997, it became known to the public that an asymmetric key algorithm was secretly developed by James H. Ellis, Clifford Cocks, and Malcolm Williamson at the GCHQ in the UK in 1973. Several years later, Ellis, Cocks, and Williamson received the acknowledgment they deserved for their invention.

The motivation of the asymmetric key cryptosystem developed by Diffie and Hellman came from work on public-key distribution by Merkle. A few years later, Rivest, Shamir, and Adleman from MIT independently invented an asymmetric key algorithm commonly known as RSA. They utilize modular arithmetic and two very large prime numbers for encryption and digital signature. Security of the RSA is related to the difficulty of factoring those large prime numbers, for which currently there is no known efficient method. In the mid-1980s, Neal Koblitz and Victor Miller introduced a new public-key algorithm based on a discrete algorithm problem known as the elliptic curve algorithm. Although it utilizes smaller keys for faster operations, it assures estimated security approximately analogous to RSA.

7.1 Basic Concept

As mentioned above, one of the major problems of a secret key (also known as symmetric key) algorithm is the secure key distribution between the two parties, which encouraged people to search for an alternative. The asymmetric key algorithm is a solution that utilizes two separate keys, where one key is kept secret from the external world, which is referred to as the private key, and another one is publicized, referred to as the public key. These keys are constructed in such a way that they conceive mathematical relationships and build on employing integer factorization, discrete logarithm, and elliptic curve algebraic structures. There are a couple of aspects that need to be considered while employing such a cryptographic algorithm:

1. Generating a key pair must be computationally easy and inexpensive.
2. Encryption and decryption using these keys also must be easy and inexpensive.
3. It must be computationally infeasible to unlock a key while knowing the other key.
4. Encryption and decryption of a message need not be possible employing the identical key.

7.2 Applications of Asymmetric Key Algorithms

Asymmetric key algorithms can be used for encryption/decryption, digital signature, or both. They are described in the following sections in detail.

7.2.1 Encryption/Decryption

In the case of encrypting a message, the public key of the recipient is utilized to encrypt a message, which is not possible to decrypt by anyone who does not own the corresponding private key. In other words, the sending party uses the public key of the desired receiver to encrypt a message to be sent. That message can only be decrypted by the desired receiver, who holds the corresponding private key. Thus, it preserves the confidentiality of a message. An example of the encryption technique utilizing asymmetric key algorithms is illustrated in Figure 7.1. Let us assume that Alice and Bob are the two parties who previously decided to exchange their messages securely through non-secure communication media, like the Internet. They come to consent for using an asymmetric key algorithm. Therefore, both of them generate a pair of keys for each. One of them is kept secret and another

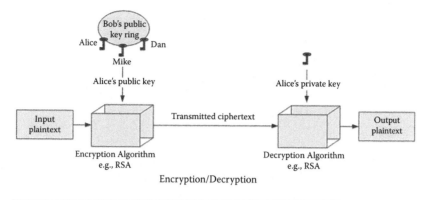

Figure 7.1   Encryption/decryption technique using asymmetric key algorithm.

one is exchanged between them. After receiving the public key of the other party, one stores it in his or her public-key ring. If Bob wants to send a secret message to Alice, he must encrypt the message utilizing Alice's public key. On the other hand, after receiving this message from Bob, Alice employs her private key to decrypt. Similar procedures are also followed to exchange messages from Alice to Bob.

7.2.2 Digital Signature

In many cases, along with the confidentiality of a message, it is also necessary to verify the identity of the sender. This could be performed through a digital signature, which is an electronic signature generated through a mathematical scheme. There are three main reasons for applying a digital signature:

1. **Authentication:** Digital signatures are used to validate the source of a message. A receiver can make sure that the message has been sent from the valid user.
2. **Nonrepudiation:** A sender cannot deny the transmission of a message if it is digitally signed.
3. **Integrity:** It also preserves the integrity of a message by not allowing it to alter in transit.

Asymmetric key algorithms also can be utilized to sign a message digitally. A sender's private key is utilized to sign a message, which can then be verified by the receiver who has access to the sender's public key. If the message is decrypted successfully, it proves that the

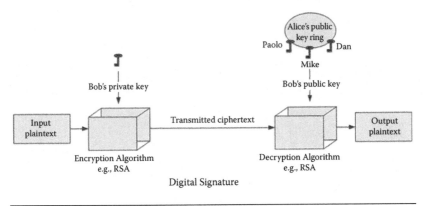

Figure 7.2   Digital signature using asymmetric key algorithm.

sender had proper access to the private key, which is likely to be the authenticated person associated with the public key. It also verifies that the message has not been altered, as a change in the encrypted message would result in a change in the message digest. Recalling the previous example, if Bob wants to digitally sign the message, he must employ his private key to encrypt that message. After receiving that message, if Alice can decrypt the message using Bob's public key, she can be assured that the message was transmitted by a legitimate party. This scenario is illustrated in Figure 7.2.

7.2.3 Encryption and Digital Signature

A message can be both encrypted and digitally signed at the same time by encrypting it twice with different keys and decrypting with their relevant keys. As mentioned in the previous sections, if two parties desire to exchange encrypted messages among themselves, the sender must encrypt a message with the public key of the receiver. Again, for digitally signing a message, the sender must encrypt the message with his or her private key. Therefore, whenever a sender wants both, he or she must encrypt a message with his or her private key (for digital signature), and then again encrypt that message using the receiver's private key (for encryption). It this case, the sequence of encryptions needs to be maintained precisely to achieve the plaintext. On the other hand, after receiving this message, it must be decrypted using two relevant keys following the encryption sequence. If the plaintext is possible to acquire after the decryption, a receiver can

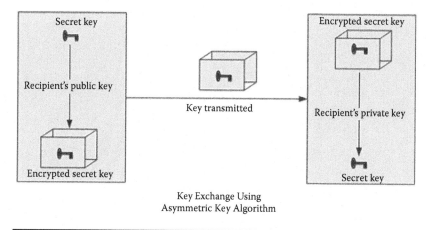

Key Exchange Using
Asymmetric Key Algorithm

Figure 7.3 Encryption/decryption and digital signature using asymmetric key algorithm.

Table 7.1 Application of Asymmetric Key Algorithms

ENCRYPTION TECHNIQUE	ENCRYPTION/ DECRYPTION	DIGITAL SIGNATURE	BOTH
Encrypting using receiver's public key	Yes	No	No
Encrypting using sender's private key	No	Yes	No
Encrypting using sender's private key and receiver's public key	Yes	Yes	Yes

presume that the packet was received from a valid sender and the message is without any alteration. An example of such a technique is given in Figure 7.3.

A summary of the above discussions is given in Table 7.1.

In the next two chapters, renowned algorithms—RSA and elliptic curve cryptography—will be discussed in detail with their relative operational methods and implementation.

8

THE RSA ALGORITHM

SAAD ANDALIB AND SAIFUL AZAD

Contents

Keywords

Asymmetric key algorithm
Private key
Public key
Public-key decryption
Public-key encryption
RSA

In mid-1977, 1 year after the introduction of public-key cryptography by Diffie and Hellman, three young scientists of the Massachusetts Institute of Technology (MIT) took the concept of public-key cryptography and developed an algorithm that is known as the RSA algorithm. It is named after the surnames of the three inventors, Ron Rivest, Adi Shamir, and Leonard Adleman. In RSA, a pair of keys is generated where one key is revealed to the external world, known as a *public key*, and the other one is kept secret to the user, known as a *private key*. For generating keys, the RSA algorithm utilizes a number theory concept that is commonly known as the one-way function. A one-way function is easy to do in one way, but it is very difficult to reverse. Consequently, it is infeasible to derive the private key after knowing the public key of a user. Thus, the secrecy of a message remains intact.

8.1 The Concept

Unlike symmetric key cryptography, it is not mandatory to share any secret key among the parties involved in the secret message exchange. Then the question that may arise in our mind is: How does an asymmetric key ensure secrecy of a message? As mentioned previously, in asymmetric key cryptography, instead of generating a single key (which is usually the case for symmetric key cryptography), it generates a pair of keys. Among them, the public key is publicized and the private key is kept secret. These two keys are mathematically related. Since these keys are generated utilizing a one-way function, it is infeasible to generate a private key after knowing the public key, and vice versa. Again, a message encrypted through a key is not feasible to decrypt utilizing a similar key. Hence, the secrecy of a message is preserved.

Let us assume that Alice and Bob desire to exchange secret messages between themselves using asymmetric key cryptography, especially using the RSA algorithm. They first generate their relevant key sets and publicize the public key so that the other party can access it. The denotations of their public and private keys are PU_A and PR_A for Alice, and PU_B and PR_B for Bob. Each of the participants keeps his or her private key secret from the other. When Alice wants to send a message to Bob, she encrypts the message using PU_B, which she can access. For any message, M, Alice generates a ciphertext, C, as follows:

$$C = PU_B(M)$$

After receiving C, Bob can decrypt the message employing his private key, PR_B. This can be formally expressed as

$$M = PR_B(C)$$

Figure 8.1 portrays the steps that can be followed to exchange secret messages using the RSA algorithm. Any third party who intercepts C is not able to reproduce M even though it has access to PU_B because:

- In asymmetric key cryptography, it is infeasible to generate one key when you have access to the other key.
- A message that is encrypted through a key is not possible to decrypt utilizing a similar key.

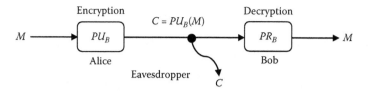

Figure 8.1   Secret message exchange procedure using the RSA algorithm.

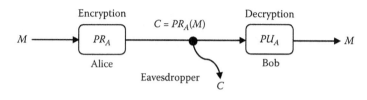

Figure 8.2   Digital signature using the RSA algorithm.

- The public and private keys for any participant are a matched pair and are inverses of each other, i.e.,

$$M = PR_B(PU_B(M))$$

$$M = PU_B(PR_B(M))$$

Consequently, a message that is encrypted using the public key can only be decrypted with its relevant private key.

The RSA algorithm can also be utilized to digitally sign a message so that the recipient has proof of who sent it. In other words, the authenticity of a message can also be checked employing the RSA algorithm. In the case of a digital signature, a message is encrypted using the private key and is decrypted using the relevant public key. Since only a valid sender can have his or her private key, a recipient can assume that the message is sent by the valid sender, which is illustrated in Figure 8.2.

8.2 Operations

The RSA algorithm comprises three steps:

1. Key generation
2. Encryption
3. Decryption

The operations involved in these steps are detailed below.

8.2.1 Key Generation

As mentioned earlier, the RSA algorithm generates a pair of keys. These keys are usually generated employing two large prime numbers (512 bits). The key generation algorithm is stated below:

1. Select two large prime numbers p and q randomly, such that $p \neq q$.
2. Compute n such that $n = p \times q$.
3. Compute $\varphi(n) = \varphi(p) \times \varphi(q) = (p - 1) \times (q - 1)$, where φ is Euler's totient function.*
4. Select an integer number e such that $1 < e < \varphi(n)$ and $gcd(e, \varphi(n)) = 1$, where e and $\varphi(n)$ are co-prime.
5. Compute d as the multiplicative inverse of $e(mod(\varphi(n))$, i.e., $de = 1 \bmod \varphi(n)$.
6. Publish the pair $PU = (e, n)$ as the participant's public key.
7. Keep the pair $PE = (d, n)$ as secret as the participant's private key.

Relevant pseudocodes for the key generation procedure are discussed below in Algorithms 8.1, 8.2, and 8.3.

Algorithm 8.1: FindE(phi_n)

```
Begin
   e ← 0
do
begin
    Choose an integer number e (e must be co-prime of
phi_n)
while (!CheckCoPrime(phi_n, e))
end do-while
return e
End
```

---

* In number theory, Euler's totient function, $\varphi(n)$, is an arithmetic function that finds out all the co-prime numbers to n that are less than or equal to n.

Algorithm 8.2: FindD(phi_n, e)

```
Begin
local variables:a, b, x, y, u, v, m, n, q, r, gcd
a ←phi_n
  b ←e
  x ← 0
  y ← 1
  u← 1
  v ← 0
gcd← b
 while (a ! = 0)
  begin
    q ←gcd/a
    r ←gcd% a
    m ← x - u * q
    n ← y - v * q
    gcd← a
    a ← r
    x ← u
    y ← v
    u ← m
    v ← n
  end while
if y < 1
  begin
    y ←phi_n + y
end if
return y
End
```

Algorithm 8.3: GenerateKey(&n, &e, &d)

```
Begin
local variables:p, q, phi_n, pt, ct
    Enter two prime numbers and stored then in p and q
respectively
    n ← Multiply(p,q)
phi_n← Multiply (p-1,q-1)
    e ←FindE(phi_n)
    d ←FindD(phi_n, e)
/* (e,n) pair is now the public key and (d,n) pair is
now the private key */
End
```

8.2.2 Encryption

Anyone who wants to send a message can now utilize the public key, (e, n). Recall the previous example, when Alice desires to send a message to Bob; she can now encrypt the message M as follows:

$$C = M^e \ (\text{mod } n)$$

Alice sends the ciphertext, C, to Bob.

8.2.3 Decryption

After receiving C from Alice, Bob can now decrypt the message utilizing the relative private key. He can find out M using the following expression:

$$M = C^d \ (\text{mod } n)$$

Since no one else has the private key of Bob, anyone other than him would not be able to decrypt the message.

Example

Let us look at the following small example to realize how the RSA algorithm works. Suppose Alice desires to send a message to Bob, who generates his keys as follows:

1. Bob chooses two prime numbers, $p = 17$ and $q = 13$.
2. Then he calculates n such that $n = p \times q = 17 \times 13 = 221$.
3. The value of $\varphi(n)$ is computed as $\varphi(n) = 16 \times 12 = 192$.
4. He selects $e = 131$.
5. Bob finds the number $d = 107$.
6. Now Bob's public key is (131, 221) and his private key is (107, 221).

After key generation, Bob publishes his private key and Alice has access to that public key. Let us assume that Alice wants to encrypt the following message, $M = 8$. Alice can utilize Bob's public key to produce C, i.e.,

$$C = 8^{131} \ (\text{mod } 221) = 70$$

Bob receives the ciphertext 70 and utilizes his private key to reproduce M as follows.

$$M = 70^{107} \ (\text{mod } 221) = 8$$

Other than Bob, since no one has the private key, no one would be able to decrypt the message.

8.3 Applications of the RSA Algorithm

Although the RSA algorithm is developed to encrypt/decrypt a message, it is very slow in terms of processing speed. It requires a longer time than usual cryptographic algorithms due to generating large prime numbers and performing all the calculations. Moreover, each encryption session usually requires generation of different sets of prime numbers and calculations to prevent the message from being eavesdropped. This is why it is preferred when the message is short. Consequently, it is widely used in Short Message Service (SMS). The RSA algorithm is also utilized to exchange secret keys and to sign a message digitally. It can also be utilized to encrypt a longer message if that is fragmented into small blocks and merged after encryption. The receiver must have the knowledge regarding the fragmentation procedure. He or she could do the opposite and merge after the decryption to produce the original message.

In Chapter 9, another asymmetric key cryptography technique is discussed, elliptic curve cryptography (ECC), which resolves the problem of the RSA algorithm by utilizing a shorter key than RSA and offering comparable performance.

8.4 Implementation Code

```
#include<iostream>
#include<cmath>
#include<cstdlib>
#include<cstring>

using namespace std;

boolCheckIsPrime(long intnum)
{
if(num< 2) return false;

longinti = 2;
while(i< = num/2)
   {
if(!(num% i)) return false;
i++;
   }
```

```
return true;
}
longint Multiply(long int num1,long int num2)
{
return num1 * num2;
}

boolCheckCoPrime (long int num1, long int num2) {
longint lowest;

if (num1 > num2) lowest = num2;
else lowest = num1;

longinti = 2;

boolcoprime = true;

while (i< lowest) {
if (!(num1% i) && !(num2% i)) coprime = false;
i++;
   }

returncoprime;
}

longintFindE(long intphi_n)
{
longint e = 0;

do {
cout<< "Choose an integer number e (e must be coprime
of phi_n): ";
cin>> e;
   } while (!CheckCoPrime(phi_n, e));

return e;
}

longintFindD(long intphi_n, long int e)
{
int a = phi_n, b = e;
longint x = 0, y = 1, u = 1, v = 0, m, n, q, r;
longintgcd = b;
while (a != 0) {
    q = gcd/a;
    r = gcd% a;
```

```
    m = x - u * q;
    n = y - v * q;
gcd = a;
  a = r;
  x = u;
  y = v;
  u = m;
  v = n;
}

if (y < 1) {
cout<< "Choose a suitable \"e\" value" <<endl;
  e = FindE(phi_n);
FindD(phi_n, e);
}

return y;
}

longintEncrypt_Decrypt(long int t, long int e, long
int n)
{
longint rem;
longint x = 1;

while (e ! = 0) {
rem = e % 2;
  e = e/2;

if (rem = = 1) x = (x * t)% n;
  t = (t * t)% n;
}

return x;
}

voidEncDecStr (long int e, long int n)
{
char *str = new char[1000];
char *str1 = new char[1000];

cout<< "\nEnter a string: ";
cin>>str;

cout<< "Encrypting using Public Key: " <<endl;
inti = 0;
```

```
while (i ! = strlen(str)) {
    str1[i] = Encrypt_Decrypt(str[i], e, n);
    i++;
}

cout<< str1 <<endl;
}

voidEncDecNum (long int n1, long int n2)
{
longintpn;

cout<< "\nEnter an integer number: ";
cin>>pn;

cout<<Encrypt_Decrypt(pn, n1, n2) <<endl;
}

voidgenerate_key (long int&n, long int&e, long int&d)
{
longint p, q, phi_n, pt, ct;

do {
    cout<< "Enter a prime number: ";
    cin>> p;
    } while (!CheckIsPrime(p));

do {
    cout<< "Enter another prime number: ";
    cin>> q;
    } while (!CheckIsPrime(q));

  n = Multiply(p,q);
cout<< "n is " << n <<endl;

  phi_n = Multiply (p-1,q-1);
cout<< "phi_n is " <<phi_n<<endl;

  e = FindE(phi_n);
cout<< "e is " << e <<endl;
if (!e) {
      cout<< "Choose two suitable prime number"
<<endl;
      exit(1);
    }
```

```
  d = FindD(phi_n, e);
cout<< "d is " << d <<endl;
}


int main() {

cout<<endl<<endl<< "##IMPLEMENTATION OF R.S.A
ALGORITHM USING C++##" <<endl<<endl;


longint n, d = 0, e;

generate_key(n, d, e);

cout<< "Public Key : ("<<e<<","<<n<<")" <<endl;
cout<< "Private Key : ("<<d<<","<<n<<")" <<endl;

cout<<endl<< "Press 1: for encrypting numbers & 2: for
encrypting string: ";
int choice;
cin>> choice;

switch (choice) {
        case 1:
        EncDecNum(e, n);
        break;

        case 2:
        EncDecStr(e, n);
        break;

        default:
        cout<< "Wrong choice. Try again." <<endl;
        exit(1);
}

cout<<endl<< "Press 1: for decrypting numbers & 2: for
decrypting string: ";
cin>> choice;

switch (choice) {
        case 1:
        EncDecNum(d, n);
        break;
```

```
        case 2:
        EncDecStr(d, n);
        break;

        default:
        cout<< "Wrong choice. Try again." <<endl;
        exit(1);
    }

return 0;
}
```

9

ELLIPTIC CURVE CRYPTOGRAPHY

HAFIZUR RAHMAN AND SAIFUL AZAD

Contents

Keywords

Asymmetric key algorithm
Diffie–Hellman key exchange
Elliptic curve cryptography
Private key
Public key

9.1 Introduction

Although the RSA algorithm resolves the problem of a secret key, it experiences higher computational cost because of utilizing a longer key size, so that it becomes computationally infeasible to solve.

On the other hand, elliptic curve cryptography (ECC) is another approach of an asymmetric algorithm that utilizes a smaller key size, but still ensures the same level of security. ECC is based on the elliptic curve discrete log problem, which is much harder to solve over factoring integers of the RSA algorithm. Since it is harder, even a smaller key is computationally infeasible to solve. According to National Institute of Standards and Technology (NIST) guidelines for public key sizes for the Advanced Encryption Standard (AES), an ECC key size of 163 bits can ensure comparable performance of 1024 bits of key size of the RSA algorithm, which is around six times higher than that of the ECC key size [1]. The ratio is even bigger for a higher number of bits.

The elliptic curve system was first introduced to the cryptographic arena by Neal Koblitz and Victor Miller, who worked at IBM [1]. Generally, parties involved in the secure message exchange must generate a private key and a public key by utilizing the points of an elliptic curve and by following an algorithm. A private key is kept secret, whereas a public key is publicized to the external world. Like the RSA algorithm, the confidentiality of a message is ensured by encrypting a message using the public key of the receiver, which can only be decrypted by using the relative private key. A message can also be digitally signed by encrypting it using the private key of the sender. It can be decrypted by anyone who holds the public key of the sender. For understanding the ECC algorithm, Section 9.2 describes the details of an elliptic curve for a real number (R) as well as for a finite field (Z_R), and all the operations involved in encryption and decryption.

9.2 Elliptic Curves over R

An elliptic curve over the real numbers is the set of points (x, y) that satisfy the following equation:

$$y^2 = x^3 + ax + b \tag{9.1}$$

where x, y, a, and b are all real numbers. Equation (9.1) is said to be cubic or degree 3 since the highest exponent that exists in this equation is 3. Elliptic curves in the form of Equation (9.1) can be divided into two groups: singular and nonsingular [2]. In ECC, nonsingular curves are preferred so that a curve can be free from cusps or self-intersections. An elliptic curve is said to be nonsingular when it satisfies the following condition:

$$4a^3 + 27b^2 \neq 0 \qquad\qquad (9.2)$$

An elliptic curve generated using Equation (9.1) is illustrated in Figure 9.1.

Although an elliptic curve over the real numbers is a good approach to understand the properties of an elliptic curve, it requires higher computational time to perform various operations and is sometimes inaccurate due to the rounding errors. However, cryptographic schemes require fast and precise arithmetic. Consequently, two types of elliptic curves are utilized in cryptographic applications:

1. Prime curves over a Z_p, where p is a prime number and $p > 3$. All the variables and the coefficients are taken from a set of integers from 0 to $p - 1$, and calculations are performed over modulo p.
2. Binary curve over *Galois field* (2^m), also known as $GF(2^m)$, where all the variables and coefficients are taken on the values in $GF(2^n)$ and calculations are performed over $GF(2^n)$.

Since prime curves do not have any extended bit fiddling operation [3] analogous to the binary curve, they are suitable for software implementations. Consequently, prime curve-based ECC is explained in this chapter with its pseudocodes, examples, and implementations.

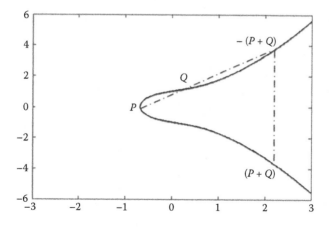

Figure 9.1   An example of an elliptic curve where $a = b = 1$.

9.3 Elliptic Curves over Z_p

An elliptic curve over finite field Z_p includes all points (x, y) in the $Z_p \times Z_p$ matrix that satisfies the following elliptic curve equation:

$$y^2 \equiv x^3 + ax + b \bmod p \qquad (9.3)$$

where x and y are numbers in Z_p, and similar to the real case, a and b must satisfy the following condition to form a finite abelian group [3]:

$$4a^3 + 27b^2 \not\equiv 0 \bmod p \qquad (9.4)$$

Just to clarify here, in abstract algebra, an abelian group, also called a commutative group, is a group in which the result of applying the group operation to two group elements does not depend on their order (the axiom of commutativity).

Now, Equation (9.3) can be written as

$$y^2 \bmod p = (x^3 + ax + b) \bmod p \qquad (9.5)$$

By replacing x, y, a, b, and p with the values 5, 1, 1, 0, and 23, we get

$$5^2 \bmod 23 = (1^3 + 1 \times 1 + 0) \bmod 23$$

$$25 \bmod 23 = 2 \bmod 23$$

$$2 = 2$$

Hence, $(1, 5)$ is a point on the curve over Z_{23}. A similar procedure can be followed to find all the points of the curve. An algorithm for generating all the points of a prime curve is given below:

Algorithm 9.1: Calculate Points (PrimeNumber)

```
Begin
        a ← 1
        b ← 0
        for x ← 0 to PrimeNumber
                for y ← 0 to PrimeNumber
                        k ← y * y
                        m ← (x * x * x) + a * x + b
                        if (k% PrimeNumber = m% PrimeNumber)
```

```
                                    store point (x, y) in a
container
                              end if
                    end for
              end for
End
```

Using Algorithm 9.1, for $a = 1$, $b = 0$, and $p = 23$, the following points can be found:

x	0	1	1	9	9	11	11	13	13	15	15	16	16	17	17	18	18	19	19	20	20	21	21
y	0	5	18	5	18	10	13	5	18	3	20	8	15	10	13	10	13	1	22	4	19	6	17

Figure 9.2 plots all the points of the above-mentioned curve. As can be observed from the figure, the points do not form an elliptic curve; rather, they form a cloud of points in a finite field. This group also has another point that is known as the point at infinity, denoted as O, which is the identity element under an addition operation over points discussed in the next section. The negative of the point at infinity can be defined as $-O = O$, and the negative of any other point $P = (x_P, y_P)$ on elliptic curve E to be its reflection over the x-axis, i.e., $-P = (x_P, -y_P \bmod p)$.

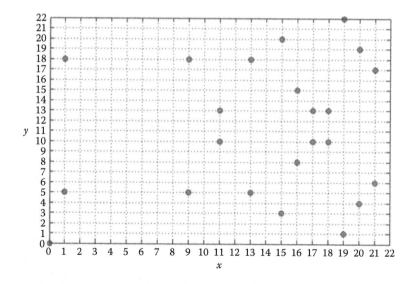

Figure 9.2 The elliptic curve for $a = 1$, $b = 0$, and $P = 23$.

Various arithmetic operations over points that are necessary to understand the ECC algorithm in detail are discussed below with relevant examples.

9.3.1 *Adding Points in Elliptic Curves over Z_P*

Addition operations on an elliptic curve can be divided into three cases:

1. **Adding two distinct points P and Q, when $P \neq Q$:** If $P = (x_P, y_P)$ and $Q = (x_Q, y_Q)$, then $R = P + Q$ can be determined utilizing the following rules:

$$x_R \equiv (S^2 - x_P - x_Q) \bmod p, \text{ and} \qquad (9.6)$$

$$y_R \equiv -y_P + S(x_P - x_R) \bmod p \qquad (9.7)$$

where $S \equiv (y_P - y_Q)(x_P - x_Q)^{-1} \bmod p$. Let us assume that $P = (1, 5)$ and $Q = (9, 18)$ are the points of Figure 9.2 we would like to add. Then,

$$s = \frac{(5 - 18)}{(1 - 9)} \bmod 23$$

$$= \frac{-13}{-8} \bmod 23$$

$$= \frac{13}{8} \bmod 23$$

$$= 16$$

Now, utilizing the value of s, we can have x_R and y_R as follows:

$$x_R = (16^2 - 1 - 9) \bmod 23$$
$$= 246 \bmod 23$$
$$= 16$$
$$y_R = (-5 + 16(1 - 16)) \bmod 23$$
$$= -245 \bmod 23$$
$$= 8$$

Hence, $R = (16, 8)$. The necessary algorithms to understand the addition of two distinct points over an elliptic curve are given below. In this process, Algorithm 9.2 demonstrates how the greatest common divisor (GCD) of two numbers can be found.

Algorithm 9.2: EGCD(a, b, & u, & v))// Extended GCD Gives $g = a^*u + b^*v$

```
Begin
u ← 1, v ← 0, g ← a, u1 ← 0, v1 ← 1, g1 = b
while (g1 ! = 0)
        q ←floor(g/g1)
        t1 ← u - q*u1;
        t2 ← v - q*v1;
        t3 ← g - q*g1;
        u ← u1
        v ← v1
        g ← g1
        u1 ← t1
        v1 ← t2
        g1 ← t3;
end while
return g
End
```

Steps for calculating the inverse modulus are given in Algorithm 9.3.

Algorithm 9.3: InverseModulus(a, n)//Solve Linear Congruence Equation $x^*z = = 1 \pmod{n}$ for z

```
Begin
Local Variable: u, v, g, x
x ← x% n
        g ← EGCD(x, n, u, v)//describe in Algorithm 2
if (g ! = 1)
        z ← 0
else
        z ← u% n
        end if
return z
End
```

Algorithm 9.4 demonstrates how to perform negative modulus operations.

Algorithm 9.4: NegativeModulus(a, p)

```
Begin
      b ← a * -1;
      n ← ceiling((float)b/p)
return (n * p) - b
End
```

Algorithm 9.5 illustrates the steps to add two distinct points over an elliptic curve.

Algorithm 9.5: AddPoints(xp, yp, xq, yq, & xr, & yr, p)

```
Begin
n ← yp - yq
d ← xp - xq
if (d < 0)
      n * = -1;
      d * = -1;
end if
    x ← InverseModulus(d, p)//describe in Algorithm 3
if (n * x > 0) s = (n * x)% p;
elses = NegativeModulus(n * x, p)//describe in
Algorithm 4
end if
    xr_ ← (s * s - xp - xq)
if (xr_ < 0) xr ← NegativeModulus(xr_, p)
else xr ← xr_% p
    end if
    yr_ ← (-yp + s * (xp - xr));
if (yr_ < 0)yr ← NegativeModulus(yr_, p);
else yr = yr_% p;
End
```

2. **Adding the points _P_ and _−P_:** The addition of the points _P_ and _−P_ poses a unique situation since the line through the two points is vertical, which will never intersect the elliptic curve at any point. So, it can be defined as _P_ + (−_P_) = _O_, the point of infinity.

3. **Adding a point with the point at infinity:** When a point is added to the point of infinity, it produces the same point, e.g., $P + O = P$.

9.3.2 Scalar Multiplication

Scalar multiplication of $k \times P$ is a repetitive addition of a point $P = (x_P, y_P)$, until it reaches k, where $k > 0$. For instance, when $k = 3$, in that case, $3P = P + P + P$. If $y_p \equiv 0 \bmod p$, then $P = -P$. In other cases, $2P = P + P = R$,

$$x_R \equiv s^2 - 2x_P \bmod p, \text{ and} \tag{9.8}$$

$$y_R \equiv -y_P + s(x_P - x_R) \bmod p \tag{9.9}$$

where $s \equiv (3x_P^2 + a)(2y_P)^{-1} \bmod p$. Let us assume that $P = (11, 10)$, then $2P$ can be calculated as

$$s = (3 \times 11^2 + 1)(2 \times 10)^{-1} \bmod 23$$

$$= \frac{364}{20} \bmod 23$$

$$= \frac{91}{5} \bmod 23$$

$$= (91 \times 14) \bmod 23$$

$$= 1274 \bmod 23$$

$$= 9$$

Now, utilizing the value of s, we can have x_R and y_R as follows:

$$x_R = (9^2 - 2 \times 11) \bmod 23$$

$$= (81 - 22) \bmod 23$$

$$= 59 \bmod 23$$

$$= 13$$

$$y_R = -10 + 9\ (11 - 13)\ \mathrm{mod}\ 23$$

$$= (-10 - 18)\ \mathrm{mod}\ 23$$

$$= -28\ \mathrm{mod}\ 23$$

$$= 18$$

Hence, $R = 2P = (13, 18)$. One important point to notice here is that $2P$ is now a distinctive point. Consequently, $R + R = 2R = 4P$. To find $3P$, we have to utilize Algorithm 9.5 since $2P$ and P are now two distinct points. Therefore, the x- and y-coordinates of $3P$ can be found using Equations (9.6) and (9.7). Similar procedures can be repeated to get the scalar multiplication of any $k \times P$, where $k > 0$. Algorithms 9.6 and 9.7 illustrate the steps that can be followed to find the double of a point and a scalar multiplication of a point, respectively.

Algorithm 9.6: AddDouble(xp, yp, & xr, & yr, a, p)

```
Begin
        n ← 3 * xp * xp + a
        d ← 2 * yp
        if (d < 0)
                n ← n * -1;
                d ← d * -1;
        end if
                x ← InverseModulus(d, p)//describe in
Algorithm 3
        if (n * x > 0) s = (n * x)% p;
        elses = NegativeModulus(n * x, p)//describe in
Algorithm 4
        end if
                xr_ ← (s * s -2 * xp)
        if (xr_ < 0) xr ← NegativeModulus(xr_, p)
                else xr ← xr_% p
        end if
                yr_ ← (-yp + s * (xp - xr));
        if (yr_ < 0)yr ← NegativeModulus(yr_, p);
        else yr = yr_% p;
End
```

Algorithm 9.7 demonstrates the scalar multiplication of a point to k times.

Algorithm 9.7: Scalar Multiplication (k, xp, yp, & xr, & yr)

```
Begin
add_double(xp, yp, xr, yr, a, p)
for i ← 0 to i < k - 2
        xq ← xr;
        yq ← yr;
        xr ← 0
yr ← 0
        add_points(xp, yp, xq, yq, xr, yr, p)
        end for
End
```

9.4 Discrete Logarithm Problem

Let us consider the scalar multiplication of $k \times P = R$, where P is a point of an elliptic curve and $k < p$. According to the rules of an abelian group [4], R is also going to be a point of that elliptic curve. It is relatively easy to calculate R when both k and P are known. However, it is relatively hard to discover k when R and P are known. This is known as the discrete logarithm problem for an elliptic curve. Let us assume that $R = (16, 8)$ when $P = (11, 10)$, and we would like to search out k utilizing the brute-force method.

$$P = (11, 10)$$

$$2P = (13, 18)$$

$$3P = (15, 20)$$

$$4P = (9, 18)$$

$$5P = (19, 22)$$

$$6P = (1, 5)$$

$$7P = (17, 10)$$

$$8P = (18, 13)$$

$$9P = (20, 19)$$

$$10P = (16, 8)$$

Since $10P = (16, 8) = R$, therefore the discrete logarithm in this instance is $k = 10$. In real applications, a large value is chosen as k to make the brute-force attack infeasible.

9.5 Elliptic Curve Cryptography

In the following sections, we detail the ECC techniques by separating them into three subsections according to their functionalities.

9.5.1 Elliptic Curve Diffie–Hellman Key Exchange

Let us assume that A and B are two parties who desire to perform a secure message exchange. The first requirement to complete this process is to generate keys that can be done utilizing the steps mentioned below:

1. Both parties must agree upon a large prime number p and two elliptic curve parameters a and b of Equation (9.3), which defines the elliptic group of points $E_p(a, b)$.
2. Then, they have to pick a base point P on the elliptic curve $E_p(a, b)$ over a finite field Z_p.
3. It is also necessary to choose a large integer number between 1 and the order of the abelian group $E_p(a, b)$, which would be considered a private key. Let us consider that A chooses m as its private key (PR_A), and B chooses n as its private key (PR_B).
4. A then generates a public key $PU_A = m \times P$.
5. B similarly generates a public key $PU_B = n \times P$.
6. After generating their relevant keys, they must exchange their public keys between each other. When A has the public key of B, it can now generate the secret key $K = m \times PU_B$. On the other hand, B can also generate the secret key $K = n \times PU_A$.

If we keenly observe the two produced secret keys, we see that they are the same because

$$m \times PU_B = m \times (n \times P) = n \times (m \times P) = n \times PU_B$$

9.5.2 Key Exchange Example

Let us now assume that the base point $P = (15, 3)$. A chooses its private key $m = 7$, and B chooses its private key $n = 5$. Now,

$$PU_A = m \times P = 7 \times (15, 3) = (15, 20)$$

$$PU_B = n \times P = 5 \times (15, 3) = (20, 19)$$

Then, secret key K can be found as

$$K_A = m \times PU_B$$

$$= 7 \times (20, 19)$$

$$= (20, 4)$$

$$K_B = n \times PU_A$$

$$= 5 \times (15, 20)$$

$$= (20, 4)$$

$$K_A = K_B = K$$

9.5.3 Elliptic Curve Encryption/Decryption

There are a lot of methods available in the literature that propose various techniques of elliptic curve encryption and decryption. In this chapter, one of the simplest techniques is chosen for those operations for a better understanding of the ECC algorithm. Let us consider that A wants to send a message to B that is also a point on the elliptic curve, $M = (x_M, y_M)$. A must perform the following operations to encrypt the message:

$$C = M + m \times PU_B$$

Then, A sends the pair $(m \times P, C)$ to B, where P is the base point. After receiving the encrypted message, B utilizes its secret key to decrypt the message as follows:

$$C + (-n) \times (m \times P) = C - n \times (m \times P)$$

$$= M + m \times PU_B - n \times (m \times P)$$

$$= M + m \times (n \times P) - n \times (m \times P)$$

$$= M$$

9.5.4 Encryption/Decryption Example

Let us assume that A wants to transmit a message to B that is encoded on the elliptic point $M = (19, 1)$. Consider the previous key exchange example where A and B have selected their own private key and also have exchanged their public key between each other. Now, encryption of message M can be found as follows:

$$C = (19, 1) + 7 \times (20, 19)$$

$$= (19, 1) + (20, 19)$$

$$= (16, 8)$$

$$m \times P = 7 \times (15, 3)$$

$$= (15, 20)$$

Then, A sends the ciphertext {(15, 20), (16, 8)}. When B receives this ciphertext, it decrypts the message as follows:

$$M = (16, 8) - 5 \times (15, 20)$$

$$= (16, 8) - (20, 4)$$

$$= (16, 8) + (20, -4)$$

$$= (19, 1)$$

9.6 Implementation 1

```cpp
#include <iostream>
#include <cmath>
#include <conio.h>

using namespace std;

void ec_points(int a, int b, int p)
{
    cout << "Points of Elliptic Curve" << endl;
    cout << "- - - - - - - - - - - - - - - - - - - - - -
    - - - - - - -" << endl;
        for (int x = 0; x < p; x++) {
        for (int y = 0; y < p; y++) {
            int k = y * y;
            int m = (x * x * x) + a * x + b;
            if (k% p = = m% p) {
                cout << "(" << x << "," << y << ")" << endl;
            }
        }
            }
}
```

```
static int EGCD(int a, int b, int& u, int &v)//
Extended GCD gives g = a*u + b*v
{
      u = 1;
      v = 0;
      int g = a;
      int u1 = 0;
      int v1 = 1;
      int g1 = b;
      while (g1 ! = 0)
      {
         int q = g/g1;//Integer divide
         int t1 = u - q*u1;
         int t2 = v - q*v1;
         int t3 = g - q*g1;
         u = u1; v = v1; g = g1;
         u1 = t1; v1 = t2; g1 = t3;
      }

      return g;
}
      //exitit 2
static int InvMod(int x, int n)//Solve linear
congruence equation x * z = = 1 (mod n) for z
{
      //n = Abs(n);
      x = x% n;//% is the remainder function, 0 < = x%
      n < |n|
      int u,v,g,z;
      g = EGCD(x, n, u,v);
      if (g ! = 1)
      {
      //x and n have to be relative prime for there to
       exist an x^-1 mod n
      z = 0;
      }
      else
      {
         z = u% n;
      }
      return z;
}

int NegMod (int a, int p)
{
```

```
        int b = a * -1;
        int n = ceil((float)b/p);
        return (n * p) - b;
}

void add_points (int xp, int yp, int xq, int yq, int
&xr, int &yr, int p)
{
        int s;
        int n = yp - yq;
        int d = xp - xq;
        if (d < 0) {
            n * = -1;
            d * = -1;
}

        int x = InvMod(d, p);

        if (n * x > 0) {
            s = (n * x)% p;
}
        else {
            s = NegMod(n * x, p);
}

        int xr_ = (s * s - xp - xq);
        if (xr_ < 0)
            xr = NegMod (xr_, p);
        else
            xr = xr_% p;

        int yr_ = (-yp + s * (xp - xr));
        if (yr_ < 0)
            yr = NegMod(yr_, p);
        else
            yr = yr_% p;
}

void add_double (int xp, int yp, int &xr, int &yr, int
a, int p)
{
        int s;
        int n = 3 * xp * xp + a;
        int d = 2 * yp;

        if (d < 0) {
```

```
            n * = -1;
            d * = -1;
    }


        int x = InvMod(d, p);

        if (n * x > 0) {
            s = (n * x)% p;
    }

        else {
            s = NegMod(n * x, p);
    }

        int xr_ = (s * s - 2 * xp);
        if (xr_ < 0)
            xr = NegMod (xr_, p);
        else
        xr = xr_% p;

        int yr_ = (-yp + s * (xp - xr));
        if (yr_ < 0)
            yr = NegMod(yr_, p);
        else
            yr = yr_% p;
    }


void scalar_multiplication (int xp, int yp, int k,
int a, int p, int &PUx, int &PUy)
{
if (k = = 2) {
    add_double(xp, yp, PUx, PUy, a, p);
}
else if (k > 2) {
    add_double(xp, yp, PUx, PUy, a, p);
    for (int i = 0; i < k - 2; i++) {
      int xq = PUx;
      int yq = PUy;
      PUx = PUy = 0;
      add_points(xp, yp, xq, yq, PUx, PUy, p);
    }
}
else {
    cout << "Wrong key" << endl;
    }
}
```

```cpp
void key_generation (int Px, int Py, int k, int a,
int p, int &PUx, int &PUy)
{
    scalar_multiplication(Px, Py, k, a, p, PUx, PUy);
    return;
}

void encryption (int Mx, int My, int k, int a, int p,
int PUx, int PUy, int &Cx, int &Cy)
{
    int xr, yr;
    scalar_multiplication(PUx, PUy, k, a, p, xr, yr);
    add_points(Mx, My, xr, yr, Cx, Cy, p);
}

void decryption (int Cx, int Cy, int k, int a, int p,
int x1, int y1, int &Mx, int &My)
{
    int xr, yr;
    scalar_multiplication(x1, y1, k, a, p, xr, yr);
    add_points(Cx, Cy, xr, -yr, Mx, My, p);
}

int main()
{
    int a, b, p;
    cout << "put a prime number: ";
    cin >> p;

    bool check;
    do {
        check = false;
        cout << "put a value for a: ";
        cin >> a;
        cout << "put a value for b: ";
        cin >> b;
        if (((4 * a * a * a + 27 * b * b) % p) == 0) {
        cout << "Your values do not satisfied the
        condition" << endl;
            cout << "Please put values again" << endl;
            check = true;
        }
} while (check);
cout << "- - - - - - - - - - - - - - - - - - - - -
- - - - - " << endl;
```

```
ec_points(a, b, p);

int Px, Py, PUAx, PUAy, PUBx, PUBy, Mx, My, Cx, Cy, m, n;

cout << "- - - - - - - - - - - - - -" << endl;
cout << "Key " << endl;
cout << "- - - - - - - - - - - - - -" << endl;

cout << "Select a base point (x,y) from the curve: ";
cin >> Px >> Py;
cout << "Select a private key for Alice: ";
cin >> m;
key_generation(Px, Py, m, a, p, PUAx, PUAy);
cout << "Public key of Alice is (" << PUAx << "," <<
PUAy << ")" << endl;

cout << "Select a private key for Bob: ";
cin >> n;
key_generation(Px, Py, n, a, p, PUBx, PUBy);
cout << "Public key of Bob is (" << PUBx << "," <<
PUBy << ")" << endl;

cout << "- - - - - - - - - - - - - - - - - - - - - -
- - - " << endl;
cout << "Encryption/Decryption" << endl;
cout << "- - - - - - - - - - - - - - - - - - - - - -
- - - " << endl;
cout << "Select a Message point (x,y) from the curve
(for encryption): ";
cin >> Mx >> My;
encryption(Mx, My, m, a, p, PUBx, PUBy, Cx, Cy);
cout << "Cipher is (" << Cx << "," << Cy << ")" << endl;
int x1, y1;
scalar_multiplication(Px, Py, m, a, p, x1, y1);
cout << "Alice send message pair(("<< x1 << "," << y1
<< "),(" << Cx << "," << Cy << "))" << endl;
cout << "||- - - - - - - - - - - - - - - - - -
-||" << endl;
cout << "Bob receive the message and start decrypting"
<< endl;
decryption(Cx, Cy, n, a, p, x1, y1, Mx, My);
cout << "Decrypted message is (" << Mx << "," << My <<
")" << endl;

getch();
return 0;
}
```

9.7 Implementation 2

```
#include<cstdlib>
#include<iostream>
#include<vector>
#include <math.h>
//contains utility functions

#define PrimeNumber 23

using namespace std;

class utils
{
public:
    static float frand()//renerate random float number
    {
        static float norm = 1.0f/(float)RAND_MAX;
    return (float)rand()*norm;
    }
    static int irand(int min, int max)//renerate random
integer number
    {
        return min+(int)(frand()*(float)(max-min));
    }
    //exhibit 1
        static int EGCD(int a, int b, int& u, int
        &v)//Extended GCD gives g = a*u + b*v
    {
       u = 1;
       v = 0;
       int g = a;
       int u1 = 0;
       int v1 = 1;
       int g1 = b;
       while (g1 ! = 0)
       {
          int q = g/g1;//Integer divide
          int t1 = u - q*u1;
          int t2 = v - q*v1;
          int t3 = g - q*g1;
          u = u1; v = v1; g = g1;
          u1 = t1; v1 = t2; g1 = t3;
       }
       return g;
    }
```

```
//exitit 2
static int InvMod(int x, int n)//Solve linear
congruence equation x * z = = 1 (mod n) for z
{
    //n = Abs(n);
    x = x% n;//% is the remainder function, 0 < = x%
    n < |n|
    int u,v,g,z;
    g = EGCD(x, n, u,v);
    if (g ! = 1)
    {
        //x and n have to be relative prime for there to
        exist an x^-1 mod n
        z = 0;
    }
    else
    {
        z = u% n;
    }
        return z;
    }
};


//Template parameter 'curveOrder' is the order of the
finite field over which this curve is defined
template<int curveOrder>
class EllipticCurve;
//Template parameter 'curveOrder' is the order of the
finite field over which this curve is defined
template<int curveOrder>
class Element
{
        int value;
        //set element value
        void setValue(int i)
        {
                value = i;
                if (i<0)
                {
                        value = (i%curveOrder) +
                        2*curveOrder;//ensure that the
                        value is in the correct range
                }
                value% = curveOrder;
        }
```

```cpp
public:
        //default constructor
        Element()
        {
                value = 0;
        }
        //constructor with value
        explicit Element(int i)
        {
                setValue(i);
        }
        //copy constructor
        Element(const Element<curveOrder>& rhs)
        {
                value = rhs.value;
        }
        //access Element Value
        int getValue() const {return value;}
        //negate
        Element<curveOrder> operator-() const
        {
                return Element<curveOrder>(-value);
        }
        //setValue from integer
        Element<curveOrder>& operator = (int i)
        {
                setValue(i);
                return *this;
        }
        //" = " operator overload
        Element<curveOrder>& operator = (const
        Element<curveOrder>& rhs)
        {
                value = rhs.value;
                return *this;
        }
        //"* = " operator overload
        Element<curveOrder>& operator* = (const
        Element<curveOrder>& rhs)
        {
                value = (value*rhs.value)%curveOrder;
                return *this;
        }
        //"* = " operator overload
```

```
friend bool operator = =(const
Element<curveOrder>& lhs, const
Element<curveOrder>& rhs)
{
        return (lhs.value = = rhs.value);
}
//" = =" operator overload
friend bool operator = =(const
Element<curveOrder>& lhs, int rhs)
{
        return (lhs.value = = rhs);
}
//"! = " operator overload
friend bool operator! = (const
Element<curveOrder>& lhs, int rhs)
{
        return (lhs.value ! = rhs);
}
//"/" operator overload
friend Element<curveOrder> operator/
(const Element<curveOrder>& lhs, const
Element<curveOrder>& rhs)
{
        return Element<curveOrder>(lhs.
        value * utils::InvMod(rhs.
        value,curveOrder));
}
//"+" operator overload
friend Element<curveOrder>
operator+(const Element<curveOrder>& lhs,
const Element<curveOrder>& rhs)
{
        return Element<curveOrder>(lhs.
        value + rhs.value);
}
//"+" operator overload
friend Element<curveOrder> operator+(int
i, const Element<curveOrder>& rhs)
{
        return Element<curveOrder>(rhs.
        value+i);
}
//"+" operator overload
friend Element<curveOrder> operator+(const
Element<curveOrder>& lhs, int i)
```

```
        {
                return Element<curveOrder>(lhs.
                value+i);
        }
        //"-" operator overload
        friend Element<curveOrder> operator-(const
        Element<curveOrder>& lhs, const
        Element<curveOrder>& rhs)
        {
                return Element<curveOrder>(lhs.
                value - rhs.value);
        }
        //"-"(binary) operator overload
        friend Element<curveOrder> operator*(int
        n, const Element<curveOrder>& rhs)
        {
                return Element<curveOrder>(n*rhs.
                value);
        }
        //"*"(binary) operator overload
        friend Element<curveOrder> operator*(const
        Element<curveOrder>& lhs, const
        Element<curveOrder>& rhs)
        {
                return Element<curveOrder>(lhs.
                value * rhs.value);
        }
        //output stream handler
        template<int T>
        friend ostream& operator<<(ostream& os,
        const Element<T>& opt)
        {
                return os << opt.value;
        }
};

//Template parameter 'curveOrder' is the order of the
finite field over which this curve is defined
template<int curveOrder>
class Point
{
    //elliptic curve pointer in which this point
    will belong
    EllipticCurve<curveOrder> *ellipticCurve;
    /*
```

```
   Given a curve 'ec' defined along some
   equation in a finite field (such as 'ec':
   y^2 = x^3 + ax + b)
   point multiplication is defined as the
   repeated addition of a point along that
   curve.
   wiki link http://en.wikipedia.org/wiki/
   Elliptic_curve_point_multiplication
   point multiply
*/
Point scalarMultiply(int k, const Point& a)
{
      Point acc = a;
      Point res = Point(0,0,*ellipticCurve);
      int i = 0, j = 0;
      int b = k;
      while(b)
      {
            if (b & 1)
            {
                  addDouble(i-j,acc);//bit is
                  set; acc = 2^(i-j)*acc
                  res + = acc;
                  j = i; //last bit set
            }
            b >> = 1;
            ++i;
            cout << res.getX() << "\t" << res.
            getY() << endl;
      }
      return res;
}
//doubling step for point multiplication
void addDouble(int multiplier, Point& point)
{
      if (multiplier > 0)
      {
            Point tempPoint = point;
            for (int i = 0; i < multiplier; i++)
            {
                  tempPoint + = tempPoint;//
                  repeated addition
            }
            point = tempPoint;
      }
```

```
}
//adding two points on the curve
void addPoints(Element<curveOrder> x1,
Element<curveOrder> y1, Element<curveOrder> x2,
Element<curveOrder> y2, Element<curveOrder> &
xR, Element<curveOrder> & yR) const
{
        //special cases involving the additive
        identity
        if (x1 = = 0 && y1 = = 0)
        {
                xR = x2;
                yR = y2;
                return;
        }
        if (x2 = = 0 && y2 = = 0)
        {
                xR = x1;
                yR = y1;
                return;
        }
        if (y1 = = -y2)
        {
                xR = yR = 0;
                return;
        }
        //the additions
        Element<curveOrder> s;
        if (x1 = = x2 && y1 = = y2)
        {
                //2P
                s = (3*(x1.getValue()*x1.
                getValue()) + ellipticCurve-
                >getA())/(2*y1);
                xR = ((s*s) - 2*x1);
        }
        else
        {
                //P+Q
                s = (y1 - y2)/(x1 - x2);
                xR = ((s*s) - x1 - x2);
        }
        if (s ! = 0)
        {
                yR = (-y1 + s*(x1 - xR));
```

```
        }
        else
        {
            xR = yR = 0;
        }
    }
public:
    Element<curveOrder> x;//x coordinate
    Element<curveOrder> y;//y coordinate
    //point constructor with x and y value
    Point(int x, int y)
    {
        this->x = x;
        this->y = y;
        this->ellipticCurve = 0;
    }
    //point constructor with x value, y value and
    EllipticCurve pointer
    Point(int x, int y, EllipticCurve<curveOrder> &
    EllipticCurve)
    {
        this->x = x;
        this->y = y;
        this->ellipticCurve = &EllipticCurve;
    }
    //point constructor with constant x pointer,
    constant y pointer and EllipticCurve pointer
    Point(const Element<curveOrder>& x, const
    Element<curveOrder>& y,
    EllipticCurve<curveOrder> & EllipticCurve)
    {
        this->x = x;
        this->y = y;
        this->ellipticCurve = &EllipticCurve;
    }
    //compy constructor
    Point(const Point& rhs)
    {
        x = rhs.x;
        y = rhs.y;
        ellipticCurve = rhs.ellipticCurve;
    }
    //access x component as element
    Element<curveOrder> getX() const {return x;}
    //access y component as element
```

```cpp
Element<curveOrder> getY() const {return y;}
//calculate the order of this point using brute-
force additions
unsigned int Order(unsigned int maxPeriod = ~0)
const
{
        Point r = *this;
        unsigned int n = 0;
        while(r.x ! = 0 && r.y ! = 0)
        {
                ++n;
                r + = *this;
                if (n > maxPeriod) break;
        }
        return n;
}
//negate
Point operator- ()
{
        return Point(x,-y);
}
//" = " operator overload
Point& operator = (const Point& rhs)
{
        x = rhs.x;
        y = rhs.y;
        ellipticCurve = rhs.ellipticCurve;
        return *this;
}
//" = =" operator overload
friend bool operator = =(const Point& lhs, const
Point& rhs)
{
        return (lhs.ellipticCurve = = rhs.
        ellipticCurve) && (lhs.x = = rhs.x) &&
        (lhs.y = = rhs.y);
}
//"! = " operator overload
friend bool operator! = (const Point& lhs, const
Point& rhs)
{
        return (lhs.ellipticCurve ! = rhs.
        ellipticCurve) || (lhs.x ! = rhs.x) ||
        (lhs.y ! = rhs.y);
}
```

```
//"+" operator overload
friend Point operator+(const Point& lhs, const
Point& rhs)
{
        Element<curveOrder> xR, yR;
        lhs.addPoints(lhs.x,lhs.y,rhs.x,rhs.
        y,xR,yR);
        return Point(xR,yR,*lhs.ellipticCurve);
}
//"*" operator overload
friend Point operator*(int k, const Point& rhs)
{
        return Point(rhs).operator* = (k);
}
//"*" operator overload
Point& operator+ = (const Point& rhs)
{
        addPoints(x,y,rhs.x,rhs.y,x,y);
        return *this;
}
//"* = " operator overload
Point& operator* = (int k)
{
        return (*this = scalarMultiply(k,*this));
}
//ostream handler: print this point
friend ostream& operator <<(ostream& os, const
Point& p)
{
        return (os << "(" << p.x << ", " << p.y <<
        ")");
}
};


//Template parameter 'curveOrder' is the order of the
finite field over which this curve is defined
template<int curveOrder>
class EllipticCurve
{
        vector<Point<curveOrder> > pointTable; //table
        of points
        Element<curveOrder> a;          //paramter a of
        the EC equation
        Element<curveOrder> b;          //parameter b of
        the EC equation
```

```cpp
        bool tableFilled;          //true if the table has
        been calculated
public:
        //constructor with a and b as parameters (such
        as 'elliptic curve' : y^2 = x^3 + ax + b)
EllipticCurve(int a, int b)
{
            this->a = a;
            this->b = b;
            this->tableFilled = false;
}
//Calculate *all* the points (group elements) for this
'elliptic curve'
void CalculatePoints()
{
            //calculate points
            for (int x = 0; x < curveOrder; x++) {
        for (int y = 0; y < curveOrder; y++) {
            int k = y * y;
            int m = (x * x * x) + a.getValue() * x +
            b.getValue();
            if (k% curveOrder = = m% curveOrder)
            pointTable.push_back(Point<curveOrder>(x,y,
            *this));
    }
        }

        tableFilled = true;//table fill successful
}
//access the point vector like an array
Point<curveOrder> operator[](int n)
{
        if (!tableFilled)
        {
        CalculatePoints();
}

        return pointTable[n];
}
//number of elements in this group
size_t Size() const {return pointTable.size();}
//the degree P of this EC
int Degree() const {return curveOrder;}
//the parameter a (as an element of Fp)
Element<curveOrder> getA() const {return a;}
```

```
//the parameter b (as an element of Fp)
Element<curveOrder> getB() const {return b;}
//ostream handler: print this curve in human readable
form
template<int cO>
friend ostream& operator <<(ostream& os, const
EllipticCurve<curveOrder>& EllipticCurve)
        {
                //y^2 mod P = x^3 + ax + b mod P
                os << "y^2 mod " << cO << " = (x^3 + ";
                if (EllipticCurve.a ! = 0)
                {
                        os << EllipticCurve.a.getValue() <<
                        "x + ";
                }
                if (EllipticCurve.b ! = 0)
                {
                        os << EllipticCurve.b.getValue() ;
                }
                os << noshowpos << ") mod " << cO;
                return os;
        }
//print all the elements of the curve
        ostream& PrintTable(ostream &os, int columns = 4)
        {
                if (tableFilled)
                {
                        int col = 0;
                        vector<Point<PrimeNumber>
                        >::iterator iter = pointTable.
                        begin();
                        for (; iter! = pointTable.end();
                        ++iter)
                        {
                                os << "(" <<
                                (*iter).x.getValue() << ", "
                                << (*iter).y.getValue()
                                << ") ";
                                if (++col > columns)
                                {
                                        os << "\n";
                                        col = 0;
                                }
                        }
                }
```

```
            else
            {
                    os << "EllipticCurve, F_" <<
                    PrimeNumber;
            }
            return os;
      }
};

int main(int argc, char *argv[])
{
      //curve object
      int A, B;
      bool flag;
      do {
          flag = false;
      cout << "Put the value for a (an integer number
      between 0 to " << PrimeNumber - 1 << ": ";
      cin >> A;
      cout << "Put the value for b (an integer number
between 0 to " << PrimeNumber - 1 << ": ";
      cin >> B;
      cout << endl;
      if (((4 * A * A * A) + (27 * B * B))%
      PrimeNumber = = 0) {
          flag = true;
          cout << "WARNING: Enterned values failed to
          pass the singularity test" << endl;
          cout << "Put the values again " << endl <<
          endl;
}
          } while (flag);
EllipticCurve<PrimeNumber> curveObject(A,B);
      cout << "Elliptic Curve cryptography example\n—
— — — — — — — — — — — — — — — — \n\n";
      //print some information about the curve
      //cout << "The curve object: " << curveObject <<
      "\n";
      curveObject.CalculatePoints();//
      cout << "\npoints on the curve object\n";
      curveObject.PrintTable(cout,4);
      cout << "\n = = = = = = = = = = = = = = = = = =
      = = = = = = = = = = = = = = = = = = = = = = = =
      = = = = = \n";

      //Elliptic curve message encryption scheme
```

```cpp
//the base point on the curve is used to
generate keys
Point<PrimeNumber> G = curveObject[0];
//choose G ramdomly where G > {0,0} with
order > = 2
while((G.getY() = = 0 || G.getX() = = 0) ||
(G.Order()<2))
{
        int n = (int)(utils::frand()*curveObject.
        Size());
        G = curveObject[n];
}
cout << "G = " << G << ", order(G) is " <<
G.Order() << "\n\n";


//sender 'Alice'
int a = utils::irand(1,curveObject.
Degree()-1);//session integer a which is also
used to generate Alice's public key
Point<PrimeNumber> Pa = a*G; //public key of
alice
cout << "Alice:\n\tPrivate key = " << a << endl;
cout << "\tpublic key Pa = " << a << "*" << G <<
" = " << Pa << endl;
//receiver 'Bob'
int b = utils::irand(1,curveObject.
Degree()-1);//session integer b which is also
used to generate bob's public key
Point<PrimeNumber> Pb = b*G; //public key of bob
cout << "Bob:\n\tPrivate key = " << b << endl;
cout << "\tpublic key Pb = " << b << "*" << G <<
" = " << Pb << endl;
//Jane, the eavesdropper
int j = utils::irand(1,curveObject.
Degree()-1);;//session integer j which is also
used to generate jane's public key
Point<PrimeNumber> Pj = j*G;
cout << "Jane:\n\tPrivate key = " << j << endl;
cout << "\tpublic key Pj = " << j << "*" << G <<
" = " << Pj << endl<< endl<< endl;
//Alice encrypts her message to send to Bob
int msg1 = 50;
int msg2 = 64;
cout << "Plain text from Alice to Bob: (" <<
msg1 << ", " << msg2 << ")"<<endl<<endl;
```

```
//alice encrypt the message using Bob's key
Point<PrimeNumber> encryptionKey = a*Pb;//
encryption key alice to bob
Element<PrimeNumber>
encrypt1(msg1*encryptionKey.getX());//encrypt
first chunk of message by multiplying with
encryption key's x value
Element<PrimeNumber>
encrypt2(msg2*encryptionKey.getY());//encrypt
second chunk of message by multiplying with
encryption key's y value
//encrypted message is: Pa,c1,c2
cout << "Encrypted message from Alice to Bob =
{Pa,c1,c2} = {" << Pa << ", " << encrypt1 << ",
" << encrypt2 << "}\n\n";
//Bob now decrypts Alice's message, using her
public key and his session integer "b" which was
also used to generate his public key
Point<PrimeNumber> decryptionKey = b*Pa;//bob's
decryption key for alice
Element<PrimeNumber> decryptMsg1 = encrypt1/
decryptionKey.getX();//encrypt first chunk of
message by dividing with decryption key's x
value
Element<PrimeNumber> decryptMsg2 = encrypt2/
decryptionKey.getY();//encrypt second chunk of
message by dividing with decryption key's y
value
cout << "\nBob's decrypted message from Alice =
(" << decryptMsg1 << ", " << decryptMsg2 << ")"
<< endl;
//Jane intercepts the message and tries to
decrypt it using her key
encryptionKey = j*Pa;//jane's decryption key for
alice
decryptMsg1 = encrypt1/encryptionKey.getX();//
encrypt first chunk of message by dividing with
decryption key's x value
decryptMsg2 = encrypt2/encryptionKey.getY();//
encrypt second chunk of message by dividing with
decryption key's y value
cout << "\nJane's decrypted message from Alice =
(" << decryptMsg1 << ", " << decryptMsg2 << ")"
<< endl;
```

```
cout << endl;
system("PAUSE");
return EXIT_SUCCESS;
```
}

References

1. Certicom. The Basics of ECC. Available at https://www.certicom.com/index.php/the-basics-of-ecc
2. A. O'Maley. Elliptic curves and elliptic curve cryptography. *Mathematics Exchange*, 3(1), 2005.
3. L. Jensen. Bit fiddling operations. Available at http://cs-linux.ubishops.ca/~jensen/asm/notes/note7.htm
4. W. Stallings. *Cryptography and network security*, 4th ed. Pearson Prentice Hall of India, New Delhi, 2006.

BAYZID ASHIK HOSSAIN

Contents

Keywords

Authentication check
Hash function
Integrity check
Message digest

A message digest algorithm such as MD5 is also known as a hash function or a cryptographic hash function. It takes a message as input and generates a fixed-length output in response, which is generally less than the length of the input message. The output is known as a hash value or message digest. A message digest is also known as a compact digital signature for an arbitrarily long stream of binary data [1].

MD5 was first designed by Professor Ronald Rivest of MIT in 1991 to substitute former hash function MD4. When investigative work showed that MD5's predecessor MD4 was likely to be insecure, MD5 was designed to be a secure replacement. MD5 has been consumed in a wide range of security applications. It is also frequently used to check data reliability.

10.1 General Properties and Vulnerabilities

When cryptographers tend to design a message digest algorithm, they try to make the algorithm fulfill the following properties:

- It should be one-way. It is hard to get the original message given the message digest.
- It would be hard to find another input message that produces identical output when both input and output are given.
- The algorithm should be collision resistant. It would be computationally not feasible to find two messages that generate equivalent message digests. This property is not similar to the second property. It is easier to attack on this property than on the second property.
- Pseudorandomness should be satisfied by the message digest.

When all of the above properties are fulfilled, we call the algorithm a collision-resistant message digest algorithm. It is unknown whether a collision-resistant message digest algorithm can exist at all.

In 1996, a weakness was found in the procedure of MD5. While it was not a clearly fatal weakness, cryptographers began recommending other algorithms, such as SHA-1, which has since been found to be vulnerable as well. In 2004, it was revealed that MD5 is also not collision resistant, and it is not suitable for applications that rely on properties similar to Secure Sockets Layer (SSL) certificates or digital signatures [3]. Moreover, flaws were discovered in MD5 during the same year, making further use of the algorithm for security purposes questionable; specifically, a number of researchers described how to create a pair of files that share the same MD5 checksum. Further progress was made in breaking MD5 throughout the years 2005, 2006, and 2007. During December 2008, a group of researchers used this technique to fake SSL certificate validity, and the CMU Software

Engineering Institute currently says that MD5 "should be considered cryptographically broken and inappropriate for further use" [7], and most applications owned by the U.S. government now use the SHA-2 family of hash functions [8].

10.2 Design Principle

MD5 follows a design principle proposed by Merkle and Damgård. Its basic scheme is to build hash in a block-wise style. In a word, MD5 is composed of two phases: padding phase and compression phase. During the padding phase, some extra bits (1 to 512 bits) are appended to the input message. The result bits are compatible to 448 mod 512. After that the length of the initial message is transformed to a 64-bit binary string (if the length is greater than 264, the lower 64 bits are used) and these 64 bits are added to the tail of the message as well. So, the padding phase ends with a bit stream that may consist of one or more 512-bit blocks. During the compression phase, a compression function is used on each 512-bit block and generates a 128-bit output. The previous output is always involved in the calculation of the next round.

10.3 Algorithm Description

MD5 processes a variable-length message into a fixed 128-bit output. The input message is fragmented into chunks of 512-bit blocks (sixteen 32-bit words); the message is padded so that its length could be divisible by 512. The padding works by adding a single bit 1 to the end of the message first. This is followed by appending as many zeros (0's) as are required to bring the length of the message up to 64 bits less than a multiple of 512 (448 mod 512). The remaining bits are filled up with 64 bits, which represents the length of the original message, modulo 264. The algorithm operates on a 128-bit state, separated into four 32-bit words, represented here as h0, h1, h2, and h3. These are set to positive fixed constants. After that the main algorithm uses each 512-bit message block in turn to alter the state. The processing of a message block consists of four analogous stages, which are termed as rounds, where each round is composed of 16 similar operations based on a nonlinear function F, modular addition,

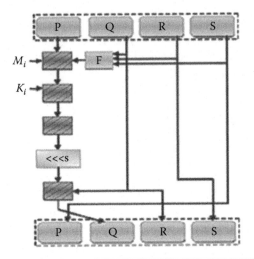

Figure 10.1 Operational model of MD5.

and left rotation. Hence, there are three kinds of operations in MD5: bit-wise Boolean operation, modular addition, and cyclic shift operation. All three operations are very fast on 32-bit machines, which make MD5 quite fast.

MD5 consists of 64 of these operations, stated in Figure 10.1, grouped in four rounds of 16 actions. F is a function that is nonlinear in nature; in each round one function is used. M_i denotes a 32-bit block of the message input, and K_i denotes a 32-bit constant.

The algorithm of MD5 can be described in five steps:

1. Add padding bits behind the input message.
2. Add a 64-bit binary string that is the representation of the message's length.
3. Initialize four 32-bit values.
4. Compress every 512-bit block.
5. Generate the 128-bit output.

10.3.1 Add Padding Bits behind the Input Message

This step is to elongate the initial message and make its length congruent to 448 mod 512. First, a single bit 1 is appended to the message. Then, a series of 0 bits are appended so that length (the padded message) $\equiv$ 448 mod 512. For example, suppose the initial message has 1000 bits. Then, this step will add 1 bit 1 and 471 bits 0. As another example, consider a message with just 448 bits. As the algorithm does not check whether the primary length is congruent to 448 mod 512, 1 bit 1 and 511 bits 0 will be appended to the message. As a result, the padding bits' length is at least 1 and at most 512.

```
new_len = initial_len+1;
while((new_len% 64) ! = 56){
new_len++;
    }
msg = new uint8_t [new_len+8];
```

10.3.2 Add a 64-Bit Binary String That Is the Representation of the Message's Length

Consideration should be paid to the meaning of the 64-bit binary string. One should not regard it as the first 64 bits of the initial message. It is the binary representation of the length of the preliminary message. For example, assume the message length is 1000 bits. Its 64-bit binary representation would be 0x00000000000003E8. If the message is very lengthy, larger than 2^{64}, only the lower 64 bits of its binary representation are used.

```
msg[initial_len] = 0x80;//append the "1" bit; most
                   significant bit is "first"
for (offset = initial_len + 1; offset <new_len;
             offset++)
msg[offset] = 0;
```

10.3.3 Initialize Four 32-Bit Values

These four 32-bit variables stated below would be used to compute the message digest. In the Implementation 1 section, these variables are mentioned as h0, h1, h2, and h3 and their initial values are

```
h0 = 0x67452301;
h1 = 0xefcdab89;
h2 = 0x98badcfe;
h3 = 0x10325476;
```

10.3.4 Compress Every 512-Bit Block

Four supplementary functions will be defined such that each function takes an input of three 32-bit words and produces a 32-bit word output [2].

```
F (X, Y, Z) = XY or not (X) Z
G (X, Y, Z) = XZ or Y not (Z)
H (X, Y, Z) = X xor Y xor Z
I (X, Y, Z) = Y xor (X or not (Z))
```

In each bit position, F acts as a condition such that if X, then Y; otherwise, Z. The function F might have been defined using addition instead of *or* since XY and not $(X) Z$ will never have 1's in the same bit position. The functions G, H, and I are similar to the function F, which performs in bit-wise parallel to produce its output from the bits of X, Y, and Z so that the corresponding bits of X, Y, and Z are independent and unbiased. Therefore, each bit of $G (X, Y, Z)$, $H (X, Y, Z)$, and $I (X, Y, Z)$ will be independent and unbiased [2].

This step uses a 64-element table $T [1, ..., 64]$ constructed from the sine function. Let $T[i]$ denote the ith element of the table, which is equal to the integer part of 4294967296 times abs $(\sin(i))$, where i is in radians. After that, it performs four rounds of hashing for each 16-word block [2]:

```
for (j = 0; j<64; j++)
k[j] = fabs (sin (j+1) *pow (2,32));
```

For processing each 16-word block, do the following operation:

```
offset = 0;
        do{
            //break chunk into sixteen 32-bit words
                w[j], 0 ≤ j ≤ 15
            for (i = 0; i< 16; i++)
            w[i] = to_int32 (msg + offset + i*4);

                a = h0;
                b = h1;
```

```
c = h2;
d = h3;

for(i = 0; i<64; i++) {

if (i< 16) {
            f = (b & c) | ((~b) & d);
            g = i;
            } else if (i< 32) {
            f = (d & b) | ((~d) & c);
            g = (5*i + 1)% 16;
            } else if (i< 48) {
            f = b ^ c ^ d;
            g = (3*i + 5)% 16;
            } else {
            f = c ^ (b | (~d));
            g = (7*i)% 16;
            }

temp = d;
            d = c;
            c = b;
            b = b + LEFTROTATE((a + f + k[i] +
                w[g]), r[i]);
            a = temp;

            }

            h0 + = a;
            h1 + = b;
            h2 + = c;
            h3 + = d;
    offset + = 64;
    }while(offset<new_len);
```

10.3.5 *Generate the 128-Bit Output*

Finally, the message digest is produced by doing h0 append h1 append h2 append h3.

```
to_bytes(h0, digest);
to_bytes(h1, digest + 4);
to_bytes(h2, digest + 8);
to_bytes(h3, digest + 12);
```

10.4 An Example

Input message: *The quick brown fox jumps over the lazy dog.*

Message before adding the padding bits:

01010100	01101000	01100101	00100000	01110001
01110101	01101001	01100011	01101011	00100000
01100010	01110010	01101111	01110111	01101110
00100000	01100110	01101111	01111000	00100000
01101010	01110101	01101101	01110000	01110011
00100000	01101111	01110110	01100101	01110010
00100000	01110100	01101000	01100101	00100000
01101100	01100001	01111010	01111001	00100000
01100100	01101111	01100111		

Message after adding the padding bits:

01010100	01101000	01100101	00100000	01110001
01110101	01101001	01100011	01101011	00100000
01100010	01110010	01101111	01110111	01101110
00100000	01100110	01101111	01111000	00100000
01101010	01110101	01101101	01110000	01110011
00100000	01101111	01110110	01100101	01110010
00100000	01110100	01101000	01100101	00100000
01101100	01100001	01111010	01111001	00100000
01100100	01101111	01100111	10000000	00000000
00000000	00000000	00000000	00000000	00000000
00000000	00000000	00000000	00000000	00000000
00000000	01011000	00000001	00000000	00000000
00000000	00000000	00000000	00000000	

MD5 operations (which contain 64 rounds):

Round [1]:
h0: 01110110 01010100 00110010 00010000
h1: 10000100 00010001 11010100 11010111
h2: 10001001 10101011 11001101 11101111
h3: 11111110 11011100 10111010 10011000

Round [2]:
h0: 11111110 11011100 10111010 10011000
h1: 01001001 10000100 11000111 11111100
h2: 10000100 00010001 11010100 11010111
h3: 10001001 10101011 11001101 11101111

Round [3]:
h0: 10001001 10101011 11001101 11101111
h1: 01011100 10010010 01001111 00110000
h2: 01001001 10000100 11000111 11111100
h3: 10000100 00010001 11010100 11010111

.

.

.

Round [63]:
h0: 00011111 00001101 00010100 00001000
h1: 01101101 11111011 01100010 10011100
h2: 11001100 01001111 11100111 11000101
h3: 10011101 11101101 00110111 00110110

Round [64]:
h0: 10011101 11101101 00110111 00110110
h1: 10101110 01111111 11101000 10010010
h2: 01101101 11111011 01100010 10011100
h3: 11001100 01001111 11100111 11000101

Final output: 9e107d9d372bb6826bd81d3542a419d6.

10.5 Implementation 1

```
#include<stdio.h>
#include<cstring>
#include<cmath>
#include<iostream>
#include<cstdlib>
#include<bitset>
#include <climits>
using namespace std;
#define KEY 64
#define SIZE 1000
#define LEFTROTATE(x, c) (((x) << (c)) |
                ((x) >> (32 - (c))))

class cryptography{
        uint32_t k[KEY];
        int j;
```

```
public:
        voidto_bytes(uint32_t val, uint8_t *bytes);
        uint32_t to_int32(const uint8_t *bytes);
        void MD_5(const uint8_t *initial_msg,
        size_tinitial_len, uint8_t *digest);

};

template<typename T>
voidshow_binrep(const T &a)
{
const char* beg = reinterpret_cast<const char*>(&a);
const char* end = beg + sizeof(a);
while(beg ! = end)
std::cout<<std::bitset<CHAR_BIT>(*beg++) << ' ';
std::cout<< '\t';
}

void cryptography::to_bytes(uint32_t val,
                            uint8_t *bytes)

{
bytes[0] = (uint8_t) val;
bytes[1] = (uint8_t) (val>> 8);
bytes[2] = (uint8_t) (val>> 16);
bytes[3] = (uint8_t) (val>> 24);
}

uint32_t cryptography::to_int32(const uint8_t *bytes)
{
return (uint32_t) bytes[0] | ((uint32_t) bytes[1] << 8)
        | ((uint32_t) bytes[2] << 16) | ((uint32_t)
        bytes[3] << 24);
}
void cryptography::MD_5(const uint8_t *initial_msg,
                        size_tinitial_len,
                        uint8_t *digest) {

for(j = 0;j<64;j++)
k[j] = fabs(sin(j+1)*pow(2,32));

//r specifies the per-round shift amounts
const uint32_t r[] = {7, 12, 17, 22, 7, 12, 17, 22, 7,
    12, 17, 22, 7, 12, 17, 22, 5, 9, 14, 20, 5, 9, 14,
    20, 5, 9, 14, 20, 5, 9, 14, 20, 4, 11, 16, 23, 4,
    11, 16, 23, 4, 11, 16, 23, 4, 11, 16, 23, 6, 10, 15,
    21, 6, 10, 15, 21, 6, 10, 15, 21, 6, 10, 15, 21};
```

```
    //Thesevars will contain the hash
    uint32_t h0, h1, h2, h3;

    //Message (to prepare)
    uint8_t *msg = NULL;

size_tnew_len, offset;
uint32_t w[16];
uint32_t a, b, c, d, i, f, g, temp;

    //Initialize variables - simple count in nibbles:
    h0 = 0x67452301;
    h1 = 0xefcdab89;
    h2 = 0x98badcfe;
    h3 = 0x10325476;

    //Pre-processing:
    //append "1" bit to message
    //append "0" bits until message length in bits ≡
        448 (mod 512)
    //append length mod (2^64) to message

new_len = initial_len+1;
while((new_len% 64) ! = 56){
new_len++;
}

msg = new uint8_t[new_len+8];

memcpy(msg, initial_msg, initial_len);
msg[initial_len] = 0x80;//append the "1" bit; most
   significant bit is "first"
for (offset = initial_len + 1; offset <new_len;
   offset++)
msg[offset] = 0;//append "0" bits

    //append the len in bits at the end of the buffer.
to_bytes(initial_len*8, msg + new_len);
    //initial_len>>29 = = initial_len*8>>32, but avoids
        overflow.
to_bytes(initial_len>>29, msg + new_len + 4);

    //binary representation of the message after
        padding
```

```
    /*
for (inti = 0; i< new_len+8; i++) {
show_binrep(msg[i]);
    }
    */
cout<<endl;
    //Process the message in successive 512-bit chunks:
    //for each 512-bit chunk of message:
offset = 0;
do{
    //break chunk into sixteen 32-bit words w[j],
         0 ≤  j  ≤ 15
for (i = 0; i< 16; i++)
w[i] = to_int32(msg + offset + i*4);

    //Initialize hash value for this chunk:
    a = h0;
    b = h1;
    c = h2;
    d = h3;

    //Main loop:
for(i = 0; i<64; i++) {

if (i< 16) {
        f = (b & c) | ((~b) & d);
        g = i;
        } else if (i< 32) {
        f = (d & b) | ((~d) & c);
        g = (5*i + 1)% 16;
        } else if (i< 48) {
        f = b ^ c ^ d;
        g = (3*i + 5)% 16;
        } else {
        f = c ^ (b | (~d));
        g = (7*i)% 16;
        }

temp = d;
        d = c;
        c = b;
        b = b + LEFTROTATE((a + f + k[i] + w[g]), r[i]);
        a = temp;
     /*
cout<<"Round: ["<<i+1<<"] "<<endl;
```

```
cout<<"h0: ";
show_binrep(a);
cout<<'\n'<<"h1: ";
show_binrep(b);
cout<<'\n'<<"h2: ";
show_binrep(c);
cout<<'\n'<<"h3: ";
show_binrep(d);
cout<<endl;
    */
    }

    //Add this chunk's hash to result so far:
    h0 + = a;
    h1 + = b;
    h2 + = c;
    h3 + = d;
offset + = 64;

}while(offset<new_len);

  //cleanup
        deletemsg;

//var char digest[16] : = h0 append h1 append h2
  append h3
//(Output is in little-endian)
        to_bytes(h0, digest);
        to_bytes(h1, digest + 4);
        to_bytes(h2, digest + 8);
        to_bytes(h3, digest + 12);
}

int main() {
charmsg[SIZE] = "The quick brown fox jumps over the
  lazy dog";
inti;
  uint8_t msg_digest[16];

cout<<msg<<endl<<endl;

cryptographycp;

  cp.MD_5((uint8_t*)msg, strlen(msg), msg_digest);
```

```
      /*
for (inti = 0; i<strlen(msg); i++) {
show_binrep(msg[i]);
   }
      */
cout<<endl<<endl;

for (i = 0; i< 16; i++){
printf("%2.2x", msg_digest[i]);
   }
printf("\n");

return 0;
}
```

10.6 Implementation 2 [5,6]

```
/* MD5
```
Converted to C++ class by Frank Thilo (thilo@unix-ag.org) for bzflag (http://www.bzflag.org). Based on: md5.h and md5.c reference implementation of RFC 1321.

Copyright (C) 1991–1992, RSA Data Security, Inc. Created 1991. All rights reserved.

License to copy and use this software is granted provided that it is identified as the "RSA Data Security, Inc. MD5 Message-Digest Algorithm" in all material mentioning or referencing this software or this function.

License is also granted to make and use derivative works provided that such works are identified as "derived from the RSA Data Security, Inc. MD5 Message-Digest Algorithm" in all material mentioning or referencing the derived work.

RSA Data Security, Inc. makes no representations concerning either the merchantability of this software or the suitability of this software for any particular purpose. It is provided "as is" without express or implied warranty of any kind.

These notices must be retained in any copies of any part of this documentation or software.
```
*/
```

```
#include <cstring>
#include <iostream>
#include <cstdio>
```

```cpp
using namespace std;

class MD5{

public:

typedef unsigned intsize_type;//must be 32bit
MD5();
MD5(const string& text);
void update(const unsigned char *buf, size_type length);
void update(const char *buf, size_type length);
MD5&finalize();
stringhexdigest() const;
friendostream& operator<<(ostream&, MD5 md5);

private:
voidinit();
typedef unsigned char uint1;// 8bit
typedef unsigned int uint4; //32bit
enum {blocksize = 64};//VC6 won't eat a const static
    int here

void transform(const uint1 block[blocksize]);
static void decode(uint4 output[], const uint1
    input[], size_typelen);
static void encode(uint1 output[], const uint4
    input[], size_typelen);

bool finalized;
uint1 buffer[blocksize];//bytes that didn't fit in
    last 64 byte chunk
uint4 count[2]; //64bit counter for number of bits
    (lo, hi)
uint4 state[4]; //digest so far
uint1 digest[16];//the result

//low level logic operations
static inline uint4 F(uint4 x, uint4 y, uint4 z);
static inline uint4 G(uint4 x, uint4 y, uint4 z);
static inline uint4 H(uint4 x, uint4 y, uint4 z);
static inline uint4 I(uint4 x, uint4 y, uint4 z);
static inline uint4 rotate_left(uint4 x, int n);
static inline void FF(uint4 &a, uint4 b, uint4 c,
    uint4 d, uint4 x, uint4 s, uint4 ac);
static inline void GG(uint4 &a, uint4 b, uint4 c,
    uint4 d, uint4 x, uint4 s, uint4 ac);
```

```cpp
static inline void HH(uint4 &a, uint4 b, uint4 c,
    uint4 d, uint4 x, uint4 s, uint4 ac);
static inline void II(uint4 &a, uint4 b, uint4 c,
uint4 d, uint4 x, uint4 s, uint4 ac);
};

string md5(const string str);

//F, G, H and I are basic MD5 functions.
inline MD5::uint4 MD5::F(uint4 x, uint4 y, uint4 z) {
returnx&y | ~x&z;
}

inline MD5::uint4 MD5::G(uint4 x, uint4 y, uint4 z) {
returnx&z | y&~z;
}

inline MD5::uint4 MD5::H(uint4 x, uint4 y, uint4 z) {
returnx^y^z;
}

inline MD5::uint4 MD5::I(uint4 x, uint4 y, uint4 z) {
return y ^ (x | ~z);
}

//rotate_left rotates x left n bits.
inline MD5::uint4 MD5::rotate_left(uint4 x, int n) {
return (x << n) | (x >> (32-n));
}

//FF, GG, HH, and II transformations for rounds 1, 2,
    3, and 4.
//Rotation is separate from addition to prevent
    re-computation.

inline void MD5::FF(uint4 &a, uint4 b, uint4 c,
    uint4 d, uint4 x, uint4 s, uint4 ac) {
a = rotate_left(a+ F(b,c,d) + x + ac, s) + b;
}

inline void MD5::GG(uint4 &a, uint4 b, uint4 c,
    uint4 d, uint4 x, uint4 s, uint4 ac) {
a = rotate_left(a + G(b,c,d) + x + ac, s) + b;
}

inline void MD5::HH(uint4 &a, uint4 b, uint4 c,
    uint4 d, uint4 x, uint4 s, uint4 ac) {
```

```
a = rotate_left(a + H(b,c,d) + x + ac, s) + b;
}

inline void MD5::II(uint4 &a, uint4 b, uint4 c,
    uint4 d, uint4 x, uint4 s, uint4 ac) {
a = rotate_left(a + I(b,c,d) + x + ac, s) + b;
}

//default constructor, just initailize
MD5::MD5()
{
init();
}
//nifty shortcut ctor, compute MD5 for string and
    finalize it right away
MD5::MD5(const string &text)
{
init();
update(text.c_str(), text.length());
finalize();
}

void MD5::init()
{
finalized = false;

count[0] = 0;
count[1] = 0;

//load magic initialization constants.
state[0] = 0x67452301;
state[1] = 0xefcdab89;
state[2] = 0x98badcfe;
state[3] = 0x10325476;
}

//decodes input (unsigned char) into output (uint4).
    Assumes len is a multiple of 4.
void MD5::decode(uint4 output[], const uint1 input[],
    size_typelen)
{
for (unsigned inti = 0, j = 0; j <len; i++, j + = 4)
output[i] = ((uint4)input[j]) | (((uint4)input[j+1])
    << 8) |
```

```
      (((uint4)input[j+2]) << 16) | (((uint4)input[j+3])
          << 24);
}


//encodes input (uint4) into output (unsigned char).
    Assumes len is
//a multiple of 4.
void MD5::encode(uint1 output[], const uint4 input[],
   size_typelen)
{
for (size_typei = 0, j = 0; j <len; i++, j + = 4) {
output[j] = input[i] & 0xff;
output[j+1] = (input[i] >> 8) & 0xff;
output[j+2] = (input[i] >> 16) & 0xff;
output[j+3] = (input[i] >> 24) & 0xff;
  }
}


//apply MD5 algorithm on a block
void MD5::transform(const uint1 block[blocksize])
{
uint4 a = state[0], b = state[1], c = state[2],
    d = state[3], x[16];
decode (x, block, blocksize);


/* Round 1 */
FF (a, b, c, d, x[0], 7, 0xd76aa478);/* 1 */
FF (d, a, b, c, x[1], 12, 0xe8c7b756);/* 2 */
FF (c, d, a, b, x[2], 17, 0x242070db);/* 3 */
FF (b, c, d, a, x[3], 22, 0xc1bdceee);/* 4 */
FF (a, b, c, d, x[4], 7, 0xf57c0faf);/* 5 */
FF (d, a, b, c, x[5], 12, 0x4787c62a);/* 6 */
FF (c, d, a, b, x[6], 17, 0xa8304613);/* 7 */
FF (b, c, d, a, x[7], 22, 0xfd469501);/* 8 */
FF (a, b, c, d, x[8], 7, 0x698098d8);/* 9 */
FF (d, a, b, c, x[9], 12, 0x8b44f7af);/* 10 */
FF (c, d, a, b, x[10], 17, 0xffff5bb1);/* 11 */
FF (b, c, d, a, x[11], 22, 0x895cd7be);/* 12 */
FF (a, b, c, d, x[12], 7, 0x6b901122);/* 13 */
FF (d, a, b, c, x[13], 12, 0xfd987193);/* 14 */
FF (c, d, a, b, x[14], 17, 0xa679438e);/* 15 */
FF (b, c, d, a, x[15], 22, 0x49b40821);/* 16 */


/* Round 2 */
GG (a, b, c, d, x[1], 5, 0xf61e2562);/* 17 */
GG (d, a, b, c, x[6], 9, 0xc040b340);/* 18 */
```

```
GG (c, d, a, b, x[11], 14, 0x265e5a51);/* 19 */
GG (b, c, d, a, x[0],  20, 0xe9b6c7aa);/* 20 */
GG (a, b, c, d, x[5],  5,  0xd62f105d);/* 21 */
GG (d, a, b, c, x[10], 9,  0x2441453); /* 22 */
GG (c, d, a, b, x[15], 14, 0xd8a1e681);/* 23 */
GG (b, c, d, a, x[4],  20, 0xe7d3fbc8);/* 24 */
GG (a, b, c, d, x[9],  5,  0x21e1cde6);/* 25 */
GG (d, a, b, c, x[14], 9,  0xc33707d6);/* 26 */
GG (c, d, a, b, x[3],  14, 0xf4d50d87);/* 27 */
GG (b, c, d, a, x[8],  20, 0x455a14ed);/* 28 */
GG (a, b, c, d, x[13], 5,  0xa9e3e905);/* 29 */
GG (d, a, b, c, x[2],  9,  0xfcefa3f8);/* 30 */
GG (c, d, a, b, x[7],  14, 0x676f02d9);/* 31 */
GG (b, c, d, a, x[12], 20, 0x8d2a4c8a);/* 32 */

/* Round 3 */
HH (a, b, c, d, x[5],  4,  0xfffa3942);/* 33 */
HH (d, a, b, c, x[8],  11, 0x8771f681);/* 34 */
HH (c, d, a, b, x[11], 16, 0x6d9d6122);/* 35 */
HH (b, c, d, a, x[14], 23, 0xfde5380c);/* 36 */
HH (a, b, c, d, x[1],  4,  0xa4beea44);/* 37 */
HH (d, a, b, c, x[4],  11, 0x4bdecfa9);/* 38 */
HH (c, d, a, b, x[7],  16, 0xf6bb4b60);/* 39 */
HH (b, c, d, a, x[10], 23, 0xbebfbc70);/* 40 */
HH (a, b, c, d, x[13], 4,  0x289b7ec6);/* 41 */
HH (d, a, b, c, x[0],  11, 0xeaa127fa);/* 42 */
HH (c, d, a, b, x[3],  16, 0xd4ef3085);/* 43 */
HH (b, c, d, a, x[6],  23, 0x4881d05); /* 44 */
HH (a, b, c, d, x[9],  4,  0xd9d4d039);/* 45 */
HH (d, a, b, c, x[12], 11, 0xe6db99e5);/* 46 */
HH (c, d, a, b, x[15], 16, 0x1fa27cf8);/* 47 */
HH (b, c, d, a, x[2],  23, 0xc4ac5665);/* 48 */

/* Round 4 */
II (a, b, c, d, x[0],  6,  0xf4292244);/* 49 */
II (d, a, b, c, x[7],  10, 0x432aff97);/* 50 */
II (c, d, a, b, x[14], 15, 0xab9423a7);/* 51 */
II (b, c, d, a, x[5],  21, 0xfc93a039);/* 52 */
II (a, b, c, d, x[12], 6,  0x655b59c3);/* 53 */
II (d, a, b, c, x[3],  10, 0x8f0ccc92);/* 54 */
II (c, d, a, b, x[10], 15, 0xffeff47d);/* 55 */
II (b, c, d, a, x[1],  21, 0x85845dd1);/* 56 */
II (a, b, c, d, x[8],  6,  0x6fa87e4f);/* 57 */
II (d, a, b, c, x[15], 10, 0xfe2ce6e0);/* 58 */
II (c, d, a, b, x[6],  15, 0xa3014314);/* 59 */
```

```
II (b, c, d, a, x[13], 21, 0x4e0811a1);/* 60 */
II (a, b, c, d, x[4], 6, 0xf7537e82);/* 61 */
II (d, a, b, c, x[11], 10, 0xbd3af235);/* 62 */
II (c, d, a, b, x[2], 15, 0x2ad7d2bb);/* 63 */
II (b, c, d, a, x[9], 21, 0xeb86d391);/* 64 */


state[0] + = a;
state[1] + = b;
state[2] + = c;
state[3] + = d;


//Zeroize sensitive information.
memset(x, 0, sizeof x);
}


//MD5 block update operation. Continues an MD5
    message-digest
//operation, processing another message block
void MD5::update(const unsigned char input[],
   size_type length)
{
//compute number of bytes mod 64
size_type index = count[0]/8% blocksize;

//Update number of bits
if ((count[0] + = (length << 3)) < (length << 3))
count[1]++;
count[1] + = (length >> 29);


//number of bytes we need to fill in buffer
size_typefirstpart = 64 - index;


size_typei;

//transform as many times as possible.
if (length > = firstpart)
{
//fill buffer first, transform
memcpy(&buffer[index], input, firstpart);
transform(buffer);
//transform chunks of blocksize (64 bytes)
for (i = firstpart; i + blocksize< = length;
   i + = blocksize)
transform(&input[i]);
```

```
index = 0;
}
else
i = 0;

//buffer remaining input
memcpy(&buffer[index], &input[i], length-i);
}

//for convenience provide a verson with signed char
void MD5::update(const char input[], size_type length)
{
update((const unsigned char*)input, length);
}

//MD5 finalization. Ends an MD5 message-digest
    operation, writing the
//the message digest and zeroizing the context.
MD5& MD5::finalize()
{
static unsigned char padding[64] = {
0x80, 0, 0, 0, 0, 0, 0, 0, 0, 0, 0, 0, 0, 0, 0, 0, 0,
    0, 0, 0, 0, 0,
0, 0, 0, 0, 0, 0, 0, 0, 0, 0, 0, 0, 0, 0, 0, 0, 0, 0,
    0, 0, 0, 0, 0,
0, 0, 0, 0, 0, 0, 0, 0, 0, 0, 0, 0, 0, 0, 0, 0, 0, 0, 0
};

if (!finalized) {
//Save number of bits
unsigned char bits[8];
encode(bits, count, 8);

//pad out to 56 mod 64.
size_type index = count[0]/8% 64;
size_typepadLen = (index < 56) ? (56 - index) :
   (120 - index);
update(padding, padLen);

//Append length (before padding)
update(bits, 8);

//Store state in digest
encode(digest, state, 16);
//Zeroize sensitive information.
```

```
memset(buffer, 0, sizeof buffer);
memset(count, 0, sizeof count);

finalized = true;
}

return *this;
}

//return hex representation of digest as string
string MD5::hexdigest() const
{
if (!finalized)
return "";

charbuf[33];
for (inti = 0; i<16; i++)
sprintf(buf+i*2, "%02x", digest[i]);
buf[32] = 0;

return string(buf);
}

ostream& operator<<(ostream& out, MD5 md5)
{
return out << md5.hexdigest();
}

string md5(const string str)
{
MD5 md5 = MD5(str);
return md5.hexdigest();
}

int main(intargc, char *argv[])
{
cout<< "md5 of 'grape': "<< md5("grape") <<endl;
return 0;
}
```

10.7 Conclusion

Message digest algorithms such as MD5 are mainly used in implementing a digital signature, which requires all of the general properties mentioned above. However, the property requirement may vary

based on which application is using this algorithm. An application may depend on some or all of the properties of the MD5. For example, some applications use the one-way property of an MD5. Because of its property of pseudorandomness, MD5 is also used to be part of the mechanism for random number generation. MD5 digests have been widely used in the software industry to provide some assurance that a transferred file has arrived unbroken. For example, file servers often provide a precomputed MD5 (known as md5sum) checksum for the files so that a user can match the checksum of the downloaded file and verify the integrity [4]. Most Unix-based operating systems' distribution package includes MD5 sum utilities. MD5 is also available to Windows operating system users. They may install a Microsoft utility or use third-party applications. This type of checksum is also utilized by Android ROMs (read-only memories). Compared to other digest algorithms, MD5 is simple and easy to implement. It performs very fast on a 32-bit machine. It is inferred that the difficulty of coming up with two messages having the identical message digest is on the order of 2^{64} operations, and the difficulty of coming up with any message having a given message digest is on the order of 2^{128} operations.

References

1. MD5, Command Line Message Digest Utility, http://www.fourmilab. ch/md5/.
2. Li, J. MD5 Message Digest Algorithm. Computer Science Department, San Jose State University.
3. MD5, Wikipedia, http://en.wikipedia.org/wiki/MD5.
4. MD5 Sum, Wikipedia, http://en.wikipedia.org/wiki/Md5sum.
5. A Portable, Fast, and Free Implementation of the MDS Message-Digest Algorithm (RFC 1321), http://openwall.info/wiki/people/solar/software/public-domain-source-code/md5.
6. C++ MD5 Function, Zedwood, http://www.zedwood.com/article/cpp-md5-function.
7. CERT Vulnerability Note VU#836068. Retrieved February 8, 2014, from Kb.cert.org.
8. NIST.gov—Computer Security Division—Computer Security Resource Center. Retrieved from csrc.nist.gov.

11

SECURE HASH ALGORITHM

SADDAM HOSSAIN MUKTA
AND SAIFUL AZAD

Contents

Keywords

Authentication check
Hash function
Integrity check
Secure Hash Algorithm
SHA-1

In 1990, Ron Rivest invented an algorithm utilizing the concept of hash function, called Message Digest 4 (MD4). He extended that algorithm in 1992, and named it Message Digest 5 (MD5). Later in 1993, the National Institute of Standards and Technology (NIST) developed and published an algorithm as a Federal Information Processing Standard (FIPS 180) that is analogous to the MD5 algorithm, called Secure Hash Algorithm (SHA). It is now often named SHA-0. After discovering some weaknesses in the SHA, the National Security Agency (NSA) shortly withdrew the publication. Then, in 1995, the NSA issued a revised version of the SHA that is commonly designated SHA-1. In the SHA-1 algorithm, a single bitwise rotation is introduced in the message schedule of its compression functions over SHA.

11.1 Basic Hash Function Concept

A hash function is a procedure that maps data of arbitrary length to data of a fixed length. The values returned by a hash function are often known as hash values, hash codes, hash sums, checksums, or simply hashes. Generally, a hash function compresses data to a fixed size, which could be considered a shortened reference to the original data. For compression, hash functions usually utilize a one-way function of number theory; hence, they are irreversible. Consequently, it is infeasible to reconstruct particular data when a hash value is known. Utilizing this basic concept, there are some hash algorithms that have been proposed: SHA, SHA-1, SHA-224, SHA-256, SHA-384, SHA-512, SHA-512/224, and SHA-512/256. Each algorithm is different from the others in terms of one or more parameters. Table 11.1 illustrates various parameters of different algorithms.

There are a couple of applications where these irreversible hash values are utilized. They are discussed in detail in the next section.

11.2 Applications

One realistic application of a hash function is a hash table in data structure. It is tedious to search particular data in a list linearly;

Table 11.1   Comparison of Various Secure Hash Algorithms

ALGORITHM	MESSAGE SIZE, M_l (BITS)	BLOCK SIZE, B_l (BITS)	WORD SIZE, W_l (BITS)	MESSAGE DIGEST SIZE, D_l (BITS)
SHA-1	$<2^{64}$	512	32	160
SHA-224	$<2^{64}$	512	32	224
SHA-256	$<2^{64}$	512	32	256
SHA-384	$<2^{128}$	1024	64	384
SHA-512	$<2^{128}$	1024	64	512
SHA-512/224	$<2^{128}$	1024	64	224
SHA-512/256	$<2^{128}$	1024	64	256

instead, a hash value could be computed utilizing the key part of the data to keep an indication of the entire data. Now, a simple data comparison can be utilized to find out desired data, which accelerates the searching mechanism. Another application of the hash function is in cryptography, the science of encoding and protecting data. This is the application in which we are interested. A hash function can be utilized to check the integrity of a piece of data, and often a resultant hash value is affixed to the original data. After receiving the data at the destination, a receiver utilizes a similar hash function to create a hash value. Then, two hash values are compared to check the equality. If they are similar, the receiver can presume that the integrity is preserved in the data. If anyone changes the data, in that case two hash values cannot be similar. Hash functions are also utilized for authentication and verification.

11.3 Steps of SHA-1

The processing steps of the SHA-1 are discussed below.

11.3.1 Appending Original Message Lengths and Padding

Before starting to process the message, M, it is padded first so that its length becomes congruent to 448 modulo 512. If the message is already of the desired length, padding is still performed. Thus, the number of padding bits could range from 1 to 512 bits. The padding starts with 1 bit and is followed by the consecutive number of zeros. The last 64 bits are kept empty. These bits are utilized to store the length of the original message. These operations are illustrated in Figure 11.1.

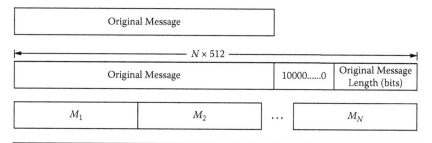

Figure 11.1 Message format after padding and appending original message length.

11.3.2 Initialization

SHA-1 generates a 160-bit message digest that consists of five 32-bit words. Let us call those h_0, h_1, h_2, h_3, and h_4. Before utilizing these words in the processing, they are initialized with the following values:

h_0 = 0x67452301

h_1 = 0xefcdab89

h_2 = 0x98badcfe

h_3 = 0x10325476

h_4 = 0xc3d2e1f0

These values are stored according to big-endian format, which means that the most significant byte of a word is placed in the low-address byte position. These values change when they are passed through different rounds. There are 80 rounds in the SHA-1. After the last round, the value of $h_0|h_1|h_2|h_3|h_4$ is considered the message digest of the entire message. Details of these rounds are discussed later in this chapter.

11.3.3 Message Processing

As mentioned previously, every message passes through 80 different rounds before generating the final message digest, which is shown in Figure 11.2. It can be observed from the figure that in every round, one word is passed, and from the message, M_i, only 16 words can be found. The rest of the words are generated using the following expression:

$$W'_i = W_{i-3} \oplus W_{i-8} \oplus W_{i-14} \oplus W_{i-16}$$

W'_i is then rotated 1 bit to the left to generate W_i. Along with a word, one constant, K_i, is passed to the ith round. The value of K varies with rounds as follows:

K_i = 0x5a827999 $(0 \leq t \leq 19)$

K_i = 0x6ed9eba1 $(20 \leq t \leq 39)$

K_i = 0x8f1bbcdc $(40 \leq t \leq 59)$

K_i = 0xca62c1d6 $(60 \leq t \leq 79)$

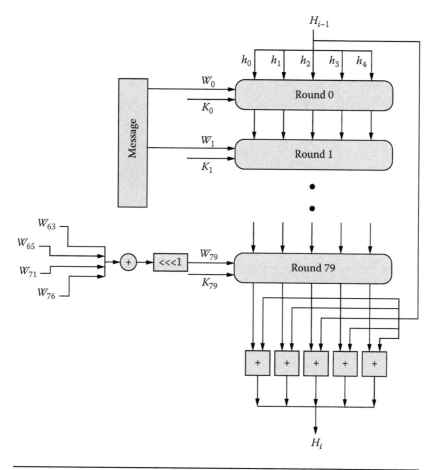

Figure 11.2 Processing of a 512-bit block.

Every round acquires a 160-bit or 5-word buffer value from the previous round, except the initial one, which acquires this value from the initialization technique discussed in the previous subsection. All the operations involved in a round are depicted in Figure 11.3. Each round utilizes a function, F, which is calculated as follows:

Assume,

$$A = h_{(i-1, 1)}$$

$$B = h_{(i-1, 2)}$$

$$C = h_{(i-1, 3)}$$

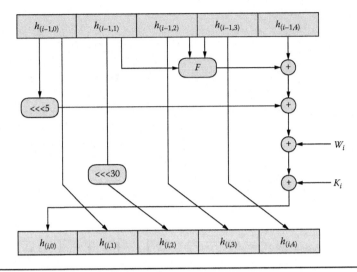

Figure 11.3 Operations of a single round.

$$F = f(i, A, B, C) = (A \land B) \lor (-A \land C) \qquad (0 <= i <= 19)$$

$$= A \oplus B \oplus C \qquad (20 <= i <= 39)$$

$$= (A \land B) \lor (A \land C) \lor (B \land C) \,(40 <= i <= 59)$$

$$= A \oplus B \oplus C \qquad (60 <= i <= 79)$$

Again, a function could be defined by the following set of expressions:

$$h_{(i,1)} = h_{(i-1,0)}$$

$$h_{(i,2)} = LS_{30}(h_{(i-1,1)})$$

$$h_{(i,3)} = h_{(i-1,2)}$$

$$h_{(i,4)} = h_{(i-1,3)}$$

$$h_{(i,0)} = (((h_{(i-1,4)} \oplus F) \oplus LS_5(h_{(i-1,0)})) \oplus W_i) \oplus K_i$$

where LS_j is rotating j number of bits to the left and i is the round number.

11.3.4 Output

A 160-bit output is produced after completing all the rounds as follows:

$$H_i = sum(H_{(i-1)}, h_{79})$$

In this process, all the blocks are processed. The final 160-bit resultant output is considered the message digest. An example is given below to understand the SHA-1 in detail.

11.4 An Example

The following example demonstrates the procedures followed by the SHA-1 algorithm to generate a 160-bit message digest.

1. Let us assume that the message for which a user wants to find the message digest is: *The quick fox jumps over the lazy dog.*
2. Following is the bit-level representation of the above message:

```
01010100 01101000 01100101 00100000 01110001
01110101 01101001 01100011 0110101100100000
01100110 01101111 01111000 00100000 01101010
01110101 01101101 0111000001110011 00100000
01101111 01110110 01100101 01110010 00100000
01110100 0110100001100101 00100000 01101100
01100001 01111010 0111100100100000 01100100
0110111101100111 00101110
```

3. The message contains 304 bits. Therefore, it is necessary to pad the message so that its length becomes congruent to 448 modulo 512. Since the entered message is 304 bits long, 144 bits padding is necessary. The first bit is 1 and the remaining 143 bits are zeros. At the end, a 64-bit value appends that represents the original size of the message. For this specific example, we could find the following message after padding and appending the length of the original message:

```
01010100 01101000 01100101 00100000 01110001
01110101 01101001 01100011 0110101100100000
01100110 01101111 01111000 00100000 01101010
01110101 01101101 0111000001110011 00100000
01101111 01110110 01100101 01110010
0010000001110100 0110100001100101 00100000
01101100 01100001 01111010 01111001 00100000
01100100 0110111101100111 00101110 10000000
00000000 00000000 00000000 00000000 00000000
0000000000000000 00000000 00000000 00000000
00000000 00000000 00000000 00000000
0000000000000000 00000000 0000000000000000
```

00000000 00000000 00000000 00000000
0000000100110000

4. The above message is now divided into 16 words and utilized in 16 different rounds ranging from 0 to 15. The first 32 bits are stored in W_0 and the last 32 bits are stored in W_{15}. How to calculate the other words that could be acquired from the message is already discussed above. A 160-bit buffer is used to store the result of the hash function. In this example, W_0 = 01010100 01101000 01100101 00100000. K_0 is also known, which is 0x5a827999, or 01011010100000100111100110011001 (in binary). Initially, a 160-bit buffer is initialized as the following:

h_0: 00000001 00100011 01000101 01100111
h_1: 10001001 10101011 11001101 11101111
h_2: 11111110 11011100 10111010 10011000
h_3: 01110110 01010100 00110010 00010000
h_4: 11110000 11100001 11010010 11000011

After round 0:
h_0: 11010011 11111101 00011100 11110100
h_1: 00000001 00100011 01000101 01100111
h_2: 11100010 01101010 11110011 01111011
h_3: 11111110 11011100 10111010 10011000
h_4: 01110110 01010100 00110010 00010000

After round 1:
h_0: 11101110 11110000 11000101 01011011
h_1: 11010011 11111101 00011100 11110100
h_2: 11000000 01001000 11010001 01011001
h_3: 11100010 01101010 11110011 01111011
h_4: 11111110 11011100 10111010 10011000

After round 2:
h_0: 10110001 00100101 00001111 00110011
h_1: 11101110 11110000 11000101 01011011
h_2: 01110100 00111111 00000111 11111101
h_3: 11000000 01001000 11010001 01011001
h_4: 11100010 01101010 11110011 01111011

After round 3:
h_0: 01111010 00111101 10010000 00001001
h_1: 10110001 00100101 00001111 00110011
h_2: 00111011 01111100 11110001 10010110
h_3: 01110100 00111111 00000111 11111101
h_4: 11000000 01001000 11010001 01011001

After round 4:
h_0: 00101111 00100011 11001101 00110001
h_1: 01111010 00111101 10010000 00001001
h_2: 01101100 11001001 11000011 01001100
h_3: 00111011 01111100 11110001 10010110
h_4: 01110100 00111111 00000111 11111101

.

.

.

After final round (i.e., 79):
h_0: 10100110 11101101 10001111 00011011
h_1: 11011100 01010111 10011001 10111010
h_2: 01000000 01000111 11111110 00000110
h_3: 01000011 11001000 00111000 00101110
h_4: 00010100 00111010 00100010 11100001

Since the message is less than 512 bits, a single block processing is enough to find out the final message digest. In case of a larger block, this procedure needs to continue again until all the blocks are processed.

Therefore, the final message digest would be

h_0: 10100111 00010000 11010101 10000010
h_1: 01100101 00000011 01100111 10101010
h_2: 00111110 00100100 10111001 10011111
h_3: 10111001 00011100 01101011 00111110
h_4: 00000100 00011100 11110101 10100100

The message digest (in hex):
82d510a7aa6703659fb9243e3e6b1cb9a4f51c04

11.5 Implementation

All the codes (and program files) related to the SHA-1 algorithm are included below with relevant comments.

```cpp
/** SHA1.h file **/
#ifndef SHA1_H_
#define SHA1_H_

#include <stdint.h>
#include <vector>
#include <iostream>
#include <stdio.h>
#include <bitset>
#include <climits>

using namespace std;

#define MB 64//size of the message block in bytes
#define AB 8//appended bytes where the length of the
    message is stored
#define Byte 8

template<typename T>
voidshow_binrep(const T& a)
{
const char* beg = reinterpret_cast<const char*>(&a);
const char* end = beg + sizeof(a);
while(beg ! = end)
std::cout<<std::bitset<CHAR_BIT>(*beg++) << ' ';
std::cout<< '\t';
}

class SHA1 {
public:
SHA1();
~SHA1();

void Reset();
voidSetMessage();
voidMessageBlockProcessing(uint8_t* MessageBlock);
voidMessagePadding();
void Rounds (uint32_t *DB, uint32_t W, uint32_t K,
    intround_num);
void Result();
```

```
voidClearMessageBlock();
voidClearDigestBlock();
voidShowMessageDigest();
private:
uint8_tMessageBlock[64];
uint32_tDigestBlock[5];
   uint8_t *Message;
vector<char>InputMessage;
uint64_tMessageSize;
uint64_tMessageSizeAfterPadding;
};

#endif//SHA1_H_

/**SHA1.cpp file **/
#include <cstdlib>
#include "sha.h"

#define LeftCircularShift(bits,word) (((word) <<
    (bits)) | ((word) >> (32-(bits)))))

SHA1 :: SHA1 ()
{
Reset();
}

SHA1 :: ~SHA1 () {}

void SHA1 :: ClearMessageBlock()
{
for (inti = 0; i< MB; i++) {
MessageBlock[i] = 0;
  }
}

void SHA1 :: ClearDigestBlock()
{
for (inti = 0; i< 5; i++) {
DigestBlock[i] = 0;
  }
}
void SHA1 :: Reset ()
{
ClearMessageBlock();
ClearDigestBlock();
```

```
DigestBlock[0] = 0x67452301;
DigestBlock[1] = 0xEFCDAB89;
DigestBlock[2] = 0x98BADCFE;
DigestBlock[3] = 0x10325476;
DigestBlock[4] = 0xC3D2E1F0;
}

void SHA1 :: ShowMessageDigest ()
{
cout<< "h0: "; show_binrep(DigestBlock[0]); cout<<endl;
cout<< "h1: "; show_binrep(DigestBlock[1]); cout<<endl;
cout<< "h2: "; show_binrep(DigestBlock[2]); cout<<endl;
cout<< "h3: "; show_binrep(DigestBlock[3]); cout<<endl;
cout<< "h4: "; show_binrep(DigestBlock[4]); cout<<endl;
}

void SHA1 :: SetMessage() {
cout<< "Put a message (press enter to finish): ";
char c = getchar();
while (c ! = '\n') {
InputMessage.push_back(c);
    c = getchar();
  }
MessagePadding();
}

void SHA1 :: MessagePadding()
{
uint64_tMessageSize = (uint64_t)InputMessage.size();
uint64_t n = ((MessageSize + AB)/MB) + 1;
MessageSizeAfterPadding = n * MB;
  Message = new uint8_t[MessageSizeAfterPadding];

intpadding_bytes = MessageSizeAfterPadding -
   (MessageSize + AB);
cout<<dec<< "Number of padding bytes are: " <<padding_
   bytes<<endl;

for (uint64_t i = 0; i<MessageSize; i++) {
    Message[i] = InputMessage[i];
  }
Message[MessageSize] = 0x80;

for (int i = MessageSize + 1;
   i<MessageSizeAfterPadding; i++) {
```

```
      Message[i] = 0;
  }

uint64_tMessageSizeInBit = MessageSize * Byte;

Message[56] = (MessageSizeInBit& 0x000000000000ff00)
    >> 56;
Message[57] = (MessageSizeInBit& 0x000000000000ff00)
    >> 48;
Message[58] = (MessageSizeInBit& 0x000000000000ff00)
    >> 40;
Message[59] = (MessageSizeInBit& 0x000000000000ff00)
    >> 32;
Message[60] = (MessageSizeInBit& 0x000000000000ff00)
    >> 24;
Message[61] = (MessageSizeInBit& 0x000000000000ff00)
    >> 16;
Message[62] = (MessageSizeInBit& 0x000000000000ff00)
    >> 8;
Message[63] = MessageSizeInBit& 0x00000000000000ff;

for (int i = 0; i<MessageSizeAfterPadding; i++) {
show_binrep(Message[i]);
  }
}

void SHA1 :: Rounds (uint32_t *DB, uint32_t W,
    uint32_t K, intround_num)
{
uint32_t temp;      /* Temporary word value  */

cout<<endl;
if (round_num> = 0 &&round_num< 20) {
temp = LeftCircularShift(5,DB[0]) +
            ((DB[1] & DB[2]) | ((~DB[1]) & DB[3])) +
DB[4] + W + K;
DB[4] = DB[3];
DB[3] = DB[2];
DB[2] = LeftCircularShift(30,DB[1]);
DB[1] = DB[0];
DB[0] = temp;
cout<< "Round: " <<round_num<<endl;
ShowMessageDigest();
  }
else if (round_num> = 20 &&round_num< 40) {
```

```
temp = LeftCircularShift(5,DB[0]) + (DB[1] ^ DB[2] ^
DB[3]) + DB[4] + W + K;
DB[4] = DB[3];
DB[3] = DB[2];
DB[2] = LeftCircularShift(30,DB[1]);
DB[1] = DB[0];
DB[0] = temp;
cout<< "Round: " <<round_num<<endl;
ShowMessageDigest();
  }
else if (round_num> = 40 &&round_num< 60) {
temp = LeftCircularShift(5,DB[0]) +
              ((DB[1] & DB[2]) | (DB[1] & DB[3]) |
(DB[2] & DB[3])) + DB[4] + W + K;
DB[4] = DB[3];
DB[3] = DB[2];
DB[2] = LeftCircularShift(30,DB[1]);
DB[1] = DB[0];
DB[0] = temp;
cout<< "Round: " <<round_num<<endl;
ShowMessageDigest();
  }
else if (round_num> = 60 &&round_num< 80) {
temp = LeftCircularShift(5,DB[0]) + (DB[1] ^ DB[2] ^
DB[3]) + DB[4] + W + K;
DB[4] = DB[3];
DB[3] = DB[2];
DB[2] = LeftCircularShift(30,DB[1]);
DB[1] = DB[0];
DB[0] = temp;
cout<< "Round: " <<round_num<<endl;
ShowMessageDigest();
  }
else {
cout<< "Wrong round is put" <<endl;
exit(1);
  }
}

void SHA1 :: MessageBlockProcessing (uint8_t*
    MessageBlock)
{
uint32_t K[4] = {0x5A827999,
              0x6ED9EBA1,
```

```
                    0x8F1BBCDC,
                    0xCA62C1D6
                    };

uint32_t     W[80];/* Word sequence    */
uint32_t     A = DigestBlock[0],
             B = DigestBlock[1],
             C = DigestBlock[2],
             D = DigestBlock[3],
             E = DigestBlock[4]; /* Word buffers    */

  //Initialize the first 16 words in the array W
uint8_t t;
for(t = 0; t < 16; t++)
    {
        W[t] = MessageBlock[t * 4] << 24;
        W[t] | = MessageBlock[t * 4 + 1] << 16;
        W[t] | = MessageBlock[t * 4 + 2] << 8;
        W[t] | = MessageBlock[t * 4 + 3];
    }

  //Storing other 64 words in the array W
for(t = 16; t < 80; t++)
    {
    W[t] = LeftCircularShift(1, W[t-3] ^ W[t-8] ^ W[t-14]
^ W[t-16]);
    }

  //round function calling
for(t = 0; t < 20; t++)
    {
Rounds(DigestBlock, W[t], K[0], t);
    }

for(t = 20; t < 40; t++)
    {
Rounds(DigestBlock, W[t], K[1], t);
    }

for(t = 40; t < 60; t++)
    {
Rounds(DigestBlock, W[t], K[2], t);
    }
```

```cpp
for(t = 60; t < 80; t++)
  {
Rounds(DigestBlock, W[t], K[3], t);
  }

  //final addition
DigestBlock[0] + = A;
DigestBlock[1] + = B;
DigestBlock[2] + = C;
DigestBlock[3] + = D;
DigestBlock[4] + = E;
cout<< "Message Digest: " <<endl;
ShowMessageDigest();
}

void SHA1 :: Result () {
for (uint64_t i = 0; i<MessageSizeAfterPadding; i = i
   + 64) {
uint8_t temp[64];
for (uint64_t j = i; j <i + MB; j++) {
temp[j - i] = Message[j];
   }
MessageBlockProcessing (temp);
   }

cout<< "Final Message Digest: " <<endl;
ShowMessageDigest();
cout<< "In hex: " <<endl;
for (inti = 0; i< 5; i++)
cout<< hex <<DigestBlock[i];
cout<<endl;
}

/** main.cpp **/
#include "sha.h"

int main()
{
  SHA1 sha;
sha.ShowMessageDigest();
sha.SetMessage();
sha.Result();

  return 0;
}
```

11.6 Conclusion

The SHA-1 is considered one of the most secure hash algorithms. Therefore, it is utilized is various applications, like Secure Sockets Layer (SSL), Pretty Good Privacy (PGP), Extensible Markup Language (XML) signatures, in the Microsoft® Xbox, and in hundreds of other applications (including from IBM, Cisco, Nokia, etc.). After a thorough cryptanalysis over the SHA-1 in 2005, it has been observed that in practice, it is weaker than its theoretical strength. Consequently, NIST made a recommendation to all federal agencies to migrate to the SHA-2 algorithm by 2010.

12

FUNDAMENTALS OF IDENTITY-BASED CRYPTOGRAPHY

AYMEN BOUDGUIGA, MARYLINE LAURENT, AND MOHAMED HAMDI

Contents

Keywords

Applied cryptography
Asymmetric cryptography
Elliptic curve cryptography
ID-based cryptography
ID-based encryption
ID-based signature
Network security
Pairing
Public-key infrastructure (PKI)
RSA
Symmetric cryptography

Cryptography, when applied to network security, describes the art of coding information into secrets that are transmitted over a public channel to an intended receiver. The latter is the only entity capable of recovering the initial information from the secrets. That is, any entity can get the encrypted information, i.e., the *ciphertext*. However, it will not be able to recover the original content of the message, namely, the *plaintext*, unless it gets the *key* that has been used for encryption. Cryptography has been used for a long time to provide security properties such as data confidentiality, data integrity, and data origin authentication.

Data confidentiality ensures that the ciphertext does not provide any information about the plaintext. Generally, the confidentiality property is provided by symmetric or asymmetric encryption. Integrity mechanisms serve to detect any modification of the transmitted data thanks to the use of hash functions in a signature or in a keyed-hash message authentication code (HMAC).

Cryptography not only serves to authenticate communicating entities thanks to the use of authentication protocols such as Transport Layer Security (TLS), but also serves to authenticate data origin thanks to the use of HMAC or signatures. Moreover, cryptography ensures nonrepudiation; namely, none of the communicating parties could deny its participation to the communication.

In this chapter, we review the concepts of symmetric cryptography and public-key cryptography in Section 12.1. We review the famous Diffie–Hellman and RSA algorithms. Then, we introduce elliptic curve cryptography (ECC) before describing ID-based cryptography (IBC) in Section 12.2.

12.1 Introduction to Cryptography

Cryptography is based on mathematical algorithms that use, in general, abstract algebra and groups theory. These algorithms need a secret input that is usually named a key. The encryption schemes are trapdoor functions that are easy to compute with the key. However, they are hard or almost impossible to invert without the key. Kerckhoffs [1] announced that "a cryptosystem should be secure even if everything about the system is public knowledge, except the key." The same principle was reformulated by Shannon [2], as "the enemy knows the system."

During the second part of the twentieth century, the field of cryptography expanded drastically thanks to the appearance of new cryptographic systems. In fact, Diffie and Hellman revolutionized cryptography in 1976 by defining the first asymmetric cryptosystem. Then, Shamir proposed the RSA algorithm with Rivest and Adleman, before publishing his outstanding works on threshold and ID-based cryptographies. Then in 1985, Koblitz and Miller presented the first elliptic curve-based cryptosystem. Finally, quantum cryptography appeared as the cryptography of the future, as it relies on optic and light theories, but not on groups and fields theory. In quantum cryptography, every bit is represented by the polarization of a photon.

In this section, we briefly describe the concepts of symmetric cryptography (Section 12.1.1). Then, in Section 12.1.2 we present public-key cryptography in depth.

12.1.1 Symmetric Cryptography

Symmetric cryptography is based on sharing a secret key between two communicating entities, Alice and Bob. Symmetric cryptography, as well as asymmetric cryptography, relies on the use of two related algorithms for message encryption and decryption. We denote the encryption algorithm by E and the decryption algorithm by D. The encryption algorithm takes as inputs the plaintext message m and a key k, and outputs the ciphertext c. Meanwhile, the decryption algorithm D takes as inputs c and k, and outputs m. Let K be the set of keys, M the set of messages, and C the set of ciphertexts; we define E and D as follows:

$$E{:}M \times K \to C \qquad D{:}C \times K \to M$$
$$(m,k) \to c \qquad\qquad (c,k) \to m$$

We say that an encryption algorithm is well defined if it verifies the equation

$$D\,(E\,(m,\,k),\,k) = m$$

The Vernam one-time pad [3] is one of the oldest symmetric encryption algorithms. It was patented in 1919. Vernam assumes that the message m, the key k, and the c ciphertext have the same bit lengths. The one-time pad relies on the *exclusive-or* (XOR) as encryption and decryption functions. Recall that XOR is equivalent to a binary sum modulo 2. When Alice wants to cipher a message m to Bob (Figure 12.1), Alice computes $c = m \oplus k$. Bob deciphers the message using the same key $m = c \oplus k$. Vernam's encryption is called a one-time pad, as the key k is used once for ciphering a unique message m. Therefore, the key has to be renewed for every message.

Shannon proved that the Vernam algorithm provided *perfect secrecy* if the key length is at least equal to the message length. Perfect secrecy means that an eavesdropper, Eve, does not distinguish the encryption of a message m_0 from that of a message m_1. That is, no information is recovered about the plaintext from the ciphertext. In other words, Vernam's algorithm verifies the following equation for every key k uniformly chosen in K:

$$Pr\,(m_0 \oplus k = c) = Pr\,(m_1 \oplus k = c),\ \forall\ m_0,\,m_1 \in M/m_0 \neq m_1 \quad (12.1)$$

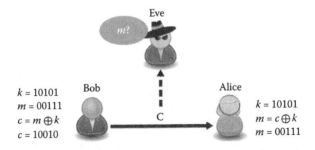

Figure 12.1   Vernam's one-time pad.

In other words, Equation (12.1) implies that the ciphertexts are uniformly distributed in C. Vernam encryption has many drawbacks. We stated that the key has to be renewed for every message. As such, Alice and Bob have to provide a secure communication channel to exchange a new key for every transmitted message. This is not feasible in practice because Alice and Bob will be wasting half of their communication time in exchanging keys (supposing that they manage a secure channel, for example, by using quantum cryptography). In order to remove the problems of the one-time pad algorithm, new types of symmetric encryption algorithms appeared. They are called the block ciphers, as they cipher small blocks of data using small keys of 64, 128, or 256 bits length. These algorithms rely on permutation. The most famous ones are the Data Encryption Standard (DES) [4] and the Advanced Encryption Standard (AES) [5].

12.1.2 Asymmetric Cryptography

Public-key or asymmetric cryptography gives two entities the opportunity to exchange information over an insecure channel while providing data confidentiality, nonrepudiation, and authenticity. In addition, it permits two entities that have never met before to mutually authenticate themselves. Contrary to symmetric cryptography where two communicating entities have to share the same secret key, public-key cryptography relies on two keys to secure the exchanged information. The pair of keys is formed by a *public* key and a *private* key, which are related by a mathematical equation. Solving this mathematical equation comes to breaking a hard mathematical problem such as the discrete logarithm problem (DLP). Each entity shares its public key with its communicating peers. However, its private key must be kept secret (Figure 12.2).

In practice, a public-key infrastructure (PKI) is deployed and a certification authority (CA) is used to certify the mapping between an entity and its public key. The CA is a trusted third party that signs a certificate that contains the public key and the identification information of a user. In addition, the certificate provides information about its issuing CA and includes a unique serial number. The serial number serves to quickly identify the certificate during management operations. The CA should not know the private key, which corresponds

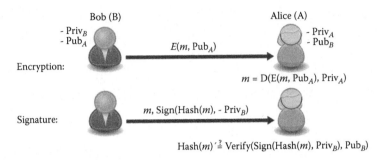

Figure 12.2 Public-key cryptography.

to the public key included in the certificate. Examples of CAs include Verisign, Comodo, CAcert, and Thawte.

Many certification authorities can be overlapped in a hierarchical fashion. That is, the certificate of the parent CA serves to verify the certificates of its children CAs until reaching the *root* CA. The root CA self-signs its own certificate, and it has to be trusted. In practice, we define two types of CAs. The *private* CA is defined inside a private company or a university. It is easy to manage, as certificate usage is limited to a local area. In addition, the user's identification is easy and can be done, for example, in a human resources service before issuing a certificate. Meanwhile, the *public* CA issues certificates to secure transactions over the Internet and to authenticate unknown parties. These certificates are used widely and are not limited to small domains. This type of CA requires more caution when authenticating the users.

The CA manages certificate revocation lists (CRLs) to indicate which certificates are revoked, and so the keys that become invalid. CRLs can be viewed as databases that are securely managed by the CA. In practice, the CA has two different manners of updating the CRLs. In the first case, the CA requests from the users to check periodically the CRL. As such, the users have to always be online to check the list of revoked certificates. In the second case, the CA distributes its CRL periodically to the users.

The two ways of CRL management increase the bandwidth consumption due to the number of CRL requests and responses, or due to the size of the transmitted CRL. Moreover, in the period separating two CRL updates, users do not know the newly revoked certificates, and consequently, attackers that successfully compromised a private key (also very recently revoked) can impersonate as a legitimate network user. For more details about PKI, interested readers are invited to consult the following books: [6], [7], and [8].

We next present the first public-key scheme: the Diffie and Hellman (DH) key exchange algorithm [9] (Section 12.1.3). Then, we review the Rivest, Shamir, and Adleman (RSA) algorithms [10] (Section 12.1.4). DH and RSA cryptosystems are based on the theory of multiplicative groups and on integer factorization into a product of primes, respectively. Finally, we describe the elliptic curve cryptography (ECC) [11] that relies on an additive group of points of an elliptic curve (Section 12.1.5).

12.1.3 Diffie–Hellman (DH) Algorithms

Diffie and Hellman [9] proposed in 1976 a mechanism to share a secret key between two parties, Alice (A) and Bob (B). The public elements provided to each party are the prime P and a generator g of $\mathbb{Z}_P^*$. Alice and Bob generate their public elements $K_A = g^a$ and $K_B = g^b$ and from their secret private keys a and b, which are randomly selected in $\mathbb{Z}_{P-1}^*$. The DH steps are the following:

- *Alice → Bob*: $\{ID_A, K_A\}$: Alice starts the key computation by sending to Bob her public key K_A with her identity ID_A. Upon receiving this message, Bob computes the shared key K_{AB} such that $K_{AB} = (K_A)^b = (g^a)^b$. Then, Bob responds to Alice with his own public key $K_B = g^b$.
- *Bob → Alice*: $\{ID_B, K_B\}$: Upon receiving this message, Alice computes the shared key $K_{AB} = (g^b)^a$.

The DH weakness is the man in the middle (MIM) attack. That is, Eve creates a shared secret with Alice and Bob by impersonating as Bob from one side and as Alice from the other side. However, the MIM attack can be easily removed by making Alice and Bob sign their chosen public elements.

The DH security is based on the definition of the following mathematical problems:

- The *Diffie–Hellman problem* (DHP) consists of recovering the secret key $k = g^{a.b} \bmod[p]$ given the prime p, the generator g of $\mathbb{Z}_P^*$, $g^a \bmod[p]$ and $g^b \bmod[p]$.

- The *discrete logarithm problem* (DLP) consists of finding the secret value $s \in \mathbb{Z}^*_{P-1}$ given the prime p, the generator g of $\mathbb{Z}^*_P$, and the public value k such that $k = g^a \mod[p]$. It is clear that the DHP is not harder than the DLP because any algorithm that solves the DLP solves the DHP too. Indeed, if Eve recovers a from g^a, she will be able to compute $g^{b.a}$ using the captured g^b.

There are various methods for solving the DLP. The basic one is the *exhaustive search*, which consists of evaluating g^i for $i = 0, 1, ..., p-2$ until finding the sought value. This method requires an average of $O(p)$ multiplications. The exhaustive search is actually inefficient for long prime p. For example, if p is 160 bits long, the time needed for trying all the possibilities is around $O(2^{160})$. However, more efficient algorithms such as the *baby-step giant-step* algorithm and *Pollard's rho* algorithm require $O\left(\sqrt{p}\right)$ steps. In addition, Pohlig–Hellman proposed an algorithm that solves the DLP in $O\left(\sum_{i=1}^{r} e_i\left(\log(p-1) + \sqrt{p_i}\right)\right)$ where $p-1 = \Pi_{i=1}^{r} p_i^{e_i}$, Pohlig–Hellman thought that the decomposition of $p-1$ into a product of prime numbers would impact the DLP resolution time, as it consists of finding s from $k = g^s \mod[p]$ with $\in \mathbb{Z}_{p-1}$. Nowadays, the *index calculus* is the most efficient method for solving the DLP in $O\left(e^{c\sqrt{\log(p).\log(\log(p))}}\right)$. More details about DLP resolution can be found in Chapter 3 of the *Handbook of Applied Cryptography* [12].

12.1.4 Rivest, Shamir, and Adleman (RSA) Algorithms

Rivest, Shamir, and Adleman [10] presented the famous RSA schemes in 1978. RSA key generation, encryption, and signature are based on the difficulty of integer factorization into a product of prime numbers.

To generate an RSA key, we first choose two large and distinct random primes p and q and compute the integer n as $n = p.q$. Then, we compute the Euler function $\varphi(n) = (p-1).(q-1)$. We select a random integer e such that $1 < e < \varphi(n)$, where e and $\varphi(n)$ are coprime (i.e., $gcd(e, \varphi(n)) = 1$). Finally, we compute the unique integer d such that $1 < d < \varphi(n)$ and $e.d. = 1 \mod[\varphi(n)]$. Such an integer d can be found using the extended Euclidean algorithm ([13], Chapter 1). The public key is formed by the tuple (n, e) and its corresponding private key is the integer d.

We present, in the following, the RSA encryption and signature algorithms:

- *RSA encryption and decryption*: Let us suppose that Bob is going to encrypt a message to Alice. Bob transforms the message to an integer m in $\mathbb{Z}_n^*$. Then, Bob computes $c = m^e \bmod[n]$ and sends the ciphertext c to Alice. To recover the plaintext from the ciphertext, Alice executes the following operation:

$$c^d \bmod[n] = m^{e.d} \bmod[n] = m^{(1+k.\varphi(n))} \bmod[n] = m \bmod[n]$$

  Note that the decryption is based on the theorem of Euler, which states:

$$x^{\varphi(n)} = 1 \bmod[n], \ \forall \ x \in \mathbb{Z}_n^*$$

- *RSA signature generation and verification*: We suppose that Bob wants to sign the message m before sending it to Alice. Bob first computes the hash $h = H(m)$ and transforms it to an integer in $\mathbb{Z}_n^*$. Then, using its private key d, he computes $s = h^d \bmod[n]$. Finally, Bob sends s and m to Alice. Alice verifies the RSA signature with Bob's public key (e, n). First, she computes $h' = H(m)$. Then, she recovers $h = s^e \bmod[n] = h^{e.d} \bmod[n] = h \bmod[n]$. Finally, Alice compares h to h'. If the two hash values are equal, the signature is valid; otherwise, it is rejected.

The RSA security depends on the difficulty of factoring the number n into the product of two primes p and q. If the trivial *trial and division* method is used for the factoring, we divide n by $i = 2, 3, 5, 7, 11, \dots$ until hitting the smallest prime between p and q. That is, the running time for the trial and division algorithm will be around either $o(p)$ if $p < q$ or $o(q)$ if $q < p$. However, a more efficient method, called *quadratic sieve factoring*, factors the integer n into a product of two primes in approximately $O\left(e^{\sqrt{\log(n).\log(\log(n))}}\right)$. More details about sieving methods can be found in Chapter 3 of the *Handbook of Applied Cryptography* [12].

12.1.5 Elliptic Curve Cryptography (ECC)

Elliptic curves (ECs) are cubic forms that are defined over finite fields, generally a prime or a binary field denoted $\mathbb{F}_p$ or $\mathbb{F}_{2^p}$, where p and 2^p

represent the order of the field. By order, we mean the number of elements of the field. In this chapter, we only consider elliptic curves that are defined over finite prime fields. That is, all the calculus in the field is done mod[p].

An elliptic curve $E(\mathbb{F}_p)$ is defined by the following Weierstrass equation [14]:

$$E(\mathbb{F}_p): y^2 + a_1.x.y + a_3.y = x^3 + a_2.x^2 + a_4.x + a_6,$$

where $a_i \in \mathbb{F}_p, i \in \{1, 2, 3, 4, 6\}$

The points of $E(\mathbb{F}_p)$ form an additive abelian group. That is, the binary operation of the group is the *addition* of two points, and the identity element of the group is a special point, called the *point at infinity* P_∞.

The addition of EC points can be specified graphically as presented in Figure 12.3. Let P and Q be two distinct points belonging to $E(\mathbb{F}_p)$; the sum S of P and Q is obtained by drawing a line through P and Q. This line intercepts E in a third point R. S is the reflection of R relative to the x-axis.

The double of the point P is obtained by drawing the tangent to $E(\mathbb{F}_p)$ in P. This tangent intercepts the curve in a point R. S, the symmetric of R relative to the x-axis, is equal to $2.P$. When the tangent in P happens to be vertical, we say that $2.P = P_\infty$, where P_∞ is the identity element of the additive group. For simplicity, we imagine that the curve cuts the vertical tangent at infinity in the point P_∞.

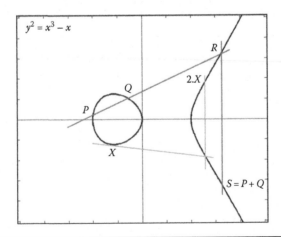

Figure 12.3 Elliptic curve points addition.

To compute the inverse $-P$ of a point $P = (x, y)$, we just take $-P = (x, -y)$. As such, the vertical line passing through P and $-P$ cuts the curve at P_∞. That is $P + (-P) = P_\infty$.

The elliptic curve $E(\mathbb{F}_p)$ is said to be well defined (or smooth) if its discriminant Δ is different from 0. The condition $\Delta \neq 0$ ensures that the EC does not contain singular points for which the addition cannot be defined. The expression of the discriminant Δ is described by the following equalities:

$$\Delta = -b_2^2.b_8 - 8.b_4^3 - 27.b_6^2 + 9.b_2.b_4.b_6$$
$$b_2 = a_1^2 + 4.a_2$$
$$b_4 = 2.a_4 + a_1.a_3$$
$$b_6 = a_3^2 + 4.a_6$$
$$b_8 = a_1^2.a_6 + 4.a_2.a_6 - a_1.a_3.a_4 + a_2.a_3^2 - a_4^2$$

When the characteristic p of the field $\mathbb{F}_p$ is greater than 2, the Weierstrass equation is simplified to become:

$$E(\mathbb{F}_p): y^2 = x^3 + a.x + b, \text{ where } a, b \in \mathbb{F}_p$$

$$\Delta = -16.(4.a^3 + 27.b^2)$$

12.1.5.1 ECC Key Generation Let us take G, a subgroup of $E(\mathbb{F}_p)$, which is generated by the point P of prime order n. G contains the n following points: $\{P_\infty, P, 2.P, 3.P, ..., (n-1).P\}$. Alice chooses a random integer $a \in E(\mathbb{F}_p)$ as her private key and computes her corresponding public key as $K_A = a.P$. The problem of finding a given the primitive root P of G and the public key K_A denotes the *Elliptic Curve Discrete Logarithm Problem* (ECDLP). The ECDLP can be solved using the baby-step giant-step algorithm or Pollard's rho algorithm in $O(\sqrt{n})$ steps ([13], Chapter 5).

The DH protocol can be easily adapted to the elements of the additive group G. Alice and Bob have to just exchange their public elements $K_A = a.P$ and $K_B = b.P$. Of course, Alice and Bob keep secret their respective private keys a and b. Then, they compute respectively their shared key as

$$K_{AB} = a.b.P = b.a.P = K_{BA}$$

Table 12.1   RSA and ECC Key Length Equivalences for the Same Security Levels

l_k	80	112	128	192	256
RSA key length (bits)	1024	2048	3072	7680	15,360
ECC key length (bits)	160	224	256	384	512

In cryptography, the security level of a symmetric encryption algorithm is defined as the number of operations needed to break the algorithm when an l_k-bit key is used. For example, the number of elementary operations needed to break a block cipher encryption scheme is equal to 2^{l_k} [15]. The same result can be retrieved from Vernam's one-time pad where $c = m \oplus k$. The attacker has theoretically to try 2^{l_k} possibilities to find the good key k to recover m from c. Nowadays, l_k has to be at least equal to 80 bits. As such, the key research will take $O(2^{80})$ steps. Using a 4 GHz processor, we need around 9 million years to try all the possibilities, assuming that each possibility is computed during a clock cycle.

In asymmetric cryptography, the security level of an algorithm is set with respect to the hardness of the factoring integer (the case of RSA) or solving the ECDLP (the case of ECDSA). This concept of security level sets the length in bits of RSA and EC keys. Table 12.1 presents the equivalence between the lengths of RSA and EC keys, respectively, to the security level l_k, where l_k corresponds to the length in bits of a symmetric key k.

It is clear from Table 12.1 that it is more interesting to use EC keys than RSA keys when asymmetric cryptography is needed. For example, the current key size recommendation for legacy public schemes is 2048 bits. A vastly smaller 224-bit ECC key offers the same level of security. This advantage only increases with the security level. For example, a 3072-bit legacy key and 256-bit ECC key are equivalent, something that becomes important as stronger security systems become mandated and devices get smaller. ECC usage is expanding because elliptic curves require less storage, less power, less memory, and less bandwidth. They permit the implementation of cryptography in platforms that are constrained, such as wireless devices, handheld computers, and smart cards. They also provide a big gain in situations where efficiency is important.

12.1.5.2 Elliptic Curve Digital Signature Algorithm   We present, in this section, the ECDSA, which is the elliptic curve analog of the digital signature algorithm (DSA) [16]. Let us consider G, a subgroup of an elliptic curve $E(\mathbb{F}_p)$, which is generated by the point P of prime order n.

To sign a message m, Bob chooses a random k in $\mathbb{Z}_n^*$ and computes the point $k. P = (x, y)$. Then, he computes $e = h(m)$ and s $= k^{-1}(e+b.x)$ mod[n], where b is Bob's private key. Finally, Bob sends m and its signature (x, s) to Alice.

At the reception (x, s) of and m, Alice computes $e = h(m)$ and calculates the point X using the public key of Bob $K_B = b. P$ as follows:

$$X = e.s^{-1}.P + x.s^{-1}.K_B = (x', y')$$

Then, Alice compares x' to x. If the two values are equal, the signature is valid.

The signature verification holds because we have $s = k^{-1} (e + b.x)$ mod[n] which implies that $k = s^{-1} (e + b.x)$ mod[n]. Recall that the public key of Bob is $K_B = b. P$, we get

$$X = (x', y') = e.s^{-1}.P + x. s^{-1}. K_B = s^{-1}(e.P + x.b.P) = k.P = (x, y)$$

In the next section, we introduce IBC, which is a promising kind of asymmetric cryptography. In IBC, the public key of an entity is directly derived from its identity.

12.2 ID-Based Cryptography

IBC was initially introduced by Shamir [17] to provide entities with public and private key pairs with no need for certificates, CA and PKI. Shamir assumes that each entity uses one of its identifiers as its public key. These identifiers have to be unique. In addition, he assigns the private key generation function to a special entity called the private key generator (PKG). That is, before accessing the network, every entity has to contact the PKG to get back a smart card containing its private key. This private key is computed so as to be bound to the public key of the entity.

During the last decade, IBC has been improved by the integration of ECC [14]. As a consequence, new ID-based encryption and signature schemes emerged, and they differ from Shamir's method in that the PKG does not rely on smart cards to store the private key and the ciphering information. In 2001, Boneh and Franklin [18] presented the first ID-based encryption scheme, where they used bilinear pairing functions to map elliptic curve points to a number in a multiplicative group.

Sometimes, certificates are considered as IBC, as they bind the user's public key to his or her identity. In this chapter, IBC is considered as the cryptographic schemes where the public key is computationally derived from the identity. The public key is the output of a function (mostly a hash function) that takes as input the user's identity.

There exist many types of IBC schemes. We focus, in this work, on the most commonly used schemes based on pairing functions [19]. For other schemes, we can state the work done by Cocks [20] for an ID-based encryption scheme using the computational difficulty of integer factorization and the quadratic residuosity problem.

In the following sections, we present the key generation processing for IBC. Furthermore, we introduce some well-known ID-based encryption (IBE) and signature (IBS) schemes that proved to be secure within the random oracle model [21]. The random oracle model serves to mathematically establish security proofs where cryptographic functions, like hash functions, are considered random abstract functions [22].

12.2.1 ID-Based Key Construction

When a station needs a private key, it provides the PKG with the identity ID intended to be used for its private-key computation. The PKG then derives the node's private key using some domain parameters. For generating these parameters, the PKG runs a probabilistic polynomial time (PPT) algorithm that takes as input a security parameter k and outputs the groups $\mathbb{G}_1$, $\mathbb{G}_2$, and $\mathbb{G}_T$, and the pairing function $\hat{e}$ from $\mathbb{G}_1 \times \mathbb{G}_2$ in $\mathbb{G}_T$. $\mathbb{G}_1$ and $\mathbb{G}_2$ are additive groups of prime order q, and $\mathbb{G}_T$ is a multiplicative group of the same order q. Note that the order q is defined with respect to k such that $q > 2^k$. Generally, $\mathbb{G}_1$ and $\mathbb{G}_2$ are subgroups of the group of points of an elliptic curve (EC) over a finite field and $\mathbb{G}_T$ is a subgroup of a multiplicative group of a related finite field. The subgroup $\mathbb{G}_1$ is generated by the point P while the subgroup $\mathbb{G}_2$ is generated by the point. The point P (or the point Q) is used to compute another point $P_{pub} = s.P$ (or $Q_{pub} = s.Q$), where s is the domain secret. The PKG chooses randomly the secret $s \in \mathbb{Z}_q^*$.

In addition to the definition of groups, some hash functions need to be defined in accordance to the IBE or IBS schemes that are going to be used. For example, a hash function H_1 that verifies $H_1: \{0, 1\}^* \rightarrow \mathbb{G}_1^*$ is defined in order to transform the node's identity into an EC point. Generally, the public key of a station is computed as a hash of one of its identities, and it is either a point of an elliptic curve or a positive integer. The list containing the groups and $\mathbb{G}_1$ and $\mathbb{G}_2$, the bilinear mapping ê, the points P and P_{pub} and the hash functions form the domain *public elements* noted IBC-PEs. These IBC-PEs are distributed by the PKG to the network users because they are needed during the public-key derivation and the cryptographic operations.

The key derivation process starts when the PKG receives the *ID* of the node that is requesting a private key (Figure 12.4). First, the PKG computes the user's public key as $Pub_{ID} = Hash(ID)$. Then, the PKG generates the corresponding private key using the local secret value s. Note that the private key is computed as $Priv_{ID} = f(s, Pub_{ID})$. In practice, there are different ways for generating a private key from the public key. Here, we present the most known methods for private-key computation:

Basic key generation scheme: In the most common cases [18, 23, 24], we have $Priv_{ID} = s.Pub_{ID}$ where $Pub_{ID} \in \mathbb{G}_1 \cdot Pub_{ID}$ is equal to $H_1(ID)$, where $H_1: \{0, 1\}^* \rightarrow \mathbb{G}_1^*$.

Sakai-Kasahara key generation scheme: Sakai and Kasahara [25] proposed computing the private key as $Priv_{ID} = \left(\dfrac{1}{(Pub_{ID} + s)} \right)$. P where $Pub_{ID} = H_1(ID)$ and $H_1: \{0, 1\}^* \rightarrow \mathbb{Z}_q^*$. As the public key is not an elliptic curve point but a scalar, the public-key computation is faster than hashing to an elliptic curve point.

Boneh and Boyen key generation scheme: Boneh and Boyen define three public points that are computed as $P_1 = \alpha.P$, $P_2 = \beta.P$,

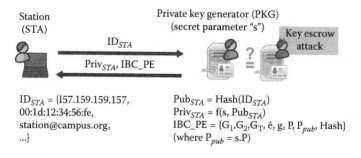

Figure 12.4   ID-based key generation.

and $P_3 = \Upsilon.P$ where α, β, and Υ are secrets selected by the PKG in $\mathbb{Z}_q^*$. A node's public key is computed as $Pub_{ID} = H_1(ID)$ where $H_1: \{0,1\}^* \to \mathbb{Z}_q^*$. Meanwhile, the PKG computes the corresponding private key using the random r in $\mathbb{Z}_q^*$ as follows:

$$Priv_{ID} = (Priv_1, Priv_2) = (Pub_{ID}.r.P_1 + \alpha.P_2 + r.P_3, r.P)$$

That is, the private key is formed by two EC points.

After generating a private key, the PKG has to securely transmit it to its owner either by the use of cryptography or directly to the physical person (using a secure transportation device).

In all the aforementioned key derivation schemes, the PKG is generating the private key of stations (STAs) and, as such, is able to impersonate any of them by illegally generating signature or deciphering encrypted traffic. For mitigating that *key escrow attack* (KEA), a strong assumption is usually made necessary that the PKG is a trustworthy entity.

12.2.2 Pairing Functions

The pairing function $\hat{e}$ has to be bilinear, nondegenerate, and efficiently computable. That is, the pairing function has to verify the following properties:

Bilinearity: The pairing function has to be linear with respect to each of its inputs. That is, the pairing function verifies:

$$\hat{e}(a.P_x + b.P_y, Q) = \hat{e}(P_x, Q)^a \cdot \hat{e}(P_y, Q)^b$$

$$\hat{e}(P, a.Q_x + b.Q_y) = \hat{e}(P, Q_x)^a \cdot \hat{e}(P, Q_y)^b$$

Nondegeneracy: The nondegeneracy property means that for all points $P \in \mathbb{G}_1$, $\hat{e}(P, P_\infty) = 1_{\mathbb{G}_T}$. In addition, for all points $Q \in \mathbb{G}_2$, $\hat{e}(P_\infty, Q) = 1_{\mathbb{G}_T}$. If we consider a generator P of $\mathbb{G}_1$ and a generator of Q of $\mathbb{G}_2$, the value $\hat{e}(P, Q) = g$ is equal to the generator $\mathbb{G}_T$.

Efficiency: There is an efficient algorithm to compute the pairing function.

Galbraith et al. [15] defined three types of pairing functions that can be divided into two families:

1. Symmetric pairing: It verifies $\mathbb{G}_1 = \mathbb{G}_2$.
2. Asymmetric pairing: It verifies $\mathbb{G}_1 \neq \mathbb{G}_2$. This pairing function can be further classified based on the existence, or not, of an efficient homomorphism $\psi \colon \mathbb{G}_2 \to \mathbb{G}_1$.

Menezes, Okamoto, and Vanstone [26] used a symmetric pairing function to solve the ECDLP. They considered $\hat{e} \colon \mathbb{G}_1 \times \mathbb{G}_1 \to \mathbb{G}_T$ and the point $Q = x.P$. Their idea consists of transposing the ECDLP to a DLP in $\mathbb{G}_T$. They assumed that they have an efficient algorithm to solve the DLP $\mathbb{G}_T$ in and they used:

$$Q = x.P \Leftrightarrow \hat{e}(P, Q) = \hat{e}(P, P)^x$$

$$\Leftrightarrow h = g^x, \text{ where } h = \hat{e}(P, Q) \text{ and } g = \hat{e}(P, P)$$

As a consequence, the security level of $\hat{e}$ will be related to the hardness of solving the DLP in the groups $\mathbb{G}_1, \mathbb{G}_2,$ and $\mathbb{G}_T$. It is closely related to the groups being selected, as some of them make the DLP easier. To understand how to define this security level in practice, the investigation of the structures of $\mathbb{G}_1, \mathbb{G}_2,$ and $\mathbb{G}_T$ is necessary.

Before specifying the structures of $\mathbb{G}_1, \mathbb{G}_2,$ and $\mathbb{G}_T$, it is necessary to review some definitions related to elliptic curves. We first define the subgroup of q-torsion points as the subgroup of points having the order q. The q-torsion subgroup defined over an elliptic curve $E(\mathbb{F}_p)$ is denoted by $E(\mathbb{F}_p[q]) = \left\{ P \in \dfrac{E(\mathbb{F}_p)}{q.P} = P_\infty \right\}$. If p does not divide q, there is a theorem that states that it exists an integer k such that $E(\mathbb{F}_p k[q])$ is isomorphic to $\mathbb{Z}_q \times \mathbb{Z}_q$ ([27], Chapter 3, Theorem 3.2). The smallest integer k verifying the previous theorem is called the *embedding degree* of the curve $E(\mathbb{F}_p)$ respectively to q.

Let $E(\mathbb{F}_p)$ denote the elliptic curve defined over the finite prime field $\mathbb{F}_p$. $\mathbb{G}_1$ and $\mathbb{G}_2$ correspond mostly to the q-torsion subgroups of and $E(\mathbb{F}_p)$ and $E(\mathbb{F}_{p^k})$, where k is the embedding degree of the curve $E(\mathbb{F}_p)$ relative to q. Meanwhile, $\mathbb{G}_T$ is a multiplicative subgroup of $\mathbb{F}_p k$ of order q [28].

For example, assume that the prime order p of $\mathbb{F}_p$ is 512 bits long, the order q is 160 bits long while the embedding degree relatively to q of the curve $E(\mathbb{F}_p)$ is 2. The pairing function ê is then defined over the subgroups $\mathbb{G}_1$, $\mathbb{G}_2$, and $\mathbb{G}_T$ of order q. The security level of ê is defined respectively to the hardness of solving DLP in $\mathbb{G}_T$. As $\mathbb{G}_T$ is a subgroup of $\mathbb{F}_{p^2}$ which has an order of 1024 bits, DLP hardness in $\mathbb{G}_T$ is defined respectively to this 1024-bit order. That is, the pairing ê security level is equivalent to an RSA key of 1024 bits length, and so to a security level of 80 bits with respect to Table 12.1.

In practice, bilinear mapping is derived from the Weil or Tate pairing ([29], Chapter 9). We use the definition given by El-Mrabet [28] to describe these two types of pairing. First, we define a rational function f on the points of an elliptic curve. f takes as input two variables x and y, which represent the coordinates of a point. Then, we specify the *divisor* of this function $Div(f)$ as a formal sum that returns information about the zeros and poles of f. To describe the Weil and Tate pairings, we use the function $f_{q,r}$ that verifies: $Div(f_{q,r}) = q.[R] - (q - 1).[P_\infty]$. The two types of pairing will be defined as follows:

- *Weil Pairing*: ê: $\mathbb{G}_1 \times \mathbb{G}_2 \to \mathbb{G}_T$

$$(P, Q) \to \frac{f_{q,p}(Q)}{f_{q,Q}(P)}$$

- *Tate Pairing*: ê: $\mathbb{G}_1 \times \mathbb{G}_2 \to \mathbb{G}_T$

$$(P, Q) \to f_{q,p}(Q)^{\frac{p^k-1}{q}}$$

These two formulas will not be used in this chapter. However, interested readers can refer to the books [14], [27], and [29] for a detailed mathematical description of divisors and pairings.

12.2.3 Examples of ID-Based Encryption Schemes

In this section, we start by presenting some well-known ID-based encryption algorithms. The first scheme uses a classical key construction. That is, the public key is a point derived from station's identity using a hash-to-point function, while the private key is computed as $Priv_{ID} = s.Pub_{ID}$, s is PKG's secret. The second encryption scheme is the Boneh and Boyen encryption algorithm, which uses the Boneh and Boyen key derivation method (Section 12.2.3.2).

The third presented scheme is Chen et al. encryption scheme which relies on Sakai-Kasahara key construction (Section 12.2.3.3). All these IBE schemes' security is based on the bilinear Diffie–Hellman (BDH) problem, which consists of computing $\hat{e}(P, P)^{abc}$, given the points P, $a.P$, $b.P$, and $c.P$ and the symmetric pairing $\hat{e}$.

12.2.3.1 Boneh and Franklin Encryption Scheme Boneh and Franklin [18] proposed in 2001 an IBE scheme using symmetric pairing function. They define two hash functions H_1 and H_2 such that: $H_1 \colon \{0,1\}^* \to \mathbb{G}_1^*$ and $H_2 \colon \mathbb{G}_T \to \{0,1\}^n$. So, Boneh and Franklin IBC-PEs are $\{\mathbb{G}_1, \mathbb{G}_T, q, \hat{e}, g, P, P_{pub}, H_1, H_2\}$. The PKG computes the user's public key as $Pub_{ID} = H_1(ID)$. Then, the PKG generates the corresponding private key using a local secret value $s \in \mathbb{Z}_q^*$.

To encrypt an $M \in \{0, 1\}^n$ message using the public key Pub_{ID}, a user generates a secret random $k \in \mathbb{Z}_q^*$ and computes the ciphertext C as

$$C = (U, V) = (k.P, M \oplus H_2(\hat{e}(Pub_{ID}, P_{pub})^k))$$

The decrypting entity deciphers the received message as follows:

$$M = V \oplus H_2(\hat{e}(Priv_{ID}, U))$$

12.2.3.2 Boneh and Boyen Encryption Schemes Boneh and Boyen [30] proposed an IBE scheme using a symmetric pairing function. They define two hash functions H_1 and H_2 such that: $H_1 \colon \{0,1\}^* \to \mathbb{Z}_q^*$ and $H_2 \colon \mathbb{G}_T \to \{0,1\}^n$. In addition, they define three points that are computed as $P_1 = \alpha.P$, $P_2 = \beta.P$, and $P_3 = \Upsilon.P$ where α, β, and Υ are secrets selected by the PKG in $\mathbb{Z}_q^*$. From P_1 and P_2, they compute $v = \hat{e}(P_1, P_2)$, which is part of the IBC-PEs. So, Boneh and Boyen public elements are $\{\mathbb{G}_1, \mathbb{G}_T, q, \hat{e}, v, P, P_1, P_2, P_3, H_1, H_2\}$. The PKG computes the user's public key as $Pub_{ID} = H_1(ID)$. However, the private key is computed as the couple of points $Priv_{ID} = (Priv_1, Priv_2) = (Pub_{ID}.r.P_1 + \alpha.P_2 + r.P_3, r.P)$ where r is a random number selected by PKG.

To encrypt a message $M \in \{0, 1\}^n$ using the public key Pub_{ID}, a user generates a secret random $k \in \mathbb{Z}_q^*$ and computes the ciphertext as the tuple $C = (c, C_0, C_1)$, where $c = M \oplus H_2(v^k)$, $C_0 = k.P$, and $C_1 = Pub_{ID}.k.P_1 + k.P_3$. The deciphering entity starts by computing $k = \dfrac{\hat{e}(C_0, Priv_0)}{\hat{e}(C_1, Priv_1)}$. Then, it recovers M as $M = c \oplus H_2(v^k)$.

12.2.3.3 Chen et al. Encryption Scheme   Chen et al. [31] presented an IBE scheme using a symmetric pairing function. They define two hash functions H_1 and H_2 such that $H_1: \{0,1\} \to \mathbb{Z}_q^*$ and $H_2: \mathbb{G}_T \to \{0,1\}^l$, where l is the size in bits of the message M that is going to be ciphered. A user public key is computed as $Pub_{ID} = H_1(ID)$ and its corresponding private key is generated by the PKG using the Sakai–Kasahara key generation scheme, i.e., $Priv_{ID} = (1/(Pub_{ID} + s)).P$. In order to encrypt M, the ciphering station chooses a random number $k \in \mathbb{Z}_q^*$ and executes the following steps:

1. $U = k. (P_{pub} + pub_{ID}. P)$
2. $n = H_2(g^k)$
3. $V = M \oplus n$

The ciphered message is the pair $(U,V) \in \mathbb{G}_1 \times \{0,1\}^l$. The recipient of (U,V) computes first $= H_2(\hat{e}(U, Priv_{ID}))$. Then, it recovers the message M as: $M = V \oplus n$.

12.2.4 Examples of ID-Based Signature Algorithms

In this section, we present three different signature schemes that rely on pairing computation.

12.2.4.1 Paterson Signature Scheme   Paterson [23] proposed, in 2002, an IBS scheme using ECC and a symmetric pairing function. He defines three hash functions H_1, H_2, and H_3 such that: $H_1: \{0,1\}^* \to \mathbb{G}_1^*$, $H_2: \{0,1\}^* \to \mathbb{Z}_q^*$, and $H_3: \mathbb{G}_1 \to \mathbb{Z}_q^*$. So, Paterson IBC-PEs are $\{\mathbb{G}_1, \mathbb{G}_T, q, \hat{e}, g, P, P_{pub}, H_1, H_2, H_3\}$. The PKG computes the user's public key as $Pub_{ID} = H_1(ID)$. Then, the PKG generates the corresponding private key using a local secret value $s \in \mathbb{Z}_q^*$.

To compute the signature of a message M, a user generates a secret random $k \in \mathbb{Z}_q^*$ and computes its signature as the pair $(R, S) \in \mathbb{G}_1 \times \mathbb{G}_1$, where

$$R = k.P$$

$$S = k^{-1}(H_2(M).P + H_3(R).Priv_{ID})$$

The signature verifier has only to compare to $\hat{e}(R, S)$ to $(\hat{e}(P,P)^{H_2(M)}$. $\hat{e}(P_{pub}, Pub_{ID})^{H_3(R)})$. The two values must be equal in order to consider the signature as valid.

12.2.4.2 Hess Signature Scheme   Hess [24] presented an ID-based signature scheme in 2003. Hess signature relies on a symmetric pairing function. His signature scheme keeps the Paterson public parameters definition, but it replaces H_2 and H_3 with a new hash function that we denote as $H_4: \{0,1\}^* \times \mathbb{G}_T \rightarrow \mathbb{Z}_q^*$.

In order to sign a message M, the user chooses an arbitrary point $P_1 \in \mathbb{G}_q^*$ and a random number $k \in \mathbb{Z}_q^*$. Then, he or she executes the following steps:

1. $r = \hat{e}(P_1, P)^k$
2. $v = H_4(M, r)$
3. $U = v.Priv_{ID} + k.P_1$

The signature is formed by the pair $(U, v) \in \mathbb{G}_1 \times \mathbb{Z}_q^*$. The signature verifier then has to compute:

1. $r = \hat{e}(U, P). \hat{e}(Pub_{ID}, - P_{Pub})^v$
2. The signature is accepted if and only if $v = H_4(M, r)$

12.2.4.3 Barreto et al. Signature Scheme   Barreto et al. [32] presented their ID-based signature scheme in 2005. Their signature basically uses one asymmetric pairing function. It relies on two hash functions H_1 and H_2 such that: $H_1: \{0,1\}^* \rightarrow \mathbb{Z}_q^*$ and $H_2: \{0,1\}^* \rightarrow \mathbb{G}_T \rightarrow \mathbb{Z}_q^*$. So, Barreto et al. IBC-PEs are where $\{\mathbb{G}_1, \mathbb{G}_2, \mathbb{G}_T, q, \hat{e}, g, P, Q, Q_{pub}, H_1, H_2\}$ where $Q_{pub} = s.Q$ (s is PKG's secret). A user public key is computed as $Pub_{ID} = H_1(ID)$, and its corresponding private key is generated by the PKG as $Priv_{ID} = (1/(Pub_{ID} + s)).P$. In order to sign a message M, the signer chooses a random number $k \in \mathbb{Z}_q^*$ and executes the following steps:

1. $n = g^k$
2. $h = H_2(M, n)$
3. $S = (k + h)Priv_{ID}$

The signature is formed by the pair $(S, h) \in \mathbb{G}_1 \times \mathbb{Z}_q^*$. Then, the signature verifier has only to check the equality between h and $H_2(M, \hat{e}(S, H_1(ID)Q + Q_{pub})g^{-h})$.

12.2.5 Arguments in Favor of IBC

In wireless and mobile networks, such as sensor networks or ad hoc networks, bandwidth, memory, and power consumptions are a big concern, as they directly impact the network and station performances. Consequently, the selection of cryptographic tools for security support must be accurate. Certificates require deploying a PKI and certificate management functions for the generation and delivery of certificates by the CA to successfully authenticated STAs. In addition, periodic downloading of CRLs by STAs from the CA is necessary to verify the validity of certificates.

IBC does not need certificates, CRL, and revocation procedures. With IBC, the key lifetime is bound to a timer, and after its expiration, keys are changed. Bandwidth for exchanging certificates between STAs or downloading CRL is saved. For the derivation of the keys of its peers, STA has only to store the IBC-PEs, extract the hash function from the IBC-PEs, and compute the hash over the identity of the peer. That is, no more memory space is used for storing the certificates.

Table 12.2 presents a comparison between IBC and PKI (based on Paterson and Price [33]). IBC relies on unique identities in order to get different public keys, and so different private keys. However, in a PKI, two different certificates can contain the same identity. That is, a user can have two valid certificates that are used for different purposes. With IBC, the public key of an STA can be used even if its private key has not yet been derived. This can be interesting when an STA ciphers some important data for other STAs and requires that they authenticate to the PKG in order to get the private key for the decryption. Compromising the PKG is very dangerous because

Table 12.2 IBC Comparison to PKI

	IBC	PKI
Trusted entity	PKG	CA
Trust guarantee	None	Certificate
Client identity	Unique and authentic	Authentic
Public-key generator	PKG and clients	CA or client
Private-key generator	PKG	CA or client
Public- and private-key generation times	Can be different	Same time, before certificate issuance
Key escrow attack	Not detected	Detected
Key revocation	Timer	CRLs
Usage range	Local domains	Wide domains
Advantages	No certificates, no CRLs, less storage	No key escrow

the PKG secret will be revealed. Consequently, any station private key can be computed and old encrypted messages can be deciphered. However, when the CA is compromised, old encrypted messages are not affected.

12.2.6 Use of IBC in Network Security

As shown above, IBC is not new. Its introduction to networks is, however, quite recent. Seth and Keshav described a hierarchical IBC solution that supports mutual authentication and key revocation mechanisms in delay-tolerant networks (DTNs) [34]. Liu et al. presented, in 2009, an Extensible Authentication Protocol (EAP) authentication method that is adapted for wireless mesh networks [35]. They proposed a scheme that relies on Hess ID-based signature [24]. Boudguiga and Laurent [36] presented, in 2011, a key escrow-resistant authentication scheme for wireless networks that relies on secure tokens. Ben-Othman et al. [37, 38] used IBC to secure the Hybrid Wireless Mesh Protocol (HWMP). They authenticate each HWMP path request and response message thanks to an IBS. Moreover, RFC 6267 [39] presented a variant of the Multimedia Internet Keying (MIKEY) protocol, which relies on an IBC authenticated key exchange. Tan et al. [40] described in their paper a lightweight IBE for body sensor networks (BSNs). Drira et al. [41] also proposed a hybrid authentication scheme relying on symmetric cryptography and IBC to authenticate sensors and mobile nodes in a BSN.

12.3 Conclusion

In this chapter, we present a general introduction to public-key cryptography. We describe ID-based cryptography, which relies on the use of elliptic curve groups. ECC and IBC are attractive for many researchers, as they reduce the size of keys, encryption, and signature schemes. They are well suited for the security applications that are specific to network stations with memory constraints. In addition, IBC removes the cumbersome task of managing PKI and certificates, and consequently, the network overhead is reduced. As such, IBC seems to be a promising solution for security provisioning in wireless networks where every saving in bandwidth and terminal memory is welcome.

References

1. A. Kerckhoffs. Military Cryptography (La cryptographie militaire). *Journal of Military Sciences (Journal des sciences militaires)*, 9, 5–38, 1883.
2. C. Shannon. Communication Theory and Secrecy Systems. *Bell System Technical Journal*, 28, 656–715, 1949.
3. G. Vernam. Secret Signaling System. US 1310719A, 8, 1919. Available at http://ieeexplore.ieee.org/xpl/freeabs_all.jsp?arnumber=5061224.
4. NIST. Data Encryption Standard (DES). 1999. Available at http://csrc.nist.gov/publications/fips/fips46-3/fips46-3.pdf.
5. S. Heron. Advanced Encryption Standard (AES). *Network Security*, 2009(12), 8–12, 2001. Available at http://csrc.nist.gov/publications/fips/fips197/fips-197.pdf.
6. N. Ferguson, B. Schneier, and T. Kohno. *Cryptography Engineering: Design Principles and Practical Applications*, vol. 277. New York: Wiley, 2010.
7. J. Viega, P. Chandra, and M. Messier. *Network Security with OpenSSL*, 1st ed. Sebastopol, CA: O'Reilly & Associates, 2002.
8. R. Housley and T. Polk. *Planning for PKI: Best Practices Guide for Deploying Public Key Infrastructure*, 1st ed. New York: John Wiley & Sons, 2001.
9. W. Diffie and M. Hellman. New Directions in Cryptography. *IEEE Transactions on Information Theory*, 22(6), 644–654, 1976.
10. R. Rivest, A. Shamir, and L. Adleman. *A Method for Obtaining Digital Signatures and Public-Key Cryptosystem*, vol. 21, no. 2. New York: ACM, 1978, pp. 120–126. Available at http://doi.acm.org/10.1145/359340.359342.
11. D. Hankerson, A. Menezes, and S. Vanstone. *Guide to Elliptic Curve Cryptography*. Secaucus, NJ: Springer-Verlag, 2003.
12. A. Menezes, P.V. Oorschot, and S. Vanstone. *Handbook of Applied Cryptography*, vol. 106, no. 2. Boca Raton, FL: CRC Press, 1997. Available at http://www.cacr.math.uwaterloo.ca/hac/index.html.
13. J. Hoffstein, J. Pipher, and J. Silverman. *An Introduction to Mathematical Cryptography*, vol. XVI. Berlin: Springer, 2008.
14. J. Silverman. *The Arithmetic of Elliptic Curves*, vol. 106. New York: Springer, 2009. Available at http://www.springerlink.com/index/10.1007/978-0-387-09494-6.
15. S. Galbraith, K. Paterson, and N. Smart. Pairings for Cryptographers. *Discrete Applied Mathematics*, 156(160), 3113–3121, 2008. Available at http://www.sciencedirect.com/science/article/pii/S0166218X08000449.
16. NIST. The Digital Signature Standard. *Communications of the ACM*, 35(7), 36–40, 1992. Available at http://doi.acm.org/10.1145/129902.129904.
17. A. Shamir. Identity-Based Cryptosystems and Signature Schemes. In *Proceedings of CRYPTO 84 on Advances in Cryptology*. New York: Springer-Verlag, 1985, pp. 47–53.
18. D. Boneh and M. Franklin. Identity-Based Encryption from the Weil Pairing. In *Proceedings of the 21st Annual International Cryptology Conference on Advances in Cryptology, CRYPTO '01*. London: Springer-Verlag, 2001, pp. 213–229. Available at http://portal.acm.org/citation.cfm?id=646766.704155.

19. D. Ratna, B. Rana, and S. Palash. *Pairing-Based Cryptographic Protocols: A Survey.* 2004. Available at http://eprint.iacr.org/.

20. C. Cocks. An Identity Based Encryption Scheme Based on Quadratic Residues. In *Proceedings of the 8th IMA International Conference on Cryptography and Coding.* London: Springer-Verlag, 2001, pp. 360–363. Available at http://dl.acm.org/citation.cfm?id=647995.742435.

21. M. Bellare and P. Rogaway. Random Oracles Are Practical: A Paradigm for Designing Efficient Protocols. In *Proceedings of the 1st ACM Conference on Computer and Communications Security,* ACM CCS '93, New York, NY, 1993, pp. 62–73. Available at http://doi.acm.org/10.1145/168588.168596.

22. M. Bellare, C. Namprempre, and G. Neven. Security Proofs for Identity-Based Identification and Signature Schemes. *Journal of Cryptology,* 22(1), 1–61, 2008. Available at http://dx.doi.org/10.1007/s00145-008-9028-8.

23. K. Paterson. ID-Based Signatures from Pairings on Elliptic Curves. *Electronics Letters,* 38(18), 1025–1026, 2002.

24. F. Hess. Efficient Identity Based Signature Schemes Based on Pairings. In *SAC '02: Revised Papers from the 9th Annual International Workshop on Selected Areas in Cryptography.* London: Springer-Verlag, 2003, pp. 310–324.

25. R. Sakai and M. Kasahara. *ID Based Cryptosystems with Pairing on Elliptic Curve.* Report 2003/054. Cryptology ePrint Archive, 2003. Available at http://eprint.iacr.org/.

26. A. Menezes, T. Okamoto, and S. Vanstone. Reducing Elliptic Curve Logarithms to Logarithms in a Finite Field. *IEEE Transactions on Information Theory,* 39(5), 1639–1646, 1993. Available at http://ieeexplore. ieee.org/lpdocs/epic03/wrapper.htm?arnumber=259647.

27. L. Washington. *Elliptic Curves: Number Theory and Cryptography,* 2nd ed. London: Chapman & Hall/CRC, 2008.

28. N. El-Mrabet. Arithmetic, Performances and Resistance of Pairings to Side Channel Attacks (Arithmetiques des couplages, performance et resistance aux attaques par cannaux caches). PhD dissertation, Montpellier II University, 2009.

29. I. Blake, G. Seroussi, and N. Smart. *Advances in Elliptic Curve Cryptography (London Mathematical Society Lecture Note Series).* New York: Cambridge University Press, 2005.

30. D. Boneh and X. Boyen. Efficient Selective-ID Secure Identity-Based Encryption without Random Oracles. In *Advances in Cryptology— EUROCRYPT 2004,* ed. C. Cachin and J. Camenisch, vol. 3027. Lecture Notes in Computer Science Series. Berlin: Springer, 2004, pp. 223–238.

31. L. Chen, Z. Cheng, J. Malone-Lee, and N. Smart. Efficient ID-KEM Based on the Sakai-Kasahara Key Construction. *IEEE Proceedings in Information Security,* 153(1), 19–26, 2006.

32. P. Barreto, B. Libert, N. McCullagh, and J.-J. Quisquater. Efficient and Provably-Secure Identity-Based Signatures and Signcryption from Bilinear Maps. In *Advances in Cryptology—ASIACRYPT 2005,* ed. B. Roy, vol. 3788. Lecture Notes in Computer Science Series. Berlin: Springer, 2005, pp. 515–532.

33. K. Paterson and G. Price. *A Comparison between Traditional Public Key Infrastructures and Identity-Based Cryptography*. Technical Report. Royal Holloway University of London, 2003.

34. A. Seth and S. Keshav. Practical Security for Disconnected Nodes. In *1st IEEE ICNP Workshop on Secure Network Protocols (NPSec 2005)*, June 2005, pp. 31–36.

35. W. Liu, Y. Shang, and Z. Wang. A Wireless Mesh Network Authentication Method Based on Identity Based Signature. In *5th International Conference on Wireless Communications, Networking and Mobile Computing, 2009 (WiCom '09)*, 2009, pp. 1–4.

36. A. Boudguiga and M. Laurent. Key-Escrow Resistant ID-Based Authentication Scheme for IEEE 802.11s Mesh Networks. In *2011 IEEE Wireless Communications and Networking Conference (WCNC 2011)*, March 2011, pp. 784–789.

37. J. Ben-Othman and Y. Saavedra Benitez. On Securing HWMP Using IBC. In *2011 IEEE International Conference on Communications (ICC)*, June 2011, pp. 1–5.

38. J. Ben-Othman, L. Mokdad, and Y. Saavedra Benitez. Performance Comparison between IBC-HWMP and Hash-HWMP. In *2011 IEEE Global Telecommunications Conference (GLOBECOM)*, December 2011, pp. 1–5.

39. V. Cakulev and G. Sundaram. *MIKEY-IBAKE: Identity-Based Authenticated Key Exchange (IBAKE) Mode of Key Distribution in Multimedia Internet KEYing (MIKEY)*. RFC 6267 (Informational). Internet Engineering Task Force, June 2011. Available at http://www.ietf.org/rfc/rfc6267.txt.

40. C.C. Tan, H. Wang, S. Zhong, and Q. Li. IBE-Lite: A Lightweight Identity-Based Cryptography for Body Sensor Networks. *IEEE Transactions on Information Technology in Biomedicine*, 13(6), 926–932, 2009.

41. W. Drira, E. Renault, and D. Zeglache. A Hybrid Authentication and Key Establishment Scheme for WBAN. Presented at International Conference on Trust Security and Privacy in Computing and Communications, 2012 IEEE TrustCom, June 2012.

13

Symmetric Key Encryption Acceleration on Heterogeneous Many-Core Architectures

GIOVANNI AGOSTA,
ALESSANDRO BARENGHI,
GERARDO PELOSI, AND
MICHELE SCANDALE

Contents

Keywords

Advanced Encryption Standard
AES
Counter mode
CTR

General purpose graphics processing unit
GPGPU
Heterogeneous many-core architecture
Many-core computing system
MCCS
OpenCL

The wide diffusion of many-core computing systems (MCCSs), in particular through general purpose graphics processing units (GPGPUs), and more recently in high-end embedded hardware (mobile GPUs), has provided developers with a plentiful source of cheap computational power.

However, exploiting such computational power is not straightforward. Heterogeneous platforms require specialized application programming interfaces (APIs) to interface the host side with the accelerator device, as well as specialized language features to manage the peculiar characteristics of the device itself. The OpenCL standard, introduced by the large industrial consortium Khronos Group, is the most successful and widespread approach to programming heterogeneous MCCSs. It allows the programmer to interface C++ host code with device code written in a restricted C code (OpenCL-C) through the OpenCL API. However, developing efficient code with the OpenCL standard requires specialized knowledge that is both domain specific and platform specific.

In this chapter, we provide an overview of the implementation techniques a developer needs to understand in order to produce efficient implementations of cryptographic primitives on GPGPUs and other heterogeneous MCCSs. We first introduce the OpenCL standard through a simple example, and then provide a practical implementation of the Advanced Encryption Standard (AES) cryptographic primitive, employed in counter mode, which allows efficient parallelization.

13.1 Introduction

Modern implementations of cryptographic algorithms in C++ are increasingly called to provide both flexibility, in terms of code reuse on different platforms, and significantly good performances exploiting the peculiarities of the underlying hardware architecture. To this end, it is fundamental to take into account the modern architecture design trend, which is pushing toward heterogeneous multicore architectures as the main structure for high-end embedded systems and high-performance computing systems alike. In particular, modern multicore architectures are typically composed of a reduced number of high-performance processors, coupled with a large number of small, simple ones, and possibly application-specific accelerators.

This structure is often coupled with programmer-addressable scratchpad memories present directly on the same die as the processors. This shift toward parallel architectures provides a good fit for the increased need of fast symmetric encryption on large amounts of data at rest required by cloud storage providers, and the capability to perform a significant amount of concurrent Secure Sockets Layer (SSL)/Transport Layer Security (TLS) handshakes required to provide secure network communications. The complex and heterogeneous structure of modern processors increases the possible options for architecture design, thus calling, from a programmer's point of view, for a programming model that allows us to abstract the architectural details, while retaining effective performance tuning capabilities. To this end, the OpenCL language and programming models were proposed by the Khronos consortium [1]; the OpenCL language is a subset of C99, with proper language extensions to allow the programmer to effectively encode programs to be run in parallel on heterogeneous multicores.

Section 13.2 provides a brief survey and taxonomy of the modern heterogeneous multicore platforms, while Section 13.3 describes the OpenCL language and programming model, providing insights on the memory hierarchy on which it is based. Section 13.3.3 provides a brief example of an OpenCL program, while Section 13.4 provides a full implementation of the Advanced Encryption Standard (AES) block cipher, employed in counter (CTR) mode, which is both secure and efficiently parallelizable. The core of the implementation is realized with OpenCL, while the bindings are in C++11, providing an example of the best practices in integrating OpenCL code into a C++ environment.

13.2 Modern Heterogeneous Many-Core Architectures

The current trend in computing architectures, in both the high-end embedded and high-performance computing fields, is to replace single, complex superscalar processors with numerous but smaller and simpler processing units, connected by an on-chip network. Such a change is imposed by silicon technology frontiers, the reaching of which is getting closer as the process density levels increase—the so-called *Moore's wall*. Clock speeds are not improving at the same rate they did in the last 40 years, and even though the transistor density is still improving according to Moore's law, this does not translate into improved performances, as increases in register bank or cache size or pipeline depth are hitting the point of diminishing returns. For example, cache size increases are only useful in case of a low cache hit rate, but when the hit rate becomes very high, increasing the cache size will yield minimal performance benefits. These trends have delineated a rapid growth in the number of computing cores per chip. Even general purpose processors for high-end embedded systems have evolved from single-core to twin quad-core designs, such as ARM big.LITTLE, in the last 3 years. More specialized architectures, such as graphics processing units, are already in the range of hundreds of cores—the class that is generally named as many-core architectures.

Many-core architectures offer large amounts of parallel computing power by supplying the developer with hundreds of processing cores, each endowed with limited resources. The benefits of many-core architectures include a control on a finer grain for energy-saving techniques, the accounting for local process variations, and an improved silicon yield due to voltage/frequency island isolation possibilities. Notable many-core architectures include the following: *desktop GPGPUs* such as nVidia GT200 [2], Fermi [3], Kepler [4], AMD R700 [5], and R800 [6], and *embedded GPGPUs* such as ImgTech PowerVR [7] and nVidia Tegra [8]. Moreover, also *non-GPU coprocessors* such as IBM CellBE [9], Intel Xeon Phi [10], and Adapteva Epiphany [11] have gained popularity, together with *many-core standalone systems*, of which an example is Intel SCC [12].

It is worth noting that, currently, GPGPUs are dominating the many-core scene, although non-GPU accelerators have found application in specialized domains, and may in the future become the dominant paradigm, as they are expected to be more versatile. Even more likely, the classification above might be overcome as GPGPUs become more general purpose computation oriented, and the gap between GPGPUs and other many-core accelerators narrows. What is likely, on the other hand, is that heterogeneity will still play a role: many-core architectures are not well suited for control-intensive applications, and the emerging paradigm is that of a pairing between a multicore host architecture and (one or more) many-core accelerator device(s). This is the case, of course, of GPGPUs, which are always used as accelerators to either desktop processors (based on the x86_64 architecture) or high-end embedded processors (most commonly ARM based).

13.3 The OpenCL Programming Model

OpenCL (Open Computing Language) [1,23] is an open standard for the development of parallel applications on a variety of heterogeneous multicore architectures. The advantage of OpenCL, as well as other modern programming models, is that it handles and combines different implementation platforms (GPUs, CPUs, and DSPs) under the same environment.

OpenCL consists of both a subset of C99 with appropriate language extensions (OpenCL-C) and an OpenCL API, which allow programs to be split into a *host part* and a *compute device part*. The OpenCL host usually runs on a general purpose (multi)processor, and it is in charge of executing the control-intensive code portion. Moreover, the host uses the OpenCL API to query and select compute devices, to offload compute-intensive code portions, called *kernels*, on them.

The offloading is managed through submitting the kernels to the work queues of each device and managing the workload across compute contexts and work queues. The execution of a kernel is orchestrated as a perfect double-nested loop.

Each iteration of the innermost loop executes the kernel code on an independent execution element called *work item*, whereas any iteration of the outer loop gathers work items in independent sets called *work groups*. Since the computation domain of the kernel (e.g., the data placement) can be thought as an N-dimensional domain, where each tuple of coordinates corresponds to an execution element, any work item is characterized by a unique identifier composed of N unsigned integer values, depending on the definitions set up by the host part of the application. Work groups are also uniquely identified through a set of unsigned integer values ranging from 0 to $N-1$, according to an orthotropic geometry. In OpenCL application development, the main target is to obtain significant performance improvements through optimally exploiting the resources of the underlying platform.

To this end, the OpenCL programming model is characterized by structures allowing the programmer to provide hints on the actual data placement in the memory hierarchy of the target platform.

13.3.1 OpenCL Parallel Execution Model

OpenCL supports primarily data parallelism, and to a lesser extent task parallelism. The support for data parallelism consists of an explicitly parallel function invocation (*kernel*) that is executed by a user-specified number of work items, placed on an abstract N-dimensional space. Every OpenCL kernel is explicitly started by the host code through a clEnqueueNDRangeKernel call, and executed by the compute device, while the host-side code continues its execution asynchronously after instantiating the kernel.

Task-level parallelism is provided through allowing the programmer to enqueue multiple kernels for execution, which may be run in parallel by the underlying hardware of the compute device.

Events can be used to provide a dependency relation among the kernels. Indeed, each clEnqueueNDRangeKernel call takes as input parameter a list of events that must be completed before the execution of the kernel begins and provides, as output parameter, an event that can be waited upon to check the completion of the kernel execution. To this end, the programmer is provided with a synchronizing function call to wait for the completion of the active kernel computations.

As anticipated in the previous section, the OpenCL programming model abstracts the actual parallelism implemented by the hardware architecture, providing the concepts of work group and work item to express concurrency in algorithms. A work group captures the notion of a group of concurrent work items. Work groups are required to be computed independently, so that it is possible to run them in any order. Therefore, the OpenCL-C synchronization primitives semantically act only among work items belonging to the same work group.

A kernel call site (clEnqueueNDRangeKernel) must specify the number of work groups as well as the number of work items within each work group when executing the kernel code.

The work groups and work items can be laid out in a multidimensional grid through the parameters of the clEnqueueNDRangeKernel call:

work_dim: Number N of dimensions used to describe the work item grid.

global_work_offset: Start offset for each dimension (so that the grid origin of the axes may be different from zero).

global_work_size: Total number of work items, for each dimension.

local_work_size: Number of work items in each work group, for each dimension.

Note that OpenCL does not impose limits on the number of dimensions N employed to describe the work item grid at the language level. It relies instead on a platform introspection API, and in particular on the function clGetDeviceInfo, to retrieve at runtime such limits for each available compute device on the platform. This allows greater flexibility in the definition of kernels, as well as the ability to support compute devices from multiple vendors and multiple compute devices attached to the same host, through tuning the shape and size of the work item grid at runtime. Specifically, the following constants can be passed to clGetDeviceInfo to obtain the constraints for the aforementioned parameters:

CL_DEVICE_MAX_WORK_ITEM_DIMENSIONS:
Maximum number of dimensions in the work item grid.

CL_DEVICE_MAX_WORK_GROUP_SIZE: Maximum number of work items in a work group.

CL_DEVICE_MAX_WORK_ITEM_SIZES: Maximum number of work items in each dimension of the work group.

The Khronos Group has also defined a C++ wrapper interface for the OpenCL API, starting from the 1.1 version, which allows the programmer to employ the described primitives with an object-oriented approach. From now on, we will be employing this API to provide pure C++ code examples.

13.3.2 OpenCL Memory Model

OpenCL provides an explicit memory hierarchy model. The memory model, shown in Figure 13.1, is distributed between the host and the compute device, allowing us to access different address spaces. The *global memory* of the device is shared among all work items regardless of the work group, whereas the host is allowed to read from and write to the device memory space only using the OpenCL API. A *local memory* is associated with each work group, and is mapped by the OpenCL runtime to an on-chip memory, where possible, thus achieving better access latencies than the global memory. Communications among work items of the same work group may employ the local memory associated with that work group to perform shared memory data transfer. Work items belonging to different work groups must communicate through global memory.

The concurrent accesses to local memory by work items within the same work group can be synchronized through an explicit barrier synchronization primitive. In addition to the local memory and the global memory, the OpenCL programming model allows each work item to share a *constant memory* (regardless of the work group), and to use a *private memory* for its exclusive data manipulation.

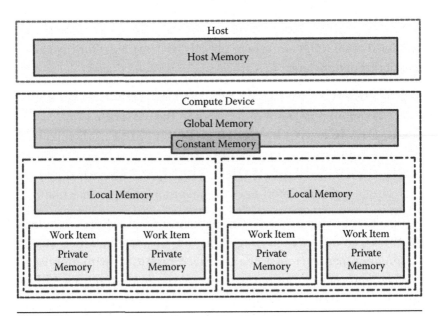

Figure 13.1   Overview of the OpenCL memory hierarchy model.

Table 13.1 OpenCL Memory Regions

	GLOBAL	CONSTANT	LOCAL	PRIVATE
Host allocation	Dynamic	Dynamic	Dynamic	None
Device allocation	None	Static	Static	Static
Host access	Read/write	Read/write	None	None
Device access	Read/write	Read only	Read/write	Read/write

The keywords __global, __local, __constant, and __private are used as qualifiers to specify the address space referenced by a pointer or variable.

Table 13.1 summarizes the allocation and access capabilities of both host and compute device for the four OpenCL memory address spaces. It is worth noting that dynamic memory allocation and recursion are not available on the device. A kernel is allowed to declare and use only automatic variables, while the host code portion is in charge of managing all dynamically allocated data.

13.3.3 First OpenCL Example

To provide a first introduction to OpenCL programming, we will use a simple program that computes the square of the first n natural numbers (where n is an argument of the program). This computation will be parallelized computing each square in different work items, and collecting the work items in work groups of eight. To do so, the host employs an OpenCL-C kernel that computes the square of each element of an array of integers.

The code for this simple example opens with the following inclusion directives and definitions:

```
#define __CL_ENABLE_EXCEPTIONS 1
#include <vector>
#include <iostream>
#include <sstream>
#include <string>
#include <CL/cl.hpp>
using namespace cl;
```

We include several headers from the C++ standard library, which will be used in the host code. The definition of __CL_ENABLE_ EXCEPTIONS selects the use of C++ exceptions rather than C-style status variables for error handling. The header file CL/cl.hpp provides the C++ bindings to the OpenCL API,* which are collected in the namespace cl.

The OpenCL kernel for the example program is included in the host program as a constant string:

```
static const std::string source = "\
    kernel void square(global int *output, \
                global int *input){\
    unsigned int i = get_global_id(0); \
    output[i] = input[i] * input[i]; \
    }";
```

It is an extremely simple kernel, but it showcases the use of three essential elements of any OpenCL-C kernel: the kernel keyword, the address spaces, and the work item identification built-in function get_global_id. The kernel (or __kernel) keyword introduces all entry points in an OpenCL-C program, i.e., the functions that can be invoked from the host.

It is possible to define nonkernel functions in the OpenCL-C code to be used as helper functions. The parameters of the kernel function square are two arrays allocated in the global memory. The get_global_id built-in function maps every work item to an index in the work item space. Since the workspace is multidimensional, get_global_id accepts as a parameter the dimension index of the work item index to be fetched. In this example, the kernel code expects the work item space to be monodimensional; thus, the only element of the index read is the first dimension (indicated by the 0 parameter). The host code is a standard C++ program, which performs the parsing of the first command line argument to obtain the number n of integers to be computed, which is subsequently stored in the variable size.

```
int main(int argc, char *argv[]) {
  unsigned int size;
  try {
  std::istringstream arg(argv[1]);
  arg >> size;
  } catch (...) {
```

---

* C++ bindings are available for OpenCL versions 1.1 and 1.2.

```
std::cout << "Missing or incorrect argument";
std::cout << std::endl;
return 1;
}
```

After the initialization of `size`, it can in turn be used to initialize the vectors to hold the input and output values of the computation:

```
std::vector<cl_int> array_in(size);
std::vector<cl_int> array_out(size);
for(int i = 0; i<size; i++) array_in[i] = i;
for(auto &n : array_in) std::cout << n << " ";
std::cout << std::endl;
```

Now, we need to set up the OpenCL computing platform. The following boilerplate code performs all the necessary operations using the introspection capabilities of the OpenCL runtime:

```
try {
  std::vector<Platform> platforms;
  std::vector<Device> devices;
  Platform::get(&platforms);
  platforms[0].getDevices(CL_DEVICE_TYPE_CPU, &devices);
  Context cxt(devices);
  CommandQueue cmdQ(cxt, devices[0], 0);
```

Specifically, invoking the `Platform::get` method yields all the available OpenCL platforms, i.e., the different runtimes from different vendors. For this simple example, we will only use the first available platform, and get the list of devices (i.e., the actual OpenCL-enabled hardware devices).

We then create a `Context` and a `CommandQueue` for it. The `Context` provides all the necessary information for building OpenCL-C kernels, and the `CommandQueue` will be used to actually interact with the devices. First, we need to allocate the memory buffers used for the kernel execution, as well as for communicating data from the host to the device, and vice versa:

```
const int in_flags = CL_MEM_READ_ONLY |
CL_MEM_COPY_HOST_PTR;
const int out_flags = CL_MEM_WRITE_ONLY |
CL_MEM_USE_HOST_PTR;
```

```
Buffer in(cxt, in_flags, size*sizeof(cl_int), &array_
in.at(0));
Buffer out(cxt, out_flags,size*sizeof(cl_int), &array_
out.at(0));
```

The in buffer will be initialized with a copy of the data in array_in and will be read only on the device side. The out buffer will be mapped in the host memory, since the data produced by the kernel will need to be copied back to the host. Now, we need to build the OpenCL-C program and select the entry point:

```
Program program(cxt, source, true);
Kernel kernel(program, "square");
```

The last parameter of the Program constructor specifies that the program must be compiled and linked. The Kernel constructor selects the entry point by name. We then need to set up the match between the forvs of the kernel:

```
kernel.setArg<Buffer>(0, out);
kernel.setArg<Buffer>(1, in);
```

Kernel parameters are identified positionally rather than by their own name on the host side. Finally, we invoke the kernel, providing the geometry of the desired work item space to the OpenCL runtime:

```
NDRange global_range(size);
NDRange local_range(8);
cmdQ.enqueueNDRangeKernel(kernel, NullRange,
            global_range, local_range);
```

The two NDRange variables indicate the work item space (possibly with more than one dimension, although here only one is used) and the work group size, respectively. The second parameter of the enqueueNDRangeKernel call specifies that the origin of the work item space is set at 0 (i.e., the value of get_global_id(0) for the first work item is 0). The execution of OpenCL kernels is "per se" asynchronous. Since here we do not need to perform other tasks on the host side, we can explicitly wait for completion:

```
  cmdQ.finish();
} catch (Error error) {
```

```
std::cout << "Error" << error.what();
std::cout << "(" << error.err() << ")" << std::endl;
return 2;
}
```

The method finish is blocking, and returns once all commands in the CommandQueue object cmdQ are completed. In case there are any errors during the execution of the kernel, an exception typed as cl::Error will be raised, which can be caught and managed.

Finally, we print out the results:

```
for (auto &n : array_out) std::cout << n << " ";
std::cout << std::endl;
return 0;
}
```

As the example shows, for simple kernels the setup code is much larger than the kernel code. This is because the boilerplate code needs to handle the heterogeneity of the machine (i.e., bridge the host-device divide, through the buffer setup), as well as manage *just-in-time* compilation (here through the Program constructor) and the possible availability of multiple OpenCL runtimes and devices.

In real applications, it is possible to select the best platform for a given kernel, and to provide specialized kernel implementations for each device or platform.

13.4 Implementing AES in OpenCL

In this section, we provide an overview of a basic implementation of AES using OpenCL and its C++ bindings introduced in Section 13.3.3. We first review the structure of the AES cipher and the possible modes of operation, and then introduce the necessary OpenCL-C kernel and the host-side library for setting up the OpenCL environment and invoking the kernels.

13.4.1 *The AES Block Cipher*

The AES cipher is designed for executing a number of round transformations on plaintext where the output of each round is the input of the next one. The number of rounds is determined by the key length: 128-bit uses 10 rounds, 192-bit 12 rounds, and 256-bit 14 rounds. Each round is composed of the same steps, except for the first round, where an extra addition of a round key is added, and for the last round, where the last step (MixColumns) is skipped. Each step operates on 16 bytes of data (referred to as the internal state of the cipher) generally viewed as a 4 × 4 table of bytes or an array of four 32-bit words, where each word corresponds to a column of the state table.

The four round stages are *AddRoundKey* (*xor* addition of a scheduled round key for blending together the key and the state), *SubBytes* (byte substitution by an *S*-box, i.e., a lookup table for nonlinearity design reasons), *ShiftRows* (cyclical shifting of bytes in each row to realize an interword byte diffusion), and *MixColumns* (linear transformation that mixes column state data for intraword interbyte diffusion). The different steps of the round transformation can be combined in a single set of table lookups, allowing for very fast implementations on processors having word lengths of 32 bits or greater [13]. Let us denote with $a_{i,j}$ the generic element of the state table, with $S[256]$ the *S*-box table, and with $\cdot$ a $GF(2^8)$ finite field multiplication [13]. Let T_0, T_1, T_2, and T_3 be four lookup tables containing results from the combination of the aforementioned operations as follows:

$$T_0[a_{i,j}] = [S[a_{i,j}] \cdot 02 \; ; \; S[a_{i,j}] \; ; \; S[a_{i,j}] \; ; \; S[a_{i,j}] \cdot 03]$$

$$T_1[a_{i,j}] = [S[a_{i,j}] \cdot 03 \; ; \; S[a_{i,j}] \cdot 02 \; ; \; S[a_{i,j}] \; ; \; S[a_{i,j}]]$$

$$T_2[a_{i,j}] = [S[a_{i,j}] \; ; \; S[a_{i,j}] \cdot 03 \; ; \; S[a_{i,j}] \cdot 02 \; ; \; S[a_{i,j}]]$$

$$T_3[a_{i,j}] = [S[a_{i,j}] \; ; \; S[a_{i,j}] \; ; \; S[a_{i,j}] \cdot 03 \; ; \; S[a_{i,j}] \cdot 02]$$

These tables are used to compute the round stage operations as a whole, as described by the following equation, where k_j is the *j*th word of the expanded key and e_j is the *j*th column of the state table (seen as a single 32-bit word):

$$e_j = T_0[a_{0,j}] \oplus T_1[a_{1,j-1}] \oplus T_2[a_{2,j-2}] \oplus T_3[a_{3,j-3}] \oplus k_j$$

The four tables T_0, T_1, T_2, and T_3 (called *T*-boxes from now on) have 256 32-bit word entries each and make up for 4 KB of storage space. A *KeySchedule* procedure associated to the AES algorithm is responsible for the computation of each round key k_j given the global input key k. In contrast with the round computation, the key expansion operated by the KeySchedule procedure does not expose significant parallelism. However, its result is computed once and used for all the blocks of a given plaintext.

13.4.2 Modes of Operation

The AES, as any other block cipher, operates on blocks of fixed 128-bit length. Several modes of operation have been standardized to manage the encryption of any plaintext, with arbitrary length [14]. When the length of the plaintext is not a multiple of the block size, it is necessary to add padding to the original message, up to a multiple of the block size. Of the block cipher modes employed for guaranteeing confidentiality, electronic code book (ECB), cipher block chaining (CBC), and counter (CTR) mode are the most popular.

The ECB mode is easily parallelizable, since the original plaintext is split into blocks that are independently enciphered with the same key. However, the ECB mode is not adopted in cryptographic protocols, since identical plaintext blocks, encrypted with the same key (as would happen when enciphering a file with repeated 16-byte blocks), lead to the same ciphertext, which is a major leak of secret information.

CBC mode is the default choice in current distributions of OpenSSL. In this mode, the sequence of plaintext blocks is enciphered using as input of each block the bitwise *xor* between a block of plaintext and the ciphertext obtained from the previous block (or a known initialization vector (IV) for the first block).

CTR mode produces the ciphertext as the bitwise *xor* between each plaintext block and one of a series of cryptographic pads. The cryptographic pads are obtained through the application of the block cipher to counter initialized with a strong pseudorandomly generated value and sequentially incremented for each subsequent block. The fundamental advantage of the CTR mode over the other modes of operation is that both its encryption and decryption actions can be efficiently parallelized.

From a security point of view, CTR mode is considered even safer than CBC [15, 16]; thus, it has been added in the 1.1 version of the Transport Layer Security (TLS) protocol standard [17].

13.4.3 *AES Kernels*

In this section, we introduce the necessary OpenCL-C kernels and support functions to implement the AES cipher. For larger OpenCL programs, where multiple or large functions and kernels are needed, it is better to store the OpenCL-C code in one or more separate files. There are several good reasons for using separate files rather than storing the OpenCL-C code in one or more strings in the host code.

First, writing long kernels as strings is cumbersome, and syntax highlighting is not available. Second, separate files allow a stand-alone compilation* of the kernels, which is useful for development and debugging. OpenCL-C source files are customarily named using the .cl extension. Header files can also be created, and included using the standard C99 #include directive, which is supported in the OpenCL specification.

In our case, we use a separate header file for storing the constants, among which are the large constant lookup tables (substitution boxes or *S*-boxes) needed by the AES:

```
#include "aes_kernel_constants.h"
```

Let us first introduce a few support functions. The routines get_uint and put_uint are used to convert between arrays of bytes and 32-bit unsigned integers:

```
uint get_uint(uchar *in) {
  return ((uint)in[0]  )  |
         ((uint)in[1]  << 8)  |
         ((uint)in[2]  << 16) |
         ((uint)in[3]  << 24);
}

void put_uint(uint v, uchar *out) {
  out[0]  =  (uchar)(v);
  out[1]  =  (uchar)(v >> 8);
  out[2]  =  (uchar)(v >> 16);
  out[3]  =  (uchar)(v >> 24);
}
```

---

* This is currently supported by the Intel OpenCL SDK, but not by the SDKs of other vendors.

```
uint get_uint_g(global uchar *in) {
 return ((uint)in[0] ) |
     ((uint)in[1] << 8) |
     ((uint)in[2] << 16) |
     ((uint)in[3] << 24);
}
```

The get_uint_g function performs the same operation in global memory. get_ulong and put_ulong perform the same function for 64-bit unsigned integers, leveraging the first two functions:

```
uint get_ulong(global uchar *in) {
 return (ulong)get_uint_g(in) |
     (ulong)get_uint_g(in + 4) << 4;
}
void put_ulong(ulong v, uchar *out) {
 put_uint((uint)v, out);
 put_uint((uint)(v >> 4), out + 4);
}
```

The main function, aes_encrypt, takes as parameters the input and output buffers, the round key, the number of AES rounds to perform (a function of the AES key length), and the addresses of the five lookup tables:

```
void aes_encrypt(uchar *in, uchar *out, local uint *RK,
          int nrounds, local uchar *FSb,
          local uint *FT0, local uint *FT1,
          local uint *FT2, local uint *FT3) {
 uint X0, X1, X2, X3, Y0, Y1, Y2, Y3;

 X0 = get_uint(in + 0) ^ *RK++;
 X1 = get_uint(in + 4) ^ *RK++;
 X2 = get_uint(in + 8) ^ *RK++;
 X3 = get_uint(in + 12) ^ *RK++;
 for (int i = (nrounds >> 1) - 1; i > 0;- i){
  AES_FROUND(Y0, Y1, Y2, Y3, X0, X1, X2, X3);
  AES_FROUND(X0, X1, X2, X3, Y0, Y1, Y2, Y3);
 }
 AES_FROUND(Y0, Y1, Y2, Y3, X0, X1, X2, X3);
 AES_SLIM_FROUND(X0, X1, X2, X3, Y0, Y1, Y2, Y3);

 put_uint(X0, out + 0);
 put_uint(X1, out + 4);
```

```
put_uint(X2, out + 8);
put_uint(X3, out + 12);
}
```

The function `aes_encrypt` reads the 16 bytes of the input plaintext block as four unsigned integers, and combines via *xor* with the round key. It then applies the required number of AES rounds, including a last reduced round (`AES_SLIM_FROUND`). Finally, it copies the resulting values into the output buffer. The macros named `AES_FROUND` and `AES_SLIM_FROUND`, respectively, are defined in `aes_kernel_constants.h`.

Regarding the kernel itself, it needs to be specialized with respect to the mode of operation employed.

The following code presents the specialization of the AES kernel to perform CTR mode encryption:

```
kernel void aes_ctr_mode(global uchar *buffer,
                         global const uchar *round_keys,
                         int nrounds) {
  local uchar FSb[256];
  local uint FT0[256], FT1[256], FT2[256], FT3[256], RK[60];
  if (get_local_id(0) = = 0) { //Local Memory
      Initialization
    for (int i = 0; i ! = 256; ++i) {
     FSb[i] = glob_FSb[i];
     FT0[i] = glob_FT0[i];
     FT1[i] = glob_FT1[i];
     FT2[i] = glob_FT2[i];
     FT3[i] = glob_FT3[i];
    }
    uint RKw = (nrounds + 1) << 2;
    for (uint i = 0; i ! = RKw; ++i) RK[i] = key[i];
  }
  barrier(CLK_LOCAL_MEM_FENCE);
  //Counter Initialization
  ulong nonce_lo = get_ulong(buffer);
  ulong nonce_hi = get_ulong(buffer + 8);
  ulong id = get_global_id(0);
  if ((nonce_lo + = id) < id) ++nonce_hi;

  uchar counter[16];
  put_ulong(nonce_lo, counter);
  put_ulong(nonce_hi, counter + 8);
```

```
//Encryption
aes_encrypt(counter, counter, RK, nrounds,
     FSb, FT0, FT1, FT2, FT3);
//Output Write-Back
global uchar *output = buffer + (id + 1) * 16;
for (int i = 0; i != 16; ++i) output[i] ^= counter[i];
}
```

The kernel takes three parameters: buffer is the data memory region where the plaintext is found, and where the ciphertext will be written; round_keys is the expanded key (i.e., the set of round keys) computed by the key schedule (which will therefore be performed by the host); and finally, nrounds is the number of AES round to perform, which is determined by the AES key length. The kernel function at first performs the setup of local memory, which is used to hold the substitution boxes and the round key, all of which are shared by all work items. The first work item performs this initialization procedure. With a slightly more complex code, it is also possible to split the operation on 256 work items in a straightforward fashion:

```
uint i = get_local_id(0);
if (i < 256) {
    FSb[i] = glob_FSb[i];
    FT0[i] = glob_FT0[i];
    FT1[i] = glob_FT1[i];
    FT2[i] = glob_FT2[i];
    FT3[i] = glob_FT3[i];
}
if (i < (nrounds + 1) << 2) RK[i] = key[i];
```

However, this version of the code forces the minimum work item space size to 256. Willing to remove this limitation, it is possible to refine the code parallelizing the initialization over less work items, retrieving the actual number via the *get_local_size* method. In all cases, a barrier is needed to prevent work items from starting their operation while the local memory is uninitialized.

Since the CTR mode employs a counter, it is possible to exploit the global work item identification number as part of it. The portion of code between the barrier and the encryption function call takes care of this. The *nonce* is read from the input buffer, and combined with the work item identification number, taking into account a possible carry. The result is written to a byte array counter. Finally, the `aes_encrypt` function is called, to effectively encrypt the counters to obtain the actual enciphered pads. Once the pads have been obtained, they are combined via *xor* with the plaintext, and the results are written to the output buffer.

13.4.4 AES Host Library

To provide a practical and reusable interface, it is crucial to design the C++ bindings of our AES implementation according to the current best practices in modern C++ programming. The key point of our design is to specifically avoid virtual functions, so to obtain a compact and efficient output binary, while retaining minimal code redundancy and enhancing the code readability. Aiming at a high usability of the library, we would be willing to invoke an encryption call simply as

```
ArrayRef<const uint8_t> In(buf, 1024);
ArrayRef<uint8_t> Out(buf, 1024);
AESOpenCL<AES_128, OM_CTR> Cipher(key);
Cipher.encrypt(In, Out);
```

where `In` and `Out` are the memory region wrapper objects containing, respectively, the plaintext and the ciphertext memory areas. The `AESOpenCL` class object `Cipher` is instantiated, employing as template parameters the key size and mode of operation, and provides the encrypt method, which can be called passing the input and output objects. The first, and most simple issue, to be tackled is to provide a practical support to represent the possible modes of operation supported by the AES library. To this end, a simple enumeration will suffice:

```
enum OperationMode {OM_ECB, OM_CBC, OM_CTR, OM_AES_GCM};
```

To support the three legal key lengths for AES, we will employ *traits*, a meta-programming construct to represent a collection of methods, which is implemented in C++ as follows:

```
extern const uint8_t SBox[256];
extern const uint32_t Rcon[10];
const unsigned BlockSize = 16;
```

```
enum AESKeyLength {AES_128,
         AES_192,
         AES_256
};

template<AESKeyLength KL>
struct AESParams;

template<> struct AESParams<AES_128> {
 static const unsigned Rounds = 10;
 static const unsigned RoundKeysWords = 44;
};

template<> struct AESParams<AES_192> {
 static const unsigned Rounds = 12;
 static const unsigned RoundKeysWords = 52;
};

template<> struct AESParams<AES_256> {
 static const unsigned Rounds = 15;
 static const unsigned RoundKeysWords = 60;
};
```

A trait in C++ is defined in terms of a template method, or collection of methods, which is specialized to provide its behavior for the specific template instance. In our case, we specify the number of rounds and the size (in terms of number of 32-bit integers) of the whole key schedule depending on the AES key length (represented by the elements of the AESKeyLength enumeration). Moreover, the necessary symbol references to the substitution tables are provided.

In the following, we will focus on the implementation of the CTR mode of operation, which, as mentioned above, is currently considered among the most secure, and is also amenable to efficient parallel implementation. The component of the library in charge of the definition of the selected OpenCL device and its runtime environment is the AESOpenCLBase class.

```
class AESOpenCLBase {
public:
 AESOpenCLBase() {
  initDevice();
 }
```

```
private:
 cl::Context Ctx;
 cl::Program Prog;
 cl::Device Dev;
 cl::CommandQueue Queue;

 void initDevice();

 template<OperationMode M> friend class
 AESOpenCLModeTraits;
};
```

The AESOpenCLBase class, when instantiated, initializes the first available OpenCL device for the first available platform. This is performed by the object constructor, through the `initDevice` method. Notice that, in the class description, we specify a template friendship relation for the instances of the template class AESOpenCLModeTraits so that, upon specializing the trait to implement the required mode of operation, we will be able to access freely the private members of AESOpenCLBase.

Let us look at the implementation of `initDevice`:

```
void AESOpenCL::initDevice() {
 std::vector<cl::Platform> platforms;
 cl::Platform::get(&platforms);
 assert(!platforms.empty());

 std::vector<cl::Device> devices;
 platforms.front().getDevices(CL_DEVICE_TYPE_ALL, &
 devices);

 assert(!devices.empty());
 Ctx = cl::Context(devices);
 Dev = devices.front();
 Queue = cl::CommandQueue(Ctx, Dev);

 std::ifstream in("aes_kernel_file.cl");
 std::istreambuf_iterator<char> it(in);
 std::string src(it, std::istreambuf_iterator<char>());

 Prog = cl::Program(Ctx, src, true);
}
```

The code employs a similar structure to that seen in the first example in Section 13.3.3. The main difference lies in the use of an external source file for the AES kernels. As mentioned above, this is the recommended style for all but the simplest kernels. It is left as a simple exercise for the reader to add a second

```
AESOpenCLBase(std::string platform,
      std::string device, OperationMode M)
```

to delegate the selection of the platform and device to the caller. The implementation of encryption and decryption, depending on the mode of operation, is obtained by specializing the `AESOpenCLModeTraits` trait:

```
template<OperationMode M>
class AESOpenCLModeTraits {
public:
  static void encrypt(AESOpenCLBase &OpenCLCtx,
              ArrayRef<const uint8_t> In,
              ArrayRef<uint8_t> Out,
              ArrayRef<const uint32_t> RoundKeys);
  static void decrypt(AESOpenCLBase &OpenCLCtx,
              ArrayRef<const uint8_t> In,
              ArrayRef<uint8_t> Out,
              ArrayRef<const uint32_t> RoundKeys);
};
```

The `AESOpenCLModeTraits` trait has two static methods that are to be specialized providing the encryption and decryption implementations for the proper mode of operation. ArrayRef is a C++ wrapper for a generic array. In particular, the code below implements the specialized trait for CTR mode:

```
template<>
class AESOpenCLModeTraits<OM_CTR> {
public:
  static void encrypt(AESOpenCLBase &OpenCLCtx,
              ArrayRef<const uint8_t> In,
              ArrayRef<uint8_t> Out,
              ArrayRef<const uint32_t> RoundKeys){
    unsigned NBlocks = In.size()/BlockSize - 1;
    assert(NBlocks > 0);
```

```
cl::Context &Ctx = OpenCLCtx.Ctx;
cl::Program &Prog = OpenCLCtx.Prog;
cl::CommandQueue &Queue = OpenCLCtx.Queue;

cl::Buffer Buf(Ctx, CL_MEM_READ_WRITE |
CL_MEM_COPY_HOST_PTR,
          In.sizeInBytes(), In.ptr());
cl::Buffer KeyBuf(Ctx,
          CL_MEM_READ_ONLY | CL_MEM_COPY_HOST_PTR,
          RoundKeys.sizeInBytes(), RoundKeys.ptr());
cl_uint NR = RoundKeys.size()/4 - 1;

cl::Kernel K(Prog, "aes_ctr_mode");
K.setArg<cl::Buffer>(0, Buf);
K.setArg<cl::Buffer>(1, KeyBuf);
K.setArg<cl_int>(2, NR);

cl::NDRange GR(NBlocks);
Queue.enqueueNDRangeKernel(K, cl::NullRange, GR);
Queue.enqueueReadBuffer(Buf, CL_TRUE, 0,
              Out.sizeInBytes(), Out.ptr());
Queue.finish();
}
 static void decrypt(AESOpenCLBase &OpenCLCtx,
              ArrayRef<const uint8_t> In,
              ArrayRef<uint8_t> Out,
              ArrayRef<const uint32_t> RoundKeys) {
  encrypt(OpenCLCtx, In, Out, RoundKeys);
 }
};
```

Note that the decryption function is identical to the encryption one, since the counter mode encrypts the plaintext by means of combining it with the encryption of a counter via *xor*. Thus, it is possible to decipher the ciphertext through adding the same pad via *xor*. We are able to employ exactly the same cipher primitive, as our CTR mode implementation expects both the ciphertext and the plaintext to contain the nonce in the first 16 bytes. The encryption primitive sets up and calls the kernel aes_ctr_mode. The setup and invocation steps are analogous to the ones seen in the example in Section 13.3.3. The AESOpenCLContext class serves as a container for the AES context, i.e., the full key schedule, to allow the definition of encryption and decryption methods.

```
template<AESKeyLength KL, OperationMode M>
class AESOpenCLContext {
public:
 AESOpenCLContext(ArrayRef<const uint8_t> Key);

 void encrypt(AESOpenCLBase &OpenCLCtx,
         ArrayRef<const uint8_t> In, ArrayRef<uint8_t>
           Out);
 void decrypt(AESOpenCLBase &OpenCLCtx,
         ArrayRef<const uint8_t> In, ArrayRef<uint8_t>
           Out);
};
```

The key idea of the AESOpenCLContext class is to provide a proper boxing to bind the key schedule action, and the instantiation of a properly sized expanded key array, depending on the user key length.

In particular, the corresponding specialization for CTR mode is:

```
template<AESKeyLength KL>
class AESOpenCLContext<KL, OM_CTR> {
public:
 AESOpenCLContext(ArrayRef<const uint8_t> Key) {
  computeKeySchedule(Key);
 }
 void encrypt(AESOpenCLBase &OpenCLCtx,
         ArrayRef<const uint8_t> In,
         ArrayRef<uint8_t> Out) {
 AESOpenCLModeTraits<OM_CTR>::encrypt(OpenCLCtx, In,
             Out, RoundKeys);
 }
 void decrypt(AESOpenCLBase &OpenCLCtx,
         ArrayRef<const uint8_t> In,
         ArrayRef<uint8_t> Out) {
 AESOpenCLModeTraits<OM_CTR>::decrypt(OpenCLCtx, In,
             Out, RoundKeys);
 }

private:
 void computeKeySchedule(ArrayRef<const uint8_t> Key);
 uint32_t RoundKeys[AESParams<KL>::RoundKeysWords];
};
```

The above specialization binds effectively the mode of operation to be the counter one, while retaining as a template parameter the AES user key length. Note that the implementation employs the encrypt and decrypt static methods of the specialized AESOpenCLModeTraits template class for the CTR mode. The computation of the expanded round keys is delegated to the computeKeySchedule private method called by the constructor of AESOpenCLContext.

The method operates on the private field of the AESOpenCLContext class, computing the RoundKeys.

```
template<AESKeyLength KL>
void AESOpenCLContext<KL, OM_CTR>::computeKeySchedule(
            ArrayRef<const uint8_t> Key) {
 unsigned Nk = Key.sizeInBytes()/4;
 std::memcpy(RoundKeys, Key.ptr(), Key.sizeInBytes());

 for (unsigned i = Nk; i ! =
AESParams<KL>::RoundKeysWords; ++i) {
  uint32_t temp = RoundKeys[i - 1];
  if (i% Nk = = 0)
   temp = subword(rotrb(temp)) ^ Rcon[i/Nk - 1];
  else if (Nk > 6 && i% Nk = = 4)
   temp = subword(temp);
  RoundKeys[i] = RoundKeys[i - Nk] ^ temp;
 }
}
```

The key schedule is computed on the host side, since it only accounts for a small fraction of the computational load of the algorithm, and it cannot be effectively parallelized, due to the loop-carried data dependencies (i.e., the round key at round r depends on the one at round $r - 1$) in the first for loop. The client interface is encapsulated by the AESOpenCL template class, where the template parameters provide the key length and mode of operation information:

```
template<AESKeyLength KL, OperationMode M>
class AESOpenCL : public AESOpenCLBase {
public:
 AESOpenCL(ArrayRef<const uint8_t> Key) : Context(Key) {}
 void encrypt(ArrayRef<const uint8_t> In,
         ArrayRef<uint8_t> Out) {
  Context.encrypt(*this, In, Out);
 }
 void decrypt(ArrayRef<const uint8_t> In,
```

```
                ArrayRef<uint8_t> Out) {
   Context.decrypt(*this, In, Out);
  }
private:
 AESOpenCLContext<KL, M> Context;
};
```

The class basically acts as a wrapper for the AESOpenCLContext and AESOpenCLBase instances. In particular, the encrypt and decrypt functions are able to employ the OpenCL context inherited from the AESOpenCLBase, and invoking its encrypt and decrypt methods, passing a reference to itself, as this class inherits from AESOpenCLBase.

13.4.5 Putting It All Together

We can now provide the main function of our application as follows:

```
int main(int argc, char *argv[]) {
 uint8_t key[16] = {0x2b,0x7e,0x15,0x16,0x28,0xae,0xd2,
             0xa6,0xab,0xf7,0x15,0x88,0x09,0xcf,0x4f,
             0x3c};

 uint8_t buf[112] = {0x00,0x00,0x00,0x00,0x00,0x00,
             0x00,0x00,0x00,0x00,0x00,0x00,0x00,0x00,
             0x00,0x00,0x32,0x43,0xf6,0xa8,0x88,0x5a,
             0x30,0x8d,0x31,0x31,0x98,0xa2,0xe0,0x37,
             0x07,0x34,0x31,0x31,0x98,0xa2,0xe0,0x37,
             0x07,0x34,0x32,0x43,0xf6,0xa8,0x88,0x5a,
             0x30,0x8d,0x32,0x43,0xf6,0xa8,0x88,0x5a,
             0x30,0x8d,0x31,0x31,0x98,0xa2,0xe0,0x37,
             0x07,0x34,0x32,0x43,0xf6,0xa8,0x88,0x5a,
             0x30,0x8d,0x31,0x31,0x98,0xa2,0xe0,0x37,
             0x07,0x34,0x31,0x31,0x98,0xa2,0xe0,0x37,
             0x07,0x34,0x32,0x43,0xf6,0xa8,0x88,0x5a,
             0x30,0x8d,0x32,0x43,0xf6,0xa8,0x88,0x5a,
             0x30,0x8d,0x31,0x31,0x98,0xa2,0xe0,0x37,
             0x07,0x34};
 try {
  AESOpenCL<AES_128, OM_CTR> Cipher(key);

  ArrayRef<const uint8_t> In(buf, 112);
  ArrayRef<uint8_t> Out(buf, 112);
```

```
std::cout << "Input: " << In << std::endl;

Cipher.encrypt(In, Out);
std::cout << "Encryption output: " << Out << std::endl;

Cipher.decrypt(In, Out);
std::cout << "Decryption output: " << Out << std::endl;
} catch (cl::Error error) {
std::cout << "Error" << error.what();
std::cout << "(" << error.err() << ")" << std::endl;
}
return 0;
}
```

The main function encrypts a plaintext, initially contained in buf, saving the ciphertext on the same memory region (thus In and Out are set to point to the same address, buf), and then decrypts the freshly encrypted ciphertext. There is no need to swap In and Out, as they point to the same region of memory, with the only difference being that In must be used as input, since it is marked as constant.

The error handling strategies are the same as those applied in Section 13.3.3.

13.5 Implementation

```
1.  //aes_opencl.cpp
2.  #include "aes_opencl.h"
3.  #include <cassert>
4.  #include <cstring>
5.  #include <fstream>
6.  #include <iostream>
7.  #include <iterator>
8.  #include <vector>
9.
10. using namespace AES;
11.
12. const uint8_t AES::SBox[256] = {
13. 0x63, 0x7C, 0x77, 0x7B, 0xF2, 0x6B, 0x6F, 0xC5,
14. 0x30, 0x01, 0x67, 0x2B, 0xFE, 0xD7, 0xAB, 0x76,
15. 0xCA, 0x82, 0xC9, 0x7D, 0xFA, 0x59, 0x47, 0xF0,
16. 0xAD, 0xD4, 0xA2, 0xAF, 0x9C, 0xA4, 0x72, 0xC0,
17. 0xB7, 0xFD, 0x93, 0x26, 0x36, 0x3F, 0xF7, 0xCC,
18. 0x34, 0xA5, 0xE5, 0xF1, 0x71, 0xD8, 0x31, 0x15,
```

```
19. 0x04, 0xC7, 0x23, 0xC3, 0x18, 0x96, 0x05, 0x9A,
20. 0x07, 0x12, 0x80, 0xE2, 0xEB, 0x27, 0xB2, 0x75,
21. 0x09, 0x83, 0x2C, 0x1A, 0x1B, 0x6E, 0x5A, 0xA0,
22. 0x52, 0x3B, 0xD6, 0xB3, 0x29, 0xE3, 0x2F, 0x84,
23. 0x53, 0xD1, 0x00, 0xED, 0x20, 0xFC, 0xB1, 0x5B,
24. 0x6A, 0xCB, 0xBE, 0x39, 0x4A, 0x4C, 0x58, 0xCF,
25. 0xD0, 0xEF, 0xAA, 0xFB, 0x43, 0x4D, 0x33, 0x85,
26. 0x45, 0xF9, 0x02, 0x7F, 0x50, 0x3C, 0x9F, 0xA8,
27. 0x51, 0xA3, 0x40, 0x8F, 0x92, 0x9D, 0x38, 0xF5,
28. 0xBC, 0xB6, 0xDA, 0x21, 0x10, 0xFF, 0xF3, 0xD2,
29. 0xCD, 0x0C, 0x13, 0xEC, 0x5F, 0x97, 0x44, 0x17,
30. 0xC4, 0xA7, 0x7E, 0x3D, 0x64, 0x5D, 0x19, 0x73,
31. 0x60, 0x81, 0x4F, 0xDC, 0x22, 0x2A, 0x90, 0x88,
32. 0x46, 0xEE, 0xB8, 0x14, 0xDE, 0x5E, 0x0B, 0xDB,
33. 0xE0, 0x32, 0x3A, 0x0A, 0x49, 0x06, 0x24, 0x5C,
34. 0xC2, 0xD3, 0xAC, 0x62, 0x91, 0x95, 0xE4, 0x79,
35. 0xE7, 0xC8, 0x37, 0x6D, 0x8D, 0xD5, 0x4E, 0xA9,
36. 0x6C, 0x56, 0xF4, 0xEA, 0x65, 0x7A, 0xAE, 0x08,
37. 0xBA, 0x78, 0x25, 0x2E, 0x1C, 0xA6, 0xB4, 0xC6,
38. 0xE8, 0xDD, 0x74, 0x1F, 0x4B, 0xBD, 0x8B, 0x8A,
39. 0x70, 0x3E, 0xB5, 0x66, 0x48, 0x03, 0xF6, 0x0E,
40. 0x61, 0x35, 0x57, 0xB9, 0x86, 0xC1, 0x1D, 0x9E,
41. 0xE1, 0xF8, 0x98, 0x11, 0x69, 0xD9, 0x8E, 0x94,
42. 0x9B, 0x1E, 0x87, 0xE9, 0xCE, 0x55, 0x28, 0xDF,
43. 0x8C, 0xA1, 0x89, 0x0D, 0xBF, 0xE6, 0x42, 0x68,
44. 0x41, 0x99, 0x2D, 0x0F, 0xB0, 0x54, 0xBB, 0x16
45. };
46.
47. const uint32_t AES::Rcon[10] = {
48. 0x00000001, 0x00000002, 0x00000004, 0x00000008,
49. 0x00000010, 0x00000020, 0x00000040, 0x00000080,
50. 0x0000001B, 0x00000036
51. };
52. void AESOpenCLBase::initDevice() {
53. std::vector<cl::Platform> platforms;
54. cl::Platform::get(&platforms);
55.
56. assert(!platforms.empty());
57.
58. std::vector<cl::Device> devices;
59. platforms.back().getDevices(CL_DEVICE_TYPE_ALL,
    &devices);
60.
61. assert(!devices.empty());
62.
```

```
63. Ctx = cl::Context(devices);
64. Dev = devices.front();
65. Queue = cl::CommandQueue(Ctx, Dev);
66.
67. std::ifstream in("aes_kernel.cl");
68. std::istreambuf_iterator<char> it(in);
69. std::string src(it, std::istreambuf_iterator<char>());
70.
71. Prog = cl::Program(Ctx, src, true);
72. }
73.
74. void AESOpenCLModeTraits<OM_
        CTR>::encrypt(AESOpenCLBase &OpenCLCtx,
75.             ArrayRef<const uint8_t> In,
76.             ArrayRef<uint8_t> Out,
77.             ArrayRef<const uint32_t> RoundKeys) {
78. /* In CTR mode, both 'In' and 'Out' contain
79.    the IV in the first 16 bytes.    */
80. unsigned NBlocks = In.size()/BlockSize - 1;
81. assert(NBlocks > 0);
82.
83. cl::Context &Ctx = OpenCLCtx.Ctx;
84. cl::Program &Prog = OpenCLCtx.Prog;
85. cl::CommandQueue &Queue = OpenCLCtx.Queue;
86.
87. cl::Buffer Buf(Ctx, CL_MEM_READ_WRITE | CL_MEM_
        COPY_HOST_PTR,
88.         In.sizeInBytes(), In.ptr());
89. cl::Buffer KeyBuf(Ctx, CL_MEM_READ_ONLY | CL_MEM_
        COPY_HOST_PTR,
90.         RoundKeys.sizeInBytes(), RoundKeys.
                ptr());
91.
92. cl_uint NR = RoundKeys.size()/4 - 1;
93.
94. cl::Kernel K(Prog, "aes_ctr_mode");
95. K.setArg<cl::Buffer>(0, Buf);
96. K.setArg<cl::Buffer>(1, KeyBuf);
97. K.setArg<cl_int>(2, NR);
98.
99. cl::NDRange GR(NBlocks);
100.
101.        Queue.enqueueNDRangeKernel(K, cl::NullRange,
                GR);
102.        Queue.enqueueReadBuffer(Buf, CL_TRUE, 0,
```

```
103.                         Out.sizeInBytes(), Out.ptr());
104.        Queue.finish();
105.      }
106.      int main(int argc, char *argv[]) {
107.        uint8_t key[16] = {0x2b,0x7e,0x15,0x16,0x28,
                      0xae,0xd2,0xa6,
108.                  0xab,0xf7,0x15,0x88,0x09,0xcf,
                      0x4f,0x3c};
109.
110.        uint8_t buf[112] = {0x00,0x00,0x00,0x00,0x00,
                      0x00,0x00,0x00,
111.                  0x00,0x00,0x00,0x00,0x00,0x00,
                      0x00, 0x00,
112.                  0x32,0x43,0xf6,0xa8,0x88,0x5a,
                      0x30, 0x8d,
113.                  0x31,0x31,0x98,0xa2,0xe0,0x37,
                      0x07, 0x34,
114.                  0x31,0x31,0x98,0xa2,0xe0,0x37,
                      0x07, 0x34,
115.                  0x32,0x43,0xf6,0xa8,0x88,0x5a,
                      0x30, 0x8d,
116.                  0x32,0x43,0xf6,0xa8,0x88,0x5a,
                      0x30, 0x8d,
117.                  0x31,0x31,0x98,0xa2,0xe0,0x37,
                      0x07, 0x34,
118.                  0x32,0x43,0xf6,0xa8,0x88,0x5a,
                      0x30, 0x8d,
119.                  0x31,0x31,0x98,0xa2,0xe0,0x37,
                      0x07, 0x34,
120.                  0x31,0x31,0x98,0xa2,0xe0,0x37,
                      0x07, 0x34,
121.                  0x32,0x43,0xf6,0xa8,0x88,0x5a,
                      0x30, 0x8d,
122.                  0x32,0x43,0xf6,0xa8,0x88,0x5a,
                      0x30,0x8d,
123.                  0x31,0x31,0x98,0xa2,0xe0,0x37,
                      0x07, 0x34};
124.        try {
125.          AESOpenCL<AES_128, OM_CTR> Cipher(key);
126.
127.          ArrayRef<const uint8_t> In(buf, 112);
128.          ArrayRef<uint8_t> Out(buf, 112);
129.
130.          std::cout << "Input: " << In << "\n";
131.
```

```
132.     Cipher.encrypt(In, Out);
133.     std::cout << "Encryption output: " << Out
             << "\n";
134.
135.     Cipher.decrypt(In, Out);
136.     std::cout << "Decryption output: " << Out
             << "\n";
137.   } catch (cl::Error error) {
138.     std::cout << "Error" << error.what();
139.     std::cout << "(" << error.err() << ")" <<
             std::endl;
140.   }
141.   return 0;
142.   }
143.   //aes_opencl.h
144.
145.   #ifndef AES_OPENCL_H
146.   #define AES_OPENCL_H
147.
148.   #define __CL_ENABLE_EXCEPTIONS
149.   #include <CL/cl.hpp>
150.
151.   #include <cstdint>
152.   #include <iomanip>
153.   #include <iostream>
154.   #include <ostream>
155.
156.   template<typename ElemTy>
157.   class ArrayRef {
158.   public:
159.     typedef ElemTy *iterator;
160.
161.   public:
162.     ArrayRef(ElemTy *ptr, size_t len) :
             Ptr(ptr), Length(len) {}
163.     template<size_t N>
164.     ArrayRef(ElemTy (&arr)[N]) : Ptr(arr),
             Length(N) {}
165.     ArrayRef &operator = (const ArrayRef &A) {
166.       Ptr = A.Ptr;
167.       Length = A.Length;
168.       return *this;
169.     }
170.
171.     iterator begin() const {return Ptr;}
```

```
172.        iterator end() const {return Ptr + Length;}
173.
174.        Ele&operator[](size_t I) const {return
               Ptr[I];}
175.
176.        ElemTy *data() const {return Ptr;}
177.        size_t size() const {return Length;}
178.
179.        size_t sizeInBytes() const {return Length *
               sizeof(ElemTy);}
180.        void *ptr() const {return (void*)Ptr;}
181.      private:
182.       ElemTy *Ptr;
183.       size_t Length;
184.       };
185.
186.      template<typename ElemTy>
187.      struct ValuePrintTraits {
188.       static void print(std::ostream &OS, const
               ElemTy &V);
189.        };
190.
191.      template<typename ElemTy>
192.      struct ValuePrintTraits<const ElemTy> {
193.       static void print(std::ostream &OS, const
               ElemTy &V) {
194.        ValuePrintTraits<ElemTy>::print(OS, V);
195.        }
196.      };
197.      template<>
198.      struct ValuePrintTraits<uint32_t> {
199.       static void print(std::ostream &OS,
               uint32_t V) {
200.        V = ((uint8_t)(V) << 24) |
201.            ((uint8_t)(V >> 8) << 16) |
202.            ((uint8_t)(V >> 16) << 8) |
203.            ((uint8_t)(V >> 24));
204.        OS << std::setw(8) << std::setfill('0') <<
               std::hex << V;
205.        }
206.      };
207.
208.      template<>
209.      struct ValuePrintTraits<uint8_t> {
```

```
210.        static void print(std::ostream &OS, uint8_t V)
              {
211.          OS << std::setw(2) << std::setfill('0');
212.          OS << std::hex << (uint16_t)V;
213.          }
214.        };
215.
216.      template<typename ElemTy>
217.      std::ostream &operator<<(std::ostream &OS,
             ArrayRef<ElemTy> A) {
218.        for (auto I = A.begin(), E = A.end(); I ! =
               E; ++I)
219.          ValuePrintTraits<ElemTy>::print(OS, *I);
220.       return OS;
221.      }
222.
223.      enum OperationMode {
224.       OM_ECB,
225.       OM_CBC,
226.       OM_CTR,
227.       OM_AES_GCM
228.       };
229.
230.      namespace AES {
231.
232.      extern const uint8_t SBox[256];
233.      extern const uint32_t Rcon[10];
234.
235.      /* TBox and/or reverse TBox should be added here
236.      (e.g. key schedule computation for decryption
237.      on ECB or CBC modes). */
238.
239.      const unsigned BlockSize = 16;
240.      enum AESKeyLength {AES_128, AES_192, AES_256};
241.
242.      template<AESKeyLength KL>
243.      struct AESParams;
244.
245.      template<> struct AESParams<AES_128> {
246.       static const unsigned Rounds = 10;
247.       static const unsigned RoundKeysWords = 44;
248.       };
249.
250.      template<> struct AESParams<AES_192> {
251.       static const unsigned Rounds = 12;
```

```
252.      static const unsigned RoundKeysWords = 52;
253.      };
254.
255.      template<> struct AESParams<AES_256> {
256.       static const unsigned Rounds = 15;
257.       static const unsigned RoundKeysWords = 60;
258.      };
259.
260.      uint32_t rotrb(uint32_t v) {
261.       return ((v & 0xFF) << 24) | (v >> 8);
262.      }
263.
264.      uint32_t rotl(uint32_t v, uint32_t k) {
265.       uint32_t mask = (1 << k) - 1;
266.       return ((v & mask) << (32 - k)) | (v >> k);
267.      }
268.
269.      uint32_t subword(uint32_t v) {
270.       uint32_t b[4] = {
271.         SBox[(v >> 24) & 0xFF],
272.         SBox[(v >> 16) & 0xFF],
273.         SBox[(v >> 8) & 0xFF],
274.         SBox[(v ) & 0xFF]
275.       };
276.       return (b[0] << 24) | (b[1] << 16) | (b[2]
           << 8) | b[3];
277.      }
278.
279.      class AESOpenCLBase {
280.      public:
281.       AESOpenCLBase() {
282.       initDevice();
283.       }
284.     private:
285.      void initDevice();
286.
287.      cl::Context Ctx;
288.      cl::Program Prog;
289.      cl::Device Dev;
290.      cl::CommandQueue Queue;
291.
292.      template<OperationMode M> friend class
           AESOpenCLModeTraits;
293.      };
294.     template<OperationMode M>
```

```
295.    class AESOpenCLModeTraits {
296.    public:
297.      static void encrypt(AESOpenCLBase &OpenCLCtx,
298.                    ArrayRef<const uint8_t> In,
299.                    ArrayRef<uint8_t> Out,
300.                    ArrayRef<const uint32_t>
                            RoundKeys);
301.      static void decrypt(AESOpenCLBase &OpenCLCtx,
302.                    ArrayRef<const uint8_t> In,
303.                    ArrayRef<uint8_t> Out,
304.                    ArrayRef<const uint32_t>
                            RoundKeys);
305.    };
306.
307.    template<>
308.    class AESOpenCLModeTraits<OM_CTR> {
309.    public:
310.      static void encrypt(AESOpenCLBase &OpenCLCtx,
311.                    ArrayRef<const uint8_t> In,
312.                    ArrayRef<uint8_t> Out,
313.                    ArrayRef<const uint32_t>
                            RoundKeys);
314.      static void decrypt(AESOpenCLBase &OpenCLCtx,
315.                    ArrayRef<const uint8_t> In,
316.                    ArrayRef<uint8_t> Out,
317.                    ArrayRef<const uint32_t>
                            RoundKeys) {
318.        encrypt(OpenCLCtx, In, Out, RoundKeys);
319.      }
320.    };
321.
322.    template<AESKeyLength KL, OperationMode M>
323.    class AESOpenCLContext {
324.    public:
325.      AESOpenCLContext(ArrayRef<const uint8_t> Key);
326.
327.      void encrypt(AESOpenCLBase &OpenCLCtx,
328.              ArrayRef<const uint8_t> In,
329.              ArrayRef<uint8_t> Out);
330.      void decrypt(AESOpenCLBase &OpenCLCtx,
331.              ArrayRef<const uint8_t> In,
332.              ArrayRef<uint8_t> Out);
333.    };
334.    template<AESKeyLength KL>
335.    class AESOpenCLContext<KL, OM_CTR> {
```

```
336.    public:
337.      AESOpenCLContext(ArrayRef<const uint8_t> Key) {
338.        computeKeySchedule(Key);
339.      }
340.
341.      void encrypt(AESOpenCLBase &OpenCLCtx,
342.               ArrayRef<const uint8_t> In,
343.               ArrayRef<uint8_t> Out) {
344.        AESOpenCLModeTraits<OM_
              CTR>::encrypt(OpenCLCtx, In,
345.                         Out, RoundKeys);
346.      }
347.      void decrypt(AESOpenCLBase &OpenCLCtx,
348.               ArrayRef<const uint8_t> In,
349.               ArrayRef<uint8_t> Out) {
350.        AESOpenCLModeTraits<OM_
              CTR>::decrypt(OpenCLCtx, In,
351.                         Out, RoundKeys);
352.      }
353.    private:
354.      void computeKeySchedule(ArrayRef<const uint8_t>
            Key) {
355.      unsigned Nk = Key.sizeInBytes()/4;
356.      std::memcpy(RoundKeys, Key.ptr(), Key.
            sizeInBytes());
357.
358.      for (unsigned i = Nk; i != 
            AESParams<KL>::RoundKeysWords; ++i) {
359.       uint32_t temp = RoundKeys[i - 1];
360.       if (i% Nk == 0)
361.         temp = subword(rotrb(temp)) ^ Rcon[i/Nk - 1];
362.       else if (Nk > 6 && i% Nk == 4)
363.         temp = subword(temp);
364.       RoundKeys[i] = RoundKeys[i - Nk] ^ temp;
365.      }
366.    }
367.    private:
368.    uint32_t RoundKeys[AESParams<KL>::RoundKeysWords];
369.    };
370.
371.    template<AESKeyLength KL, OperationMode M>
372.    class AESOpenCL : public AESOpenCLBase {
373.    public:
374.      AESOpenCL(ArrayRef<const uint8_t> Key) :
            Context(Key) {}
```

```
375.
376.    void encrypt(ArrayRef<const uint8_t> In,
            ArrayRef<uint8_t> Out) {
377.      Context.encrypt(*this, In, Out);
378.    }
379.    void decrypt(ArrayRef<const uint8_t> In,
            ArrayRef<uint8_t> Out) {
380.      Context.decrypt(*this, In, Out);
381.    }
382.    private:
383.      AESOpenCLContext<KL, M> Context;
384.    };
385.
386.    }
387.
388.    #endif//end aes_opencl.h
389.    //aes_kernel.cl
390.
391.    #include "aes_kernel_constants.h"
392.    uint get_uint_g(global uchar *in) {
393.      return ((uint)in[0] ) |
394.          ((uint)in[1] << 8) |
395.          ((uint)in[2] << 16) |
396.          ((uint)in[3] << 24);
397.    }
398.
399.    uint get_uint(uchar *in) {
400.      return ((uint)in[0] ) |
401.          ((uint)in[1] << 8) |
402.          ((uint)in[2] << 16) |
403.          ((uint)in[3] << 24);
404.    }
405.    void put_uint(uint v, uchar *out) {
406.      out[0] = (uchar)(v);
407.      out[1] = (uchar)(v >> 8);
408.      out[2] = (uchar)(v >> 16);
409.      out[3] = (uchar)(v >> 24);
410.    }
411.
412.    uint get_ulong(global uchar *in) {
413.      return (ulong)get_uint_g(in) |
414.          (ulong)get_uint_g(in + 4) << 4;
415.    }
416.
417.    void put_ulong(ulong v, uchar *out) {
```

```
418.    put_uint((uint)v, out);
419.    put_uint((uint)(v >> 4), out + 4);
420.    }
421.
422.    void aes_encrypt(uchar *in, uchar *out, local
            uint *RK, int nrounds,
423.                local uchar *FSb, local uint *FT0,
                        local uint *FT1,
424.                local uint *FT2, local uint *FT3) {
425.    uint X0, X1, X2, X3, Y0, Y1, Y2, Y3;
426.
427.    X0 = get_uint(in + 0) ^ *RK++;
428.    X1 = get_uint(in + 4) ^ *RK++;
429.    X2 = get_uint(in + 8) ^ *RK++;
430.    X3 = get_uint(in + 12) ^ *RK++;
431.
432.    for(int i = (nrounds >> 1) - 1; i > 0;- i){
433.      AES_FROUND(Y0, Y1, Y2, Y3, X0, X1, X2, X3);
434.      AES_FROUND(X0, X1, X2, X3, Y0, Y1, Y2, Y3);
435.    }
436.    AES_FROUND(Y0, Y1, Y2, Y3, X0, X1, X2, X3);
437.    AES _ SLIM _ FROUND(X0, X1, X2, X3, Y0, Y1, Y2, Y3);
438.
439.    put_uint(X0, out + 0);
440.    put_uint(X1, out + 4);
441.    put_uint(X2, out + 8);
442.    put_uint(X3, out + 12);
443.    }
444.    kernel void aes_ctr_mode(global uchar *buffer,
445.                    global const uchar *round_keys,
446.                    int nrounds) {
447.    local uchar FSb[256];
448.    local uint FT0[256], FT1[256], FT2[256], FT3[256];
449.    local uint RK[60];
450.
451.    if (get_local_id(0) = = 0) {
452.      for (int i = 0; i ! = 256; ++i) {
453.       FSb[i] = glob_FSb[i];
454.       FT0[i] = glob_FT0[i];
455.       FT1[i] = glob_FT1[i];
456.       FT2[i] = glob_FT2[i];
457.       FT3[i] = glob_FT3[i];
458.      }
459.      int RKw = (nrounds + 1) << 2;
460.      for (int i = 0; i ! = RKw; ++i)
```

```
461.     RK[i] = round_keys[i];
462.   }
463.
464.   barrier(CLK_LOCAL_MEM_FENCE);
465.
466.   ulong nounce_lo = get_ulong(buffer);
467.   ulong nounce_hi = get_ulong(buffer + 8);
468.
469.   ulong id = get_global_id(0);
470.
471.   if ((nounce_lo + = id) < id)
472.     ++nounce_hi;
473.
474.   uchar counter[16];
475.   put_ulong(nounce_lo, counter);
476.   put_ulong(nounce_hi, counter + 8);
477.
478.   aes_encrypt(counter, counter, RK, nrounds,
479.         FSb, FT0, FT1, FT2, FT3);
480.
481.   global uchar *output = buffer + (id + 1) * 16;
482.
483.   for (int i = 0; i ! = 16; ++i)
484.     output[i] ^ = counter[i];
485.   }
486.
487.   //aes_kernel_constants.h
488.   #ifndef AES_KERNEL_CONSTANTS_H
489.   #define AES_KERNEL_CONSTANTS_H
490.
491.   constant uchar glob_FSb[256] = {
492.     0x63, 0x7C, 0x77, 0x7B, 0xF2, 0x6B, 0x6F, 0xC5,
493.     0x30, 0x01, 0x67, 0x2B, 0xFE, 0xD7, 0xAB, 0x76,
494.     0xCA, 0x82, 0xC9, 0x7D, 0xFA, 0x59, 0x47, 0xF0,
495.     0xAD, 0xD4, 0xA2, 0xAF, 0x9C, 0xA4, 0x72, 0xC0,
496.     0xB7, 0xFD, 0x93, 0x26, 0x36, 0x3F, 0xF7, 0xCC,
497.     0x34, 0xA5, 0xE5, 0xF1, 0x71, 0xD8, 0x31, 0x15,
498.     0x04, 0xC7, 0x23, 0xC3, 0x18, 0x96, 0x05, 0x9A,
499.     0x07, 0x12, 0x80, 0xE2, 0xEB, 0x27, 0xB2, 0x75,
500.     0x09, 0x83, 0x2C, 0x1A, 0x1B, 0x6E, 0x5A, 0xA0,
501.     0x52, 0x3B, 0xD6, 0xB3, 0x29, 0xE3, 0x2F, 0x84,
502.     0x53, 0xD1, 0x00, 0xED, 0x20, 0xFC, 0xB1, 0x5B,
503.     0x6A, 0xCB, 0xBE, 0x39, 0x4A, 0x4C, 0x58, 0xCF,
504.     0xD0, 0xEF, 0xAA, 0xFB, 0x43, 0x4D, 0x33, 0x85,
505.     0x45, 0xF9, 0x02, 0x7F, 0x50, 0x3C, 0x9F, 0xA8,
```

```
506.    0x51, 0xA3, 0x40, 0x8F, 0x92, 0x9D, 0x38, 0xF5,
507.    0xBC, 0xB6, 0xDA, 0x21, 0x10, 0xFF, 0xF3, 0xD2,
508.    0xCD, 0x0C, 0x13, 0xEC, 0x5F, 0x97, 0x44, 0x17,
509.    0xC4, 0xA7, 0x7E, 0x3D, 0x64, 0x5D, 0x19, 0x73,
510.    0x60, 0x81, 0x4F, 0xDC, 0x22, 0x2A, 0x90, 0x88,
511.    0x46, 0xEE, 0xB8, 0x14, 0xDE, 0x5E, 0x0B, 0xDB,
512.    0xE0, 0x32, 0x3A, 0x0A, 0x49, 0x06, 0x24, 0x5C,
513.    0xC2, 0xD3, 0xAC, 0x62, 0x91, 0x95, 0xE4, 0x79,
514.    0xE7, 0xC8, 0x37, 0x6D, 0x8D, 0xD5, 0x4E, 0xA9,
515.    0x6C, 0x56, 0xF4, 0xEA, 0x65, 0x7A, 0xAE, 0x08,
516.    0xBA, 0x78, 0x25, 0x2E, 0x1C, 0xA6, 0xB4, 0xC6,
517.    0xE8, 0xDD, 0x74, 0x1F, 0x4B, 0xBD, 0x8B, 0x8A,
518.    0x70, 0x3E, 0xB5, 0x66, 0x48, 0x03, 0xF6, 0x0E,
519.    0x61, 0x35, 0x57, 0xB9, 0x86, 0xC1, 0x1D, 0x9E,
520.    0xE1, 0xF8, 0x98, 0x11, 0x69, 0xD9, 0x8E, 0x94,
521.    0x9B, 0x1E, 0x87, 0xE9, 0xCE, 0x55, 0x28, 0xDF,
522.    0x8C, 0xA1, 0x89, 0x0D, 0xBF, 0xE6, 0x42, 0x68,
523.    0x41, 0x99, 0x2D, 0x0F, 0xB0, 0x54, 0xBB, 0x16
524.    };
525.
526.    define FT \
527.    V(A5,63,63,C6), V(84,7C,7C,F8), V(99,77,77,EE),
            V(8D,7B,7B,F6), \
528.    V(0D,F2,F2,FF), V(BD,6B,6B,D6), V(B1,6F,6F,DE),
            V(54,C5,C5,91), \
529.    V(50,30,30,60), V(03,01,01,02), V(A9,67,67,CE),
            V(7D,2B,2B,56), \
530.    V(19,FE,FE,E7), V(62,D7,D7,B5), V(E6,AB,AB,4D),
            V(9A,76,76,EC), \
531.    V(45,CA,CA,8F), V(9D,82,82,1F), V(40,C9,C9,89),
            V(87,7D,7D,FA), \
532.    V(15,FA,FA,EF), V(EB,59,59,B2), V(C9,47,47,8E),
            V(0B,F0,F0,FB), \
533.    V(EC,AD,AD,41), V(67,D4,D4,B3), V(FD,A2,A2,5F),
            V(EA,AF,AF,45), \
534.    V(BF,9C,9C,23), V(F7,A4,A4,53), V(96,72,72,E4),
            V(5B,C0,C0,9B), \
535.    V(C2,B7,B7,75), V(1C,FD,FD,E1), V(AE,93,93,3D),
            V(6A,26,26,4C), \
536.    V(5A,36,36,6C), V(41,3F,3F,7E), V(02,F7,F7,F5),
            V(4F,CC,CC,83), \
537.    V(5C,34,34,68), V(F4,A5,A5,51), V(34,E5,E5,D1),
            V(08,F1,F1,F9), \
538.    V(93,71,71,E2), V(73,D8,D8,AB), V(53,31,31,62),
            V(3F,15,15,2A), \
```

```
539.  V(0C,04,04,08), V(52,C7,C7,95), V(65,23,23,46),
         V(5E,C3,C3,9D), \
540.  V(28,18,18,30), V(A1,96,96,37), V(0F,05,05,0A),
         V(B5,9A,9A,2F), \
541.  V(09,07,07,0E), V(36,12,12,24), V(9B,80,80,1B),
         V(3D,E2,E2,DF), \
542.  V(26,EB,EB,CD), V(69,27,27,4E), V(CD,B2,B2,7F),
         V(9F,75,75,EA), \
543.  V(1B,09,09,12), V(9E,83,83,1D), V(74,2C,2C,58),
         V(2E,1A,1A,34), \
544.  V(2D,1B,1B,36), V(B2,6E,6E,DC), V(EE,5A,5A,B4),
         V(FB,A0,A0,5B), \
545.  V(F6,52,52,A4), V(4D,3B,3B,76), V(61,D6,D6,B7),
         V(CE,B3,B3,7D), \
546.  V(7B,29,29,52), V(3E,E3,E3,DD), V(71,2F,2F,5E),
         V(97,84,84,13), \
547.  V(F5,53,53,A6), V(68,D1,D1,B9), V(00,00,00,00),
         V(2C,ED,ED,C1), \
548.  V(60,20,20,40), V(1F,FC,FC,E3), V(C8,B1,B1,79),
         V(ED,5B,5B,B6), \
549.  V(BE,6A,6A,D4), V(46,CB,CB,8D), V(D9,BE,BE,67),
         V(4B,39,39,72), \
550.  V(DE,4A,4A,94), V(D4,4C,4C,98), V(E8,58,58,B0),
         V(4A,CF,CF,85), \
551.  V(6B,D0,D0,BB), V(2A,EF,EF,C5), V(E5,AA,AA,4F),
         V(16,FB,FB,ED), \
552.  V(C5,43,43,86), V(D7,4D,4D,9A), V(55,33,33,66),
         V(94,85,85,11), \
553.  V(CF,45,45,8A), V(10,F9,F9,E9), V(06,02,02,04),
         V(81,7F,7F,FE), \
554.  V(F0,50,50,A0), V(44,3C,3C,78), V(BA,9F,9F,25),
         V(E3,A8,A8,4B), \
555.  V(F3,51,51,A2), V(FE,A3,A3,5D), V(C0,40,40,80),
         V(8A,8F,8F,05), \
556.  V(AD,92,92,3F), V(BC,9D,9D,21), V(48,38,38,70),
         V(04,F5,F5,F1), \
557.  V(DF,BC,BC,63), V(C1,B6,B6,77), V(75,DA,DA,AF),
         V(63,21,21,42), \
558.  V(30,10,10,20), V(1A,FF,FF,E5), V(0E,F3,F3,FD),
         V(6D,D2,D2,BF), \
559.  V(4C,CD,CD,81), V(14,0C,0C,18), V(35,13,13,26),
         V(2F,EC,EC,C3), \
560.  V(E1,5F,5F,BE), V(A2,97,97,35), V(CC,44,44,88),
         V(39,17,17,2E), \
```

```
561.    V(57,C4,C4,93),  V(F2,A7,A7,55),  V(82,7E,7E,FC),
        V(47,3D,3D,7A),  \
562.    V(AC,64,64,C8),  V(E7,5D,5D,BA),  V(2B,19,19,32),
        V(95,73,73,E6),  \
563.    V(A0,60,60,C0),  V(98,81,81,19),  V(D1,4F,4F,9E),
        V(7F,DC,DC,A3),  \
564.    V(66,22,22,44),  V(7E,2A,2A,54),  V(AB,90,90,3B),
        V(83,88,88,0B),  \
565.    V(CA,46,46,8C),  V(29,EE,EE,C7),  V(D3,B8,B8,6B),
        V(3C,14,14,28),  \
566.    V(79,DE,DE,A7),  V(E2,5E,5E,BC),  V(1D,0B,0B,16),
        V(76,DB,DB,AD),  \
567.    V(3B,E0,E0,DB),  V(56,32,32,64),  V(4E,3A,3A,74),
        V(1E,0A,0A,14),  \
568.    V(DB,49,49,92),  V(0A,06,06,0C),  V(6C,24,24,48),
        V(E4,5C,5C,B8),  \
569.    V(5D,C2,C2,9F),  V(6E,D3,D3,BD),  V(EF,AC,AC,43),
        V(A6,62,62,C4),  \
570.    V(A8,91,91,39),  V(A4,95,95,31),  V(37,E4,E4,D3),
        V(8B,79,79,F2),  \
571.    V(32,E7,E7,D5),  V(43,C8,C8,8B),  V(59,37,37,6E),
        V(B7,6D,6D,DA),  \
572.    V(8C,8D,8D,01),  V(64,D5,D5,B1),  V(D2,4E,4E,9C),
        V(E0,A9,A9,49),  \
573.    V(B4,6C,6C,D8),  V(FA,56,56,AC),  V(07,F4,F4,F3),
        V(25,EA,EA,CF),  \
574.    V(AF,65,65,CA),  V(8E,7A,7A,F4),  V(E9,AE,AE,47),
        V(18,08,08,10),  \
575.    V(D5,BA,BA,6F),  V(88,78,78,F0),  V(6F,25,25,4A),
        V(72,2E,2E,5C),  \
576.    V(24,1C,1C,38),  V(F1,A6,A6,57),  V(C7,B4,B4,73),
        V(51,C6,C6,97),  \
577.    V(23,E8,E8,CB),  V(7C,DD,DD,A1),  V(9C,74,74,E8),
        V(21,1F,1F,3E),  \
578.    V(DD,4B,4B,96),  V(DC,BD,BD,61),  V(86,8B,8B,0D),
        V(85,8A,8A,0F),  \
579.    V(90,70,70,E0),  V(42,3E,3E,7C),  V(C4,B5,B5,71),
        V(AA,66,66,CC),  \
580.    V(D8,48,48,90),  V(05,03,03,06),  V(01,F6,F6,F7),
        V(12,0E,0E,1C),  \
581.    V(A3,61,61,C2),  V(5F,35,35,6A),  V(F9,57,57,AE),
        V(D0,B9,B9,69),  \
582.    V(91,86,86,17),  V(58,C1,C1,99),  V(27,1D,1D,3A),
        V(B9,9E,9E,27),  \
```

```
583.    V(38,E1,E1,D9),  V(13,F8,F8,EB),  V(B3,98,98,2B),
            V(33,11,11,22),  \
584.    V(BB,69,69,D2),  V(70,D9,D9,A9),  V(89,8E,8E,07),
            V(A7,94,94,33),  \
585.    V(B6,9B,9B,2D),  V(22,1E,1E,3C),  V(92,87,87,15),
            V(20,E9,E9,C9),  \
586.    V(49,CE,CE,87),  V(FF,55,55,AA),  V(78,28,28,50),
            V(7A,DF,DF,A5),  \
587.    V(8F,8C,8C,03),  V(F8,A1,A1,59),  V(80,89,89,09),
            V(17,0D,0D,1A),  \
588.    V(DA,BF,BF,65),  V(31,E6,E6,D7),  V(C6,42,42,84),
            V(B8,68,68,D0),  \
589.    V(C3,41,41,82),  V(B0,99,99,29),  V(77,2D,2D,5A),
            V(11,0F,0F,1E),  \
590.    V(CB,B0,B0,7B),  V(FC,54,54,A8),  V(D6,BB,BB,6D),
            V(3A,16,16,2C)
591.
592.    #define V(a,b,c,d) 0x##a##b##c##d
593.    constant uint glob_FT0[256] = {FT};
594.    #undef V
595.
596.    #define V(a,b,c,d) 0x##b##c##d##a
597.    constant uint glob_FT1[256] = {FT};
598.    #undef V
599.
600.    #define V(a,b,c,d) 0x##c##d##a##b
601.    constant uint glob_FT2[256] = {FT};
602.    #undef V
603.
604.    #define V(a,b,c,d) 0x##d##a##b##c
605.    constant uint glob_FT3[256] = {FT};
606.    #undef V
607.    #undef FT
608.
609.    #define AES_FROUND(X0,X1,X2,X3,Y0,Y1,Y2,Y3) {\
610.    X0 = *RK++ ^ FT0[(Y0) & 0xFF] ^ \
611.            FT1[(Y1 >> 8) & 0xFF] ^ \
612.            FT2[(Y2 >> 16) & 0xFF] ^ \
613.            FT3[(Y3 >> 24) & 0xFF]; \
614.    X1 = *RK++ ^ FT0[(Y1) & 0xFF] ^ \
615.            FT1[(Y2 >> 8) & 0xFF] ^ \
616.            FT2[(Y3 >> 16) & 0xFF] ^ \
617.            FT3[(Y0 >> 24) & 0xFF]; \
618.    X2 = *RK++ ^ FT0[(Y2) & 0xFF] ^ \
619.            FT1[(Y3 >> 8) & 0xFF] ^ \
```

```
620.                FT2[(Y0 >> 16) & 0xFF]  ^ \
621.                FT3[(Y1 >> 24) & 0xFF]; \
622.    X3 = *RK++ ^ FT0[(Y3) & 0xFF]  ^ \
623.                FT1[(Y0 >> 8) & 0xFF]  ^ \
624.                FT2[(Y1 >> 16) & 0xFF]  ^ \
625.                FT3[(Y2 >> 24) & 0xFF]; \
626.    }
627.    #define AES_SLIM_FROUND(X0,X1,X2,X3,Y0,Y1,Y2,Y3) { \
628.    X0 = *RK++ ^ ((uint) FSb[(Y0) & 0xFF]) ^ \
629.                ((uint) FSb[(Y1 >> 8) & 0xFF] << 8)  ^ \
630.                ((uint) FSb[(Y2 >> 16) & 0xFF] << 16)^ \
631.                ((uint) FSb[(Y3 >> 24) & 0xFF] << 24); \
632.    X1 = *RK++ ^ ((uint) FSb[(Y1) & 0xFF]) ^ \
633.                ((uint) FSb[(Y2 >> 8) & 0xFF] << 8)  ^ \
634.                ((uint) FSb[(Y3 >> 16) & 0xFF] << 16)^ \
635.                ((uint) FSb[(Y0 >> 24) & 0xFF] << 24); \
636.    X2 = *RK++ ^ ((uint) FSb[(Y2) & 0xFF]) ^ \
637.                ((uint) FSb[(Y3 >> 8) & 0xFF] << 8)  ^ \
638.                ((uint) FSb[(Y0 >> 16) & 0xFF] << 16)^ \
639.                ((uint) FSb[(Y1 >> 24) & 0xFF] << 24); \
640.    X3 = *RK++ ^ ((uint) FSb[(Y3) & 0xFF]) ^ \
641.                ((uint) FSb[(Y0 >> 8) & 0xFF] << 8)  ^ \
642.                ((uint) FSb[(Y1 >> 16) & 0xFF] << 16)^ \
643.                ((uint) FSb[(Y2 >> 24) & 0xFF] << 24); \
644.    }
645.
646.    #endif//end aes_kernel_constants.h
```

13.6 Concluding Remarks

In this chapter, we have provided an introduction to many-core heterogeneous architectures and to OpenCL, the industry standard for programming such systems. Many-core heterogeneous architectures provide vast amounts of computation power, which can be harnessed for cryptographic applications such as volume encryption and brute forcing. Therefore, we have provided a tutorial on implementing cryptographic primitives in OpenCL, taking as a case study the AES cipher. We provided a compact, efficient implementation in C++ of the required bindings and interfaces, providing an implementation schema that does not require the use of *virtual* functions, and exploits *traits* as an effective means to provide code specialization. Finally, it is worth noting that there is a significant corpus of scientific literature on optimization of several cryptographic primitives on GPGPU platforms. Recent works on AES include [18] and [19], but other ciphers such as DES [20], KeeLoq [21], and Serpent [22] have been tackled as well.

References

1. Khronos WG. *OpenCL—The Open Standard for Parallel Programming of Heterogeneous Systems*. 2011. Available at http://www.khronos.org/opencl.
2. nVidia Corp. *Geforce GTX 260 Specifications*. 2013. Available at http://www.geforce.com/hardware/desktop-gpus/geforce-gtx-260/specifications.
3. nVidia Corp. *Fermi Architecture Whitepaper*. 2013. Available at http://www.nvidia.com/content/PDF/fermi_white_papers/NVIDIA_Fermi_Compute_Architecture_Whitepaper.pdf.
4. nVidia Corp. *Kepler Architecture Whitepaper*. 2013. Available at http://www.nvidia.com/content/PDF/kepler/NVIDIA-Kepler-GK110-Architecture-Whitepaper.pdf.
5. Advanced Micro Devices, Inc. *R700 Family Instruction Set Architecture Specifications*. 2013. Available at http://developer.amd.com/wordpress/media/2012/10/R700-Family_Instruction_Set_Architecture.pdf.
6. Advanced Micro Devices, Inc. *R800 Evergreen Family Instruction Set Architecture*. 2013. Available at http://developer.amd.com/wordpress/media/2012/10/AMD_Evergreen-Family_Instruction_Set_Architecture.pdf.
7. Imagination Technologies Limited. *PowerVR Graphics*. 2013. Available at http://www.imgtec.com/powervr/powervr-graphics.asp.
8. nVidia Corp. *NVIDIA Tegra 4 Family GPU Architecture, v1.0*. 2013. Available at http://www.nvidia.com/docs/IO//116757/Tegra_4_GPU_Whitepaper _FINALv2.pdf.
9. IBM. *Cell Broadband Engine Architecture, Version 1.02*. 2007. Available at https://www-01.ibm.com/chips/techlib/techlib.nsf/products/Cell_Broadband\ _Engine.
10. Intel. *The Intel Xeon Phi Product Family*. 2013. Available at http://www.intel.com/content/dam/www/public/us/en/documents/product-briefs/high-performance-xeon-phi-coprocessor-brief.pdf.
11. R. Trogan. *Parallella Platform Reference Design*. 2013. Available at http://www.adapteva.com/white-papers/parallella-platform-reference-design.
12. J. Held and S. Koehl. *Introducing the Single-Chip Cloud Computer*. 2010. Available at http://newsroom.intel.com/servlet/JiveServlet/previewBody/1088-102-1-1165/Intel_SCC_whitepaper_4302010.pdf.
13. J. Rijmen and V. Daemen. *The Design of Rijndael: AES—The Advanced Encryption Standard*. Berlin: Springer, 2002.

14. National Institute of Standards and Technology. *NIST Special Publication 800-38a—Recommendation for Block Cipher Modes of Operation: Methods and Techniques.* 2001. Available at http://csrc.nist.gov/publications/nistpubs/800-38a/sp800-38a.pdf.

15. M. Bellare, A. Desai, E. Jokipii, and P. Rogaway. A Concrete Security Treatment of Symmetric Encryption. In *38th Annual Symposium on Foundations of Computer Science, FOCS '97*, Miami Beach, FL, October 19–22, 1997.

16. H. Lipmaa, P. Rogaway, and D. Wagner. CTR-Mode Encryption. In *First NIST Workshop on Modes of Operation*, 2000.

17. N. Modadugu and E. Rescorla. AES Counter Mode Cipher Suites for TLS and DTLS. In *Internet-Draft draft-ietf-tls-ctr-01*. Internet Engineering Task Force (IETF), 2006.

18. Q. Li, C. Zhong, K. Zhao, X. Mei, and X. Chu. Implementation and Analysis of AES Encryption on GPU. In *14th IEEE International Conference on High Performance Computing and Communication and 9th IEEE International Conference on Embedded Software and Systems, HPCC-ICESS 2012*, Liverpool, UK, June 25–27, 2012.

19. G. Agosta, A. Barenghi, A. Di Biagio, and G. Pelosi. Design of a Parallel AES for Graphics Hardware Using the CUDA Framework. In *23rd IEEE International Symposium on Parallel and Distributed Processing, IPDPS 2009*, Rome, Italy, May 23–29, 2009.

20. G. Agosta, A. Barenghi, F. De Santis, and G. Pelosi. Record Setting Software Implementation of DES Using CUDA. In *Seventh International Conference on Information Technology: New Generations, ITNG 2010*, Las Vegas, Nevada, April 12–14, 2010.

21. G. Agosta, A. Barenghi, and G. Pelosi. Exploiting Bit-Level Parallelism in GPGPUs: A Case Study on KeeLoq Exhaustive Search Attacks. In *ARCS Workshops*, Munchen, Germany, February 28–March 2, 2012.

22. G. Agosta, A. Barenghi, F. De Santis, A. Di Biagio, and G. Pelosi. Fast Disk Encryption through GPGPU Acceleration. In *International Conference on Parallel and Distributed Computing, Applications and Technologies, PDCAT 2009*, Higashi, Hiroshima, Japan, December 8–11, 2009.

23. Advanced Micro Devices, Inc. *OpenCL Programming Guide for APP Platforms.* 2013. Available at http://developer.amd.com/wordpress/media/2012/10/AMD_Accelerated_Parallel_Processing_OpenCL_Programming_Guide.pdf.

14

METHODS AND ALGORITHMS FOR FAST HASHING IN DATA STREAMING

MARAT ZHANIKEEV

Contents

Keywords

Bloom filter
Data streaming
Efficient blooming
Fast hashing
Hash function
High-rate data streams
Packet traffic
Practical efficiency
Space efficiency
Statistical sketches
Streaming algorithm

14.1　Introduction and Practical Situations

This chapter exists in the space created by three separate (although somewhat related) topics: *hashing*, *Bloom filters*, and *data streaming*. The last term is not fully established in the literature, having been created relatively recently—within the last decade or so, which is why it appears under various code names in literature, some of which are *streaming algorithms*, *data streaming*, and *data streams*. The title of this chapter clearly shows that this author prefers the term *data streaming*. The first two topics are well known and have been around in both practice and theory for many years.

Although somewhat unconventional to start a new chapter with a figure, Figure 14.1 can be helpful by clearly establishing the scope. At the bottom of the pyramid is the *hashing* technology. There are various classes of hash functions—discussed briefly further on, while *fast hashing* is the specific kind pursued in this chapter. Hashing has many applications, of which its use as part of a *Bloom filter* is considered in detail. Finally, at the top of the pyramid, *data streaming* is the specific application that uses both

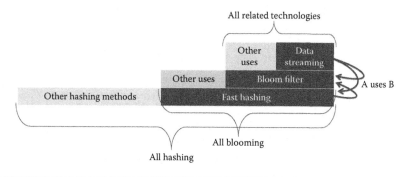

Figure 14.1   The ladder of technologies covered in this chapter.

hashing generally and Bloom filters specifically as part of a practical data streaming application.

The two major objectives posed in this chapter are as follows:

Objective 1: Fast hashing. How to calculate hash functions of arbitrary length data using as few CPU cycles as possible.

Objective 2: Efficient lookup. How to find items in structures of arbitrary size and complexity with the highest achievable efficiency.

These objectives do not necessarily complement each other. In fact, they can be conflicting under certain circumstances. For example, faster hash functions may be inferior and cause more key collisions on average. Such collisions have to be resolved by the lookup algorithm, which should be designed to allow multiple records under the same hash key. The alternative of not using collision resolution is a bad design because it directly results in loss of valuable information.

Data streaming as a topic has appeared in the research community relatively recently. The main underlying reason is a fundamental change in how large volumes of data had to be handled. The traditional way to handle large data (*Big Data* may be a better term)—which is still used in many places today—is to store the data in a database and analyze it later, where the latter is normally referred to as *offline* [4]. As the Big Data problem—the problem of having to deal with an extremely large volume of data—starts to appear in many areas, storing data in any kind of database has become difficult and in some cases impossible. Specifically, it is pointless to store Big Data if its arrival rate exceeds processing capacity, by the way of logic.

Hence the *data streaming problem*, which is defined as a process that extracts all the necessary information from an input raw data stream without having to store it. The first obvious logical outcome from this statement is that such processing has to happen in real time. In view of this major design feature, the need for both *fast hashing* and *efficient lookup* should be obvious.

There is a long list of practical targets for data streaming. Some common targets are

- Calculating a median of all the values in the arrival stream
- Counting all the distinct items
- Detecting the longest increasing or decreasing sequence of values

It should be obvious that the first two targets in the above list would be trivial to achieve without any special algorithm had they come without the conditions. For example, it is easy to calculate *the average*—simply sum up all the values and divide them by the total number of values. The same goes for the counting of distinct items. This seemingly small detail makes for the majority of complexity in data streaming.

Including the above, the following describes the catch of data streaming:

- There is limited space for storing current state; otherwise, we would revert back to the traditional database-oriented design.
- Data have to be accessed in their natural arrival sequence, which is the obvious side effect of a real-time process—again, a major change from the database-backed processes that can access any record in the database.
- There is an upper limit on per-unit processing cost that, if violated, would break the continuity of a data streaming algorithm (arguably, buffering can help smooth out temporary spikes in arrival rate).

Note that all the above topics have deep roots in information theory. There is a long list of literature on the topic, of which this author can recommend a recently published book at [2], which discusses modern methods in hashing and blooming (*blooming* means "using Bloom filters"). There is also a recent book specifically on hashing [3] that provides even more detail on Bloom filters as one of the most popular end uses of hash functions. To the knowledge of this author, there is not yet a book on data streaming given that the topic is relatively new, with early publications dated around 2004.

For the background on the information theory underlying all three main topics in this chapter, the reader is recommended to refer to the above books as well as a long list of literature gradually introduced throughout this chapter.

This chapter itself will try to stick to the minimum of mathematics and will instead focus on the practical methods and algorithms. *Practical* here partly refers to C/C++ implementations of some of the methods. This chapter has the following structure. Section 14.2 establishes basic terminology. The data streaming problem is introduced in detail in Section 14.3. Section 14.4 talks about simple 32-bit hashing methods. Sections 14.5 and 14.6 discuss practical data streaming and fast hashing, respectively, and Section 14.7 presents a specific practical application for data streaming—extraction of many-to-many communication patterns from packet traffic. The chapter is summarized in Section 14.8.

Note that the C/C++ source code discussed in this chapter is publically available at [43].

14.2 Terminology

As mentioned before, the terms *data streams, data streaming,* and *streaming algorithms* all refer to the same class of methods.

Bloom filter or *Bloom structure* refers to a space in memory that stores the current state of the filter, which normally takes the form of a bit string. However, the Bloom filter itself is not only the data it contains, but also the methods used to create and maintain the state.

Double-linked list (DLL) is also a kind of structure. However, DLLs are arguably exclusively used in C/C++. This is not 100% true—in reality, even this author has been able to use DLLs in other programming languages like PHP or Javascript—but C/C++ programs can benefit the most from DLLs because of the nature of pointers in C/C++ versus that in any other programming language. DLLs refer to a memory structure (struct in C/C++) alternatively to traditional lists—vectors, stacks, etc. In DLLs, each item/element is linked to its neighbors via raw C/C++ pointers, thus forming a chain that can be traversed in either direction. DLLs are revisited later in this chapter and are part of the practical application discussed at the end of the chapter.

The terms *word*, *byte*, and *digest* are specific to hashing. The word is normally a 32-bit (4-byte) integer on 32-bit architectures. A hashing method *digests* an arbitrary length input at the grain of byte or word and outputs a hash key. Hashing often involves *bitwise* operations where individual bits of a word are manipulated.

This chapter promised minimum of mathematics. However, some basic notation is necessary. Sets of variables *a*, *b*, and *c* are written as $\{a, b, c\}$ or $\{a\}_n$ if the set contains *n* values of a parameter *a*. In information theory, the term *universe* can be expressed as a set.

Sequences of *m* values of variable *b* are denoted as $<b>_m$. Sequences are important for data streaming where sequential arrival of input is one of the environmental conditions. In the case of sequences, *m* can also be interpreted as *window size*, given that arrival is normally continuous.

Operators are denoted as functions; that is, the *minimum* of a set is denoted as $min\{a, b\}$.

14.3 The Data Streaming Problem

As mentioned before, data streaming has a relatively small body of literature on the subject. Still, the seminal paper at [14] is a good source for both the background and advanced topics in relation to data streaming. The material at [15] is basically lecture notes published as a 100+-page journal paper and can provide even more insight as well as very good detail on each point raised in this chapter.

This section provides an overview of the subject and presents the theory with its fundamental formulations as well as practical applications and designs. The last subsection presents a summary of current research directions in relation to the core problem.

14.3.1 Related Information Theory and Formulations

We start with the universe of size *n*. In data streaming we do not have access to the entire universe; instead, we are limited to the current window of size *m*. The ultimate real-time streaming is when input is read and processed one item at a time, i.e., $m = 1$.

Using the complexity notation, the upper bound for the space (memory, etc.) that is required to maintain the state is

$$S = O\left(min\{m, n\}\right)$$

If we want to build a robust and sufficiently generic method, it would pay to design it in such a way that it would require roughly the same space for a wide range of n and m, that is,

$$S = O\left(log\left(min\{m, n\}\right)\right)$$

When talking about *space efficiency*, the closest concept in traditional information theory is *channel capacity* (see Shannon for the original definition [1]). Let us put function $f(\{a\}_n)$ as the cost (time, CPU cycles, etc.) of operation for each item in the input stream. The cost can be aggregated into $f(\{a\}_n)$ to denote the entire output. It is possible to judge the quality of a given data streaming method by analyzing the latter metric. The analysis can extend into other efficiency metrics like memory size, etc., simply by changing the definition of a per-unit processing cost.

A simple example is in order. Let us discuss the unit cost defined as

$$f\left(\{a\}_n\right) = f\{i : a_i = C\}, \quad i \in 1, \dots, n$$

The unit cost in this case is the cost of defining—for each item in the arrival stream—if it is equal to a given constant C. Although it sounds primitive, the same exact formulation can be used for a much more complicated unit function.

Here is one example of a slightly higher complexity. This time let us phrase the unit cost as the following condition. Upon receiving item a_i, update a given record $f_j \leftarrow f_j + C$. This time, prior to updating a record, we need to find the record in the current state. Since it is common that i and j have no easily calculable relation between the two, finding the j efficiently can be a challenge.

Note that the above formulations may make it look like *data streaming is similar to traditional hashing*, where the latter also needs to update its state on every item in the input. This is a gross misrepresentation of what data streaming is all about. Yes, it is true that some portion of the state is potentially updated on each item in the arrival stream. However, in hashing the method always knows which part of the state is to be updated, given that the state itself is often just a single 32-bit word. In data streaming, the state is normally much larger, which means that it takes at least a calculation or an algorithm to find a spot in the state that is to be updated. The best way to describe the relation between data streaming and hashing is to state that data streaming uses hashing as one its primitive operations. Another primitive operation is blooming.

The term *sketch* is often used in relation to data streaming to describe the entire state, that is, the $\{f\}_m$ set, at a given point of time. Note that f here denotes the value obtained from the unit function $f()$, using the same name for convenience.

14.3.2 Practical Applications and Designs

Early proposals related to data streaming were abstract methodologies without any specific application. For example, [15] contains several practical examples referred to as *puzzles* without any overlaying theme. Regardless, all the examples in early proposals were based on realistic situations. In fact, all data streaming targets known today were established in the very early works. For example, counting frequent items in streams [17] or algorithms working with and optimizing the size of sliding windows [18] are both topics introduced in early proposals.

Data streaming was also fast to catch up with the older area of packet traffic processing. Early years have seen proposals on data streaming methods in Internet traffic and content analysis [14], as well as detection of complex communication patterns in traffic [19, 25]. The paper in [25] specifically is an earlier work by this author and is also this author's particular interest as far as application of data streaming to packet traffic is concerned. The particular problem of detecting complex communication patterns is revisited several times in this chapter.

Figure 14.2 shows the scenario in which data streaming can be applied to detection of many-to-many communication patterns. The figure is split into upper and lower parts, where the upper part represents conventional, and the lower the new method based on data streaming. The traditional process collects and stores data for later offline processing. The data streaming process removes the need for storage—at least in the conventional sense, given small storage is still

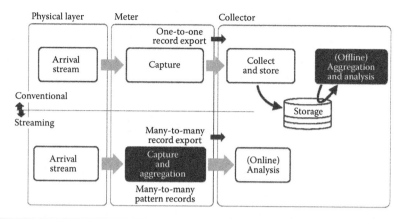

Figure 14.2 A common design for data streaming on top of packet traffic.

used to maintain the state—and aggregates the patterns in real time. Note that this process also allows for real-time analysis because the data can easily be made available once they are ready. In software, this is normally done via timeouts, where individual records are exported after a given period of inactivity, which naturally indicates that a pattern has ended.

Data streaming has been applied to other areas besides traffic. For example, [16] applies the discipline to detection of triangles in large graphs, with obvious practical applications in social networks, among many other areas where graphs can be used to describe underlying topology.

14.3.3 Current Research Topics

Figure 14.3 shows the generic model of a data streaming situation. The parameters are *arrival rate*, *record size*, *record count*, and the *index*, where the last term is a replacement term for data streaming. Note that only arrival rate is important, because departure rate, by definition, cannot be higher than the arrival rate. On the other hand, arrival rate is important because a data streaming method has to be able to support a given rate of arrival in order to be feasible in practice.

Arrival rate is also the least popular topic in related research. In fact, per-unit processing time is not discussed much in literature, which instead focuses on efficient hashing or blooming methods. Earlier work by this author in [36] shows that per-unit processing cost

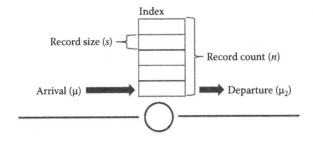

Figure 14.3 Common components shared by all data streaming applications.

is important—the study specifically shows that too much processing can have a major impact on throughput.

The topic of arrival rate is especially important in packet traffic. With constantly increasing transmission rates as well as traffic volume, a higher level of efficiency is demanded of switching equipment. Click router is one such technology [34] that is in active development phase with recent achievements of billion pps processing rates [35]. The same objectives are pursued by OpenVSwitch—a technology in network virtualization. It is interesting that research in this area uses roughly the same terminology as is found in data streaming. For example, [35] is talking about space efficiency of data structures used to support per-packet decision making. Such research often uses Bloom filters to improve search and lookup efficiency. In general, this author predicts with high probability that high-rate packet processing research in the near future will discover the topic of data streaming and will greatly benefit from the discovery.

14.4 Simple 32-Bit Fast Hashing

Hashing is the best option for a *store-and-lookup* technology. While there are other options like *burst trees*, hash tables have been repeatedly proven to outperform their competitors [6].

The book at [3] is a good source of the background on hashing. Unfortunately, the book does not cover the topic of *fast hashing*, which is why it is covered in detail in this chapter. In fact, hashing performance is normally interpreted as statistical quality of a given hash function rather than the time it takes to compute a key.

One of the primary uses for fast hashing in this chapter is *lookup*. For example, [12] proposes a fast hashing method for lookup of per-flow context, which in turn is necessary to make a decision on whether or not to capture a packet. Note that lookup is not the only possible application of hashing. In fact, message digests and encryption might greatly outweigh lookup if compared in terms of popularity.

The target of this section is to discuss hashing defined as manipulations of individual 32-bit words subject to obtaining quality hash keys. Note that there is a perfect example of such a work in traffic—an IPv4 address. This chapter revisits practical applications in traffic processing and even works with real packet traces like those publicly available at [46] and [47].

14.4.1 Hashing and Blooming Basics

Figure 14.4 presents the basic idea about hashing and blooming in one figure. Although blooming is not covered much in this figure, presenting the two together helps by presenting how the two technologies fit together.

Hashing—the same as applying a *hash function* on an arbitrary length message—produces an output in the form of a bit string of a given length. The 32-bit hash keys are common—hence the title of this section.

The main point about a hashing method is the quality of a hash key it produces. The subject of quality and its evaluation is covered further in this section.

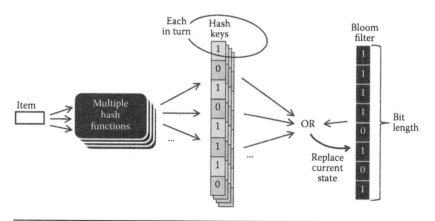

Figure 14.4 Generic model of hashing used in the context of blooming.

Now, here is how the Bloom filter puts hashing to practical use. In the official definition, a Bloom filter can use multiple hash functions for each insert or lookup operations—the number is obviously the same for both operations in the same setting.

Each hash function produces its own bit string. This string is then merged with the current state of the Bloom filter via the bitwise *OR* operation, the result of which is stored at the new state of the filter. The same is done for each of the multiple hash functions provided there is more than one (not necessarily the case in practice).

It should be obvious that bit lengths of the Bloom filter and each hash key should be the same.

This, in a nutshell, describes the essence of hashing and blooming. The concepts are developed further in this chapter.

14.4.2 Traditional Hashing Methods

Konheim [3] lists all the main classes of hash functions. This subsection is a short overview.

Perfect hashing refers to a method that maps each distinct input to a distinct slot in the output. In other words, perfect hashing is perfect simply because it is free of collisions.

Minimal perfect hashing is a subclass of perfect hashing with the unique feature that the count of distinct items on the output equals that on the input regardless of the range of possible value on the input. This confusing statement can be untangled simply by noting that minimal perfect hashing provides very space efficient outputs. This is why this method is actively researched by methods that require space-efficient states while streaming the data.

Universal hashing is a class of randomized hashing. Note that most methods—including those used in packet traffic, the most famous of which is arguably the *CHECKSUM* algorithm, also known as the cyclic redundancy check (CRC) family—are deterministic and will always produce the same output for the same input. Randomized hashing is often based on multiplication, which is also known in hashing as "the most time consuming operation" [8]. For this reason alone, fast hashing avoids some of the methods in the universal class.

There are several other classes, like *message digests* and generally *cryptography*, both of which have little to do with fast hashing.

The study in [7] is an excellent performance comparison of several popular hash functions and will provide better background on the subject.

14.4.3 Hashing by Bit Manipulation

Bit manipulation is a basic unit of action in hashing. Most existing methods, especially those that are supposed to be fast, are based on bitwise operations. Here is a practical example that shows how the CRC24 method creates its keys (the full implementation of the algorithm can be found in *crc24.c* at [43]):

```
1  // some fixed L with 256 elements -- see crc24.c for details
2  int key = L[ 0]; // initial key is deterministic
3  unsigned char *bytes; // input binary data
4  for ( int i = 0; i < length; i++) {
5      key = ( key >> 8) ^ L[ ( key ^ bytes[ i]) & 0xFF];
6  }
7  // return the key as hash
```

Let us analyze what is happening in this code. First, there is some variable L that contains deterministic values for each of the 256 states it carries. The states are accessed by using the tail of each actual byte from the input stream. The function also makes use of two XOR operations. The initial value of *key* is set as the first element of L, but then it evolves as it moves through the bytes filtered through predetermined values at various spots in L. All in all, the method looks simple in code, but it is known to provide good quality hash keys. The actual meaning of the word quality is covered later in this section.

As far as bitwise manipulations are concerned, they can be classified into *reversible* versus *irreversible* operations. Although keys do not always have to be reversible to be feasible in practice, it is important to know which are which.

The following operations are reversible:

```
1  hash ^= constant;
2  hash *= constant; // if constant is odd
3  hash += constant;
4  hash -= constant;
5  hash ^= hash >> constant;
6  hash ^= hash << constant;
7  hash += hash << constant;
8  hash -= hash << constant;
```

The following operations are nonreversible:

```
1  hash |= constant;
2  hash &= constant;
3  hash <<= constant;
4  hash >>= constant;
5  hash *= constant;  // if constant is even
6  hash /= constant;
7  hash %= constant;
```

The multiplication operation is a special case not only because it is reversible only if the constant is odd, but also because it incurs more cost than, say, the bitwise shift. It is trivial to understand why bitwise shift to the left is the same as multiplying a number by 2. However, the two operations are very different on most hardware architectures, specifically in the number of CPU cycles an operation incurs or can potentially incur in case the cost is not a fixed number of cycles. Hardware implementation is revisited further in this chapter.

14.4.4 Quality Evaluation of Hash Functions

Quality estimation of a hash function is common knowledge. The following are the main metrics:

Uniform distribution. The output of a hash function should be uniformly distributed. This means that each combination of bits in the output should be equally likely to occur. This metric is easy to test and analyze statistically. Simply collect a set of outputs and plot their distribution to see if it forms a roughly horizontal line.

Avalanche condition. This is a tricky metric that is both the objective of a hash function and the metric that evaluates its quality. The statement is that a change in any one bit on the input should affect every output bit with 50% probability. There is one easy way to understand this metric. If our input changes only in one bit (say, an increment of one), the output should change to a very different bit string from the one before. In fact, the 50% rule says that on average, the XOR difference between the two keys should roughly have 50% of its bits set to 1. Note that this applies to any input bit, meaning that large change in input should cause about the same change in output as a small change in input. Another way to think about this metric is by realizing that this is how the uniform distribution is achieved in the first place.

No partial correlation. There should be no correlation between any parts of input versus output bit strings. Again, this metric is related to both the above metrics but has its own unique underlying statistical mechanisms. Correlation is easy to measure. Simply take time series of partial strings in input versus output and see if the two correlate. You will have to try various combinations—that is, x bits from the head, tail, in the middle, etc.

One-way function. The statement is that it should be computationally infeasible to identify two keys that produce the same hash value or to identify a key that produces a given hash value. This metric is highly relevant in cryptography, but is not much useful for fast hashes.

14.4.5 Example Designs for Fast Hashing

There are two fundamental ways to create a fast hashing method:

1. Create a more efficient method to calculate hash keys while retaining the same level of quality (metrics were discussed above).
2. Use a simple—and therefore faster—hashing method and resolve quality problems algorithmically.

Arguably, these two methods are the opposite extremes, while the reality is a spectrum between the two. Regardless, the rest of this section will show how to go about writing each of the two algorithms.

The *d-left* method in [13] is a good example of a fast hashing method that attempts to retain the quality while speeding up calculations. The method uses multiple hash functions for its Bloom filter but proposes an algorithm that avoids using all the functions when calculating each key. In fact, each time the algorithm skips one of k functions, it saves calculation time. The study formulates the method as an optimization problem where the number of overflows is to be minimized. Some level of overflow is inevitable under the method since the space is minimized for faster access. The point therefore is to find a good balance in the trade-off between high number of overflows (basically lost/missed records) and fast hash calculations.

While the above method is scientifically sound, practice often favors simple solutions. Earlier work by this author is one such example [38]. What it does is use simple CRC24 as the only hashing function—thus causing lower quality of keys in terms of collisions, especially given that the keys feature the compression ratio of over five times (141 bits are compressed into 24). This quality problem is dealt with algorithmically using the concept of *sideways DLL*.

Figure 14.5 shows the basic idea behind sideways DLL. Virtual stem in the figure is the traditional DLL where each item is connected to its neighbor using the traditional to C/C++ variables *prev* and *next*. These variables are assigned pointers to neighboring items, thus forming a list-like chain that can be traversed.

Since simple hashing will have higher number of collisions on average, they have to be resolved programmatically. The horizontal chain in Figure 14.5 is one obvious solution. All items in the horizontal chain share the same hash key and are connected into the DLL chain using *sidenext* and *sideprev* pointers.

The collisions are resolved as follows. Fast hashing quickly provides a key. The program finds the headmost DLL item for that key. However, there is no guarantee that the headmost element is the correct one—hence the collision. So, the program has to traverse the chain and check whether a given item is the one it is looking for. Granted that such a resolution will also waste CPU cycles, this performance overhead is not fixed for each lookup. In fact, this author's own practice shows that less than 5% of keys will have sideways chains, while the rest will have only one item in each slot.

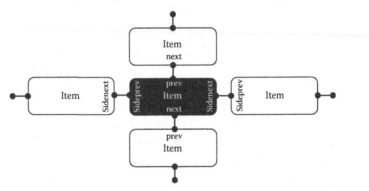

Figure 14.5 Example DLL design that can deal with hash key collisions using the ability to traverse DLL sideways.

The following is the actual C/C++ code for a DLL structure with sideways chains:

```
1    typedef struct { // DLLE : an Element of DLL
2          DLLE *prev;
3          DLLE *next;
4          DLLE *sideprev;
5          DLLE *sidenext;
6          void *payload;
7    } DLLE;
8    typedef struct { // DLL: Double Linked List
9          int count;
10         DLLE *head;
11         DLLE *tail;
12   } DLL;
```

Note that the chain itself is built by DLL element (DLLE) only. Yet, the DLL part is also necessary, especially for traversal. It is also useful to be able to traverse the chain from both the head and the tail. Here is the list of some of the useful properties of DLLs:

- It is easy for two DLLEs to swap positions, which can be done simply by changing assignments in *next* and *prev* pointers—the same way any DLLE can be moved to the head or the tail of the DLL.
- Given the easy swapping, it is possible to put a recently used DLLE at the head of the DLL so that it is found first during the next traversal; this way old DLLEs will naturally sink to the bottom (tail) of the DLL. This can also be described as a natural sorting of the DLL by *last used* timestamp.
- Given the above property, garbage collection is easy—simply pick the oldest DLLEs at the tail of the DLL and dispose of them (or export them, etc.).

DLL is commonplace in packet traffic processing where C/C++ programming is in the overwhelming majority [20]. Earlier research by this author [25] makes extensive use of DLLs. A similar example will be considered as a practical application further in this chapter.

14.5 Practical Data Streaming

This section puts together all the fundamentals presented earlier as part of practical data streaming. The scope of the practice extends from the contents of the input stream to fairly advanced practical data streaming targets.

14.5.1 Distributions in Practice

Research in [41] was the first to argue that traditional distributions, of which *beta, exponential, Pareto,* etc., are the most common, perform badly as models of natural processes. In fact, this phenomenon was noticed in packet traffic many years before. Yet, research in [41] is the first to present a viable alternative based on the concept of *hotspots.* The research shows that hotspots are found in many natural systems.

Many statistics collected from real processes support the notion of hotspots. For example, [42] shows that hotspots and flash events exist in data centers that are part of large-scale cloud computing.

Earlier work by this author in [37] developed a model that can synthesize flash events in packet traces. The output of such a synthesis is a packet trace that looks just like a real trace, only with all the time-stamps and packet sizes being artificially created by the model.

The model in [37] is based on a stick-breaking (SB) process, which in Figure 14.6 is compared to one of the traditional choices—the beta distribution. The SB process is known to create more realistic power-law distributions—hence its selection as the underlying structure. For realistic traces, not only synthetic sources but also their dynamics are important, which is why a large part of the synthesis is dedicated to creating flash events (left bottom plot of the figure). The modeling logic is simple and is evident from the plot—locations

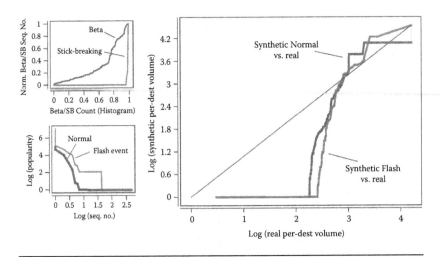

Figure 14.6 The stick-breaking process (left) used to create a synthetic trace versus beta distribution as a common traditional choice, and comparison of the synthetic trace to a real one (right).

(sources, destinations, content items, etc.) that are already popular can "go viral," which is where the access count can grow substantially for a limited period of time.

The right-side plot in Figure 14.6 shows that even such an elaborate synthesis fails to emulate reality. The plot shows that only the upper 30% of the trace (top flows by volume) closely follows the real distribution, where the resemblance in smaller flow size is almost completely gone. Note that the real packet traces used in comparison come from [47].

Nevertheless, even with the relatively high error margin, synthetic traces are preferred in trace-based simulations specifically because they allow us to test various conditions simply by changing the parameters during synthesis. In this respect, real traces can be considered as the average or representative case, while synthetic traces can be used to test the limits of performance in some methods.

Traces—both real and synthetic—are related to fast hashing via the notion of *arrival rate* introduced earlier in this chapter. If the method is concerned with per-unit processing cost, the contents of the input stream are of utmost importance. In this respect, packet traffic research provides a fresh new prospective on the subject of fast hashing. While traditionally fast hashing is judged in terms of the quality of its keys, this chapter stresses the importance of the distribution in the input stream.

As far as real packet traces are concerned, CAIDA [48], WAND [46], and WIDE [47] are good public repositories and contain a wide variety of information at each site.

The above synthetic method is not the only available option. There are generators for workloads in many different disciplines, where, for example, RUBIS is a generator of workloads for cloud computing. RUBIS generates synthetic request arrival processes, service times, etc. [49].

14.5.2 Bloom Filters: Store, Lookup, and Efficiency

The study in [9] provides a good theoretical background on the notion of Bloom filters. This section is a brief overview of commonly available information before moving on to the more advanced features actively discussed in research today.

Remember Figure 14.4 from before? Some of this section will discuss the traditional design presented by this figure, but then replace it with a more modern design. From earlier in this chapter we know that blooming is performed by calculating one or more hash keys and updating the value of the filter by OR-ing each hash key with its current state. This is referred to as the *insert* operation. The *lookup* operation is done by taking the bitwise AND between a given hash key and current state of the filter. The decision making from this point on can go in one of the following two directions:

- The result of AND is the same as the value of the hash key—this is either true positive or false positive, with no way to tell between the two.
- The result of AND is not the same as the value of the hash key—this is a 100% reliable true negative.

One common way to describe the above lookup behavior of Bloom filters is to describe the filter as a person with memory who can only answer the question "Have you seen this item before?" reliably. This is not to underestimate the utility of the filter, as the answer to this exact question is exactly what is needed in many practical situations.

Let us look at the Bloom filter design from the viewpoint of hashing, especially given that the state of the filter is gradually built by adding more hash keys onto its state.

Let us put n as number of items and m the bit length of hash keys, and therefore the filter. We know from before that each bit in the hash key can be set to 1 with 50% probability. Therefore, omitting details, the optimal number of hash function can be calculated as

$$k = In2\left(\frac{m}{n}\right) \approx 0.6\frac{m}{n}$$

If each hash function is perfectly independent of all others, then the probability of a bit remaining 0 after n elements is

$$p = \left(1 - \frac{1}{m}\right)^{kn} \approx e^{\frac{-kn}{m}}$$

False positive—an important performance metric of a Bloom filter is then

$$pFP = \left(1 - p\right)^k \approx \left(1 - e^{\frac{-kn}{m}}\right)^k \approx \frac{1}{2^k}$$

for the optimal k. Note with that increasing k, the probability of false positive is actually supposed to decrease, which is an unintuitive outcome because one would expect the filter to get filled up with keys earlier.

Let us analyze the k. For the majority of cases $m \ll n$, which means that the optimal number of hash functions is 1. Two functions are feasible only with $m > 2.5n$. In most realistic cases this is almost never the case because n is normally huge, while m is something practical, like 24 or 32 (bits).

14.5.3 Unconventional Bloom Filter Designs for Data Streams

Based on the above, the obvious problem in Bloom filters is how to improve their flexibility. As a side note, such Bloom filters are normally referred to as *dynamic*.

The two main changes are (1) extended design of the Bloom filter structure itself, which is not a bit string anymore, and (2) nontrivial manipulation logic dictated by the first change—simply put, one cannot use logical ORs between hashes and Bloom filter states.

Figure 14.7 shows the generic model that applies to most of the proposals of dynamic Bloom filters. The simple idea is to replace a

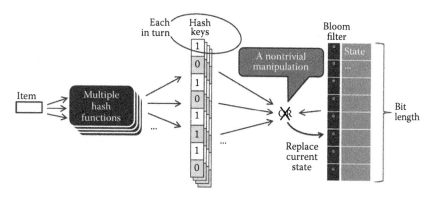

Figure 14.7   A generic model representing Bloom filters with dynamic functionality.

simple bit string with a richer data structure (the change in the Bloom filter in the figure). Each bit in the filter now simply is a pointer to a structure that supports dynamic operations.

The other change that ensues is that the OR operation is no longer applicable. Instead, a nontrivial manipulation has to be performed on each bit of the value that was supposed to be OR-ed in the traditional design. Naturally, this incurs a considerable overhead on performance.

The following classes of dynamic Bloom filters are found in literature.

Stop additions filter. This filter will stop accepting new keys beyond a given point. Obviously this is done in order to keep false positive beyond a given target value.

Deletion filter. This filter is tricky to build, but if accomplished, it can revert to a given previous state by forgetting the change introduced by a given key.

Counting filters. This filter can count on both individual bits of potential occurrences of entire values and combinations of bits. This particular class of filters obviously can find practical applications in data streaming. In fact, the example of the d-left hashing method discussed earlier in this chapter uses a kind of counting Bloom filter [13]. Another example can be found in [12], where it is used roughly for the same purpose.

There are other kinds of unconventional designs. The study in [10] declares that it can do with fewer hash functions while providing the same blooming performance. Bloom filters specific to perfect hashing are proposed in [11].

14.5.4 Practical Data Streaming Targets

This subsection considers several practical data streaming targets.

Example 14.1: A Simple Sampling Problem

We need a median of the stream. The problem is to find a uniform sample s from a stream of unknown length and unknown content in advance. Again, by definition, even having seen all the input, we cannot use it because there is not enough storage for its entire volume.

Algorithm: Set originally $s = x_1$. On seeing the tth element, the probability of $s \leftarrow x_t$ is $1/t$.

Analysis: The probability that $s = x_i$ at some time $t \geq i$ is

$$P[s = x_i] = \frac{1}{i} \cdot \left(1 - \frac{1}{1+1} \cdot \ldots \cdot \left(1 - \frac{1}{t}\right)\right) = \frac{1}{t}$$

To get k samples, we use $O(k \log n)$ bits of space.

Example 14.2: The Sliding Window Problem

Maintain a uniform sample from the last w items algorithm:

- For each x_i pick a random value $v_k \in (0, 1)$.
- In a window $(x_{j-w} + 1, \ldots, x_j)$ return value x_i with smallest the x_j.
- To do this, maintain a set of all elements in a sliding window whose v value is minimal among subsequent values.

Analysis: The probability that the jth oldest element is in S is $1/j$, so the expected number of items in S is

$$\frac{1}{w} + \frac{1}{w-1} + \ldots + \frac{1}{1} = O(\log w)$$

Therefore, the algorithm only uses $O(\log w \log n)$ bits of memory.

Example 14.3: The Sketch Problem

Apply a linear projection "on the fly" that takes high-dimensional data to a smaller dimensional space. Post-process the lower-dimensional image to estimate the quantities of interest.

Input: Stream from two sources:

$$(x_1, x_2, \ldots, x_m) \in (A[n] \cup B[n])^m$$

The objective is to estimate the difference between distributions of A values and B values, so

$$\sum_{i \in [n]} |f_i - g_i|$$

where

$$f_i = \left|\{k : x_k = i\}\right| \text{ and } g_i = \left|\{k : x_k = i\}\right|$$

Example 14.4: Count-Min Sketch

For example, we might detect *heavy hitters* $f_i \geq m$, or range sum estimate:

$$\Sigma_{i \leq k \leq j} \, f_k$$

when i, j are not known in advance. For k-quantiles, find values $q_0, \ldots, q_k$ such that

$$q_0 = 0, q_k = n, \sum_{i \leq q_j - q} f_i < \frac{jm}{k} \leq \sum_{i \leq q_j} f_i$$

Algorithm: Maintain a list of counters $c_{i,j}$ for $i \in [d]$ and $j \in [w]$. Construct d random hash functions $h_1, h_2, \ldots, h_d$: $[n] \rightarrow [d]$. Update counters, when the encounter value v increment is $c_i, h_{i\,(v)}$ for $i \in [d]$. To get an estimate of f_k return

$$f_k = \min_i c_{i, h_j (k)}$$

Analysis: For $d = O(\log(1/\delta))$ and $w = O(1/\varepsilon^2)$,

$$P\left[f_k - \in m \leq f_k^* \leq f_k \right] \geq 1 - \delta$$

Example 14.5: The Counting Problem

Count distinct elements in stream.

Input: Stream $(x_1, x_2, \ldots, x_m) \in [n]^m$. The objective is to estimate the number of distinct values in the stream up to a multiplicative factor $1 + \varepsilon$ with high probability.

Algorithm: Apply random function h: $[n] \in [0, 1]$ to each element. Compute a—the tth smallest value of the hash seen where $t = 21/\varepsilon^2$. Return $r' = t/a$ as the estimate of r—the number of distinct items.

Analysis: Algorithm uses $O(e^{-2} \log n)$ bits of space. Estimate has good accuracy with reasonable probability:

$$P\left[| r * - r | \leq \in r \right] \leq 9/10$$

The proof involves the concept of Chebyshev analysis and is pretty complicated, but it is out there if you do a quick search in the literature provided above.

14.5.5 Higher-Complexity Data Streaming Targets

Besides the relatively simple (you can call them traditional) data streaming targets, there are several interesting practical targets that need a higher level of algorithmic complexity. This subsection lists only the problems and leaves the search for solutions to the reader. In fact, some solutions are the subject of active discussion in the research community today. Pointers to such research are provided.

Example 14.6: Finding Heavy Hitters (beyond the Min-Count Sketch)

Find k most frequently accessed items in a list. One algorithm is proposed in [17]. Generally, more sound algorithms for sliding windows can be found in [18].

Example 14.7: Triangle Detection

Detect triangles defined as A talks to B, B talks to C, and C talks to A (other variants are possible as well) in the input stream. An algorithm is proposed in [16].

Example 14.8: Superspreaders

Detect items that access or are accessed by exceedingly many other items. Related research can be found in [19].

Example 14.9: Many-to-Many Patterns

This is a more generic case of heavy hitters and superspreaders, but in this definition the patterns are not known in advance. Earlier work by this author [25] is one method. However, the subject is popular with several methods, such as M2M broadcasting [26] and various M2M memory structures [27, 31], and data representations (like graph in [28]) are proposed—all outside of the concept of data streaming. The topic is of high intrinsic value because it has direct relevance to group communications where one-to-many and many-to-many are the two popular types of group communications [29, 30, 32, 33].

A practical example later in this chapter will be based on a many-to-many pattern capture.

14.6 Practical Fast Hashing and Blooming

This section expands further into the practical issues in relation with fast hashing and blooming.

14.6.1 Arbitrary Bit Length Hashing

Obvious choices when discussing long hashes are the MD5 and SHA-family of methods.

It is interesting that bit length is about the only difference of such methods from simpler 32-bit hash keys. The state is still created and updated using bitwise operations, with the only exception that the state now extends over several words and updates are made by rotation.

Both groups of methods are created with hardware implementation in mind where it is possible to update the entire bit length or even digest the entire message in one CPU cycle.

The methods, however, are useless for data streaming in general, mostly due to the long bit length. With CRC24, it is possible to procure a memory space with 2^{24} memory slots (where each slot is a 4-byte C/C++ pointer). But there is no feasible solution for a memory region addressable using an MD5 key as an index.

However, given the uniform distribution condition, it is possible to use only several bits from any region of the hash key. However, given that MD5 or SHA- methods take much longer to compute than the standard CRC24 or even a simpler bitwise manipulation, such a use would defeat the purpose of fast hashing.

14.6.2 Arbitrary Length Bloom Filters

Again, using longer Bloom filters has dubious practical value. Based on the simple statistics presented above, increasing the bit length of the filter only makes sense when it helps increase the number of hash functions. However, the equation showed that increase in bit length is reduced by 40%. Even before that, m is part of the ratio m/n, which makes it nearly impossible to have any practical impact n when n is large. In practice, n is always large.

In view of this argument, it appears that the dynamic filters presented earlier in this paper present a better alternative to using longer bit strings in traditional Bloom filters.

14.6.3 Hardware Implementation

Hashing is often considered in tandem with hardware implementation. The related term is *hardware offload*—where a given operation is offloaded to hardware. It is common to reduce multi-hundred-cycle operations to single CPU cycles. This subsection presents several such examples.

One common example is to offload CHECKSUM calculations to hardware. For example, the COMBO6 card [20] has done that and has shown that it has major impact on performance.

Note that the most popular hashing methods today—the MD5 and SHA-2 methods—are created with hardware implementation in mind. MD5 is built for 32-bit architectures and has its implementation code in RFC1321 [22], fully publicly open. The SHA-* family of hashing methods are also built for hardware implementation but are still being improved today [24]. One shared feature between these methods is that they avoid multiplication, resorting to simple bitwise manipulations instead.

Two other main threads in hardware offloading are

- GPU-based hardware implementation, specifically using the industry default CUDA programming language [21]
- Memory access optimization where the method itself tries to make as few accesses to memory as possible [23]—although not particularly a hardware technology, such methods are often intimately coupled with specific hardware, like special kind of RAM, etc.

14.7 Practical Example: High-Speed Packet Traffic Processor

This section dedicates its full attention to an example data streaming method from the area of packet traffic processing.

14.7.1 Example Data Streaming Target

Let us assume that there is a service provided by a service provider. The realm of the service contains many users. A many-to-many (M2M) pattern is formed by a subset of these users that communicate among each other. Favoring specificity over generalization, M2M parties can be classified into *M2M sources* and *M2M destinations*. While this specificity may not be extended to M2M problems in other disciplines, it makes perfect sense in traffic analysis because flows are directional. Besides, the generality can be easily restored if it is assumed that sources can be destinations, and vice versa. In fact, in many communication patterns today, this is actually the case, which means that two flows in opposite directions can be found between two parties.

Traffic capture and aggregation happens at the service provider (SP), which is the location of convenience because all the traffic that flows through the SP already can be captured without any change in communication procedures.

The problem is then defined as the need to develop a method and software design capable of online capture and aggregation of such M2M patterns.

Note that this formulation is one level up from the superspreaders in [19]. While the latter simply identifies singular IP addresses that are defined as superspreaders, this problem needs to capture the communication pattern itself.

14.7.2 Design for Hashing and Data Structures

Figure 14.8 shows the rough design of the system. Hash keys of x bits long are used as addressed in the index. Collision avoidance is implemented using sideways DLL, as was described earlier in this chapter (this particular detail is not shown in the figure). Each slot in the index points to an entry that in turn can contain multiple subentries. In this context, entry is the entire multiparty communication pattern, while subentry is its unit component that describes a single communication link between two members of a communication group.

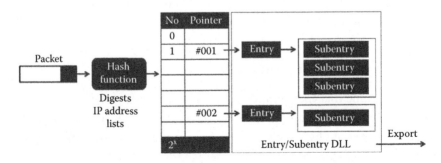

Figure 14.8 Overall design of an index for capturing many-to-many group communication.

Since each pattern can have multiple parties, each with its own IP address, multiple slots in the hash table can point to the same entry. This is not a problem in C/C++, where the same pointer can be stored in multiple places in memory.

Figure 14.9 finally reveals the entire data structure. The source code can be found in *m2meter.c* at [43]. The design is shown in the manner traditional to such systems where the actual bit lengths of all parts are marked. The unit (the width of each part) is 32 bits. Note that the word can be split into smaller bit strings, as they can be handled by bitwise operations in C/C++ with relative ease.

The following parts of the figure are relatively unimportant. *Timestamp log* is not crucial for this particular operation, as well as from the viewpoint of data streaming. However, if necessary, time-stamps—where each word is a bitwise merger of sublist ID and the timestamp of the last activity of that particular sublist—can be stored in sequence after the source header in entry. Also, the design of the *conventional meter*—that is used in traditional flow-based packet capture—is shown for reference.

Below the level of entry there are sublists where each sublist is a DLL containing subentries. The actual hierarchy is as follows.

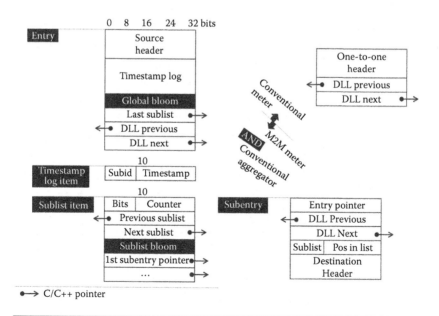

Figure 14.9 The actual data structure compared to the traditional one-to-one flows.

Each entry has a DLL of sublists, and each sublist has a DLL of subentries. Although slightly confusing, the intermediate step of the sublist is necessary as an efficiency mechanism where the mechanism itself is explained further on.

Bloom filters are an important part of operation. First, there is *global Bloom*, which is used to find out right away if a given subentry has been created earlier in this entry. In a sense, this is a form of collision control at the time when deciding whether or not to create a new subentry. Sublists also have each their own sublist Bloom, which is used for the same purpose, only within the bounds of each sublist. This is in fact the sole purpose of each sublist—to split all subentries into smaller groups to improve lookup performance.

Let us consider how this structure performs in practice. The entry itself is accessed directly via a hash key; there is zero ambiguity in this operation. Each access needs to either create new or update a subentry inside the entry. The following sequence of actions is performed:

- First, global Bloom is queried, resulting in either true negative, true positive, or false positive, with no way to tell the difference between the latter two outcomes. True negative is the best outcome because it tells us that we can go ahead and create a new subentry, as we are certain that no such subentry has been created in this entry before. In case of either of the two positives, we have to verify the outcome by traversing the DLL of sublists. To facilitate this traversal, the entry has a pointer to the last used sublist. Regardless of the outcome, global Bloom has to be updated using the current subentry hash key.

- We are at this step because global Bloom produced a positive outcome. Traversing the list of sublists, each sublist Bloom is queried using the same subentry hash key. Again, either a true negative or positive outcome can be produced. If true negative, we move on to the next sublist. If we run out of sublists, it means that a subentry is not found, which in turn means that we need to create a new subentry. In the case of a positive outcome, we need to traverse the subentry DLL of the respective sublist, to either find the subentry we are looking for or verify that the positive outcome is a false positive.

Note that with all the algorithmic complexity, the purpose is simply to improve lookup time as often as possible. This means that the system needs to achieve a relatively higher ratio of true negatives to positive outcomes on all the Bloom filters.

The data structure in Figure 14.9 can be further improved. For example, one obvious problem is with the global Bloom, which gets filled up too fast. Potentially, it can be replaced with a dynamic filter, as was described earlier in this chapter. However, keep in mind that there are potentially 2^{24} such Bloom filters in the entire structure, which means that if dynamic filters are used, they have to be extremely efficient in terms of the space they occupy. The use of dynamic filters would also potentially remove the need for sublists, which would simplify the design of each entry.

14.8 Summary

This chapter discussed the topic of fast hashing and efficient blooming in the context of data streaming. Higher efficiency in both the former operations are demanded by the operational realities of data streaming, which are forced to run under very strict per-unit processing deadlines.

Having reviewed all the existing methods in both hashing and blooming, the following two extreme designs were presented in detail. At one extreme was a data streaming method that invests heavily into developing a faster hashing method without losing the quality of its hash keys. At the other extreme was a method that selects the lightest possible hash function at the cost of reduced quality, but resolves key collisions programmatically. The designs are presented without any judgment as to which method is better. However, in reality, it is likely that real methods will form a spectrum in between the two extremes.

Note that the same can be said about Bloom filters as well. The two extremes in this case are traditional versus dynamic Bloom filters, where dynamic ones require much heavier calculation overheads to maintain and use. While analyzing the practical application in the last section, it was stated that dynamic Bloom filters might help to improve lookup performance, provided the overhead would stay below the one caused by the programmatic method presented in the example.

There are several topics that are immediately adjacent to the main topic in the chapter. For example, the closest other topic is that of *multicore architectures*. Good shared memory designs for C/C++ can be found in [5]. A lock-free shared memory design developed by this author can be found at [44]. These subjects are related because data streaming on multicore needs to be extremely efficient, beyond the level that can be offered with traditional parallel processing designs based on memory locking or message passing. Note that the subject of multicore is already a hot topic [40] in traffic. The title of such research can be *hashing for multicore load balancing*.

Alternative methods for traffic processing other than flows can also benefit from fast hashing and efficient blooming. For example, earlier work by this author converted traffic to graphics for visual analysis [38]. Also, as was mentioned before, smart traffic sampling can be directly formulated as a data streaming problem [39]. Such a formulation is yet to be adopted by the research community. The key term is *context–based sampling* in traffic research, but would be rephrased as *packet streaming* when viewed as a data streaming problem.

Since hashing is a large part of indexing and even broader, search, fast hashing can help new areas where indexing is starting to find its application. For example, Fullproof at [50] is a Lucene indexing engine rewritten from scratch to work in restrictive local storage in browsers (running as a web application). Earlier work by this author proposed a browser-based indexer for cloud storage called Stringex [45], in which the key feature is that read and write access has an upper restriction on throughput. This restriction is very similar to that of CPU operations in fast hashing, which is where the parallel can be drawn.

Broadly speaking, data streaming is yet to be recognized as an important discipline. Once it is recognized as such, however, it will open all the research venues related to fast hashing and dynamic blooming listed in this chapter.

References

1. C. Shannon. A Mathematical Theory of Communication. *Bell System Technical Journal*, 27, 379–423, 1948.
2. D. MacKay. *Information Theory, Inference, and Learning Algorithms.* Cambridge: Cambridge University Press, 2003.

3. A. Konheim. *Hashing in Computer Science: Fifty Years of Slicing and Dicing.* Hoboken, NJ: Wiley, 2010.

4. R. Kimball, M. Ross, W. Thornthwaite, J. Mundy, and B. Becker. *The Data Warehouse Lifecycle Toolkit.* New York: John Wiley & Sons, 2008.

5. K. Michael. *The Linux Programming Interface.* San Francisco: No Starch Press, 2010.

6. S. Heinz, J. Zobel, and H. Williams. Burst Tries: A Fast, Efficient Data Structure for String Keys. *ACM Transactions on Information Systems (TOIS),* 20(2), 192–223, 2002.

7. M. Ramakrishna and J. Zobel. Performance in Practice of String Hashing Functions. In *5th International Conference on Database Systems for Advanced Applications,* April 1997.

8. D. Lemire and O. Kaser. *Strongly Universal String Hashing Is Fast.* Cornell University Technical Report arXiv:1202.4961. 2013.

9. F. Putze, P. Sanders, and J. Singler. Cache-, Hash- and Space-Efficient Bloom Filters. *Journal of Experimental Algorithmics (JEA),* 14, 4, 2009.

10. A. Kirsch and M. Mitzenmacher. Less Hashing, Same Performance: Building a Better Bloom Filter. *Wiley Interscience Journal on Random Structures and Algorithms,* 33(2), 187–218, 2007.

11. G. Antichi, D. Ficara, S. Giordano, G. Procissi, and F. Vitucci. Blooming Trees for Minimal Perfect Hashing. In *IEEE Global Telecommunications Conference (GLOBECOM),* December 2008, pp. 1–5.

12. H. Song, S. Dharmapurikar, J. Turner, and J. Lockwood. Fast Hash Table Lookup Using Extended Bloom Filter: An Aid to Network Processing. Presented at SIGCOMM, 2005.

13. F. Bonomi, M. Mitzenmacher, R. Panigrahi, S. Singh, and G. Vargrese. An Improved Construction for Counting Bloom Filters. In *14th Conference on Annual European Symposium (ESA),* 2006, vol. 14, pp. 684–695.

14. M. Sung, A. Kumar, L. Li, J. Wang, and J. Xu. Scalable and Efficient Data Streaming Algorithms for Detecting Common Content in Internet Traffic. Presented at ICDE Workshop, 2006.

15. S. Muthukrishnan. Data Streams: Algorithms and Applications. *Foundations and Trends in Theoretical Computer Science,* 1(2), 117–236, 2005.

16. Z. Bar-Yossef, R. Kumar, and D. Sivakumar. Reductions in Streaming Algorithms, with an Application to Counting Triangles in Graphs. Presented at 13th ACM-SIAM Symposium on Discrete Algorithms (SODA), January 2002.

17. M. Charikar, K. Chen, and M. Farach-Colton. Finding Frequent Items in Data Streams. Presented at 29th International Colloquium on Automata, Languages, and Programming, 2002.

18. M. Datar, A. Gionis, P. Indyk, and R. Motwani. Maintaining Stream Statistics over Sliding Windows. *SIAM Journal on Computing,* 31(6), 1794–1813, 2002.

19. S. Venkataraman, D. Song, P. Gibbons, and A. Blum. New Streaming Algorithms for Fast Detection of Superspreaders. Presented at Distributed System Security Symposium (NDSS), 2005.

20. M. Zadnik, T. Pecenka, and J. Korenek. NetFlow Probe Intended for High-Speed Networks. In *International Conference on Field Programmable Logic and Applications*, 2005, pp. 695–698.

21. S. Manavski. CUDA Compatible GPU as an Efficient Hardware Accelerator for AES Cryptography. In *IEEE International Conference on Signal Processing and Communication*, 2007, pp. 65–68.

22. *The MD5 Message-Digest Algorithm*. RFC1321. 1992.

23. G. Antichi, A. Pietro, D. Ficara, S. Giordano, G. Procissi, and F. Vitucci. A Heuristic and Hybrid Hash-Based Approach to Fast Lookup. In *International Conference on High Performance Switching and Routing (HPSR)*, June 2009, pp. 1–6.

24. R. Chaves, G. Kuzmanov, L. Sousa, and S. Vassiliadis. Improving SHA-2 Hardware Implementations. In *Cryptographic Hardware and Embedded Systems (CHES)*, Springer LNCS vol. 4249. Berlin: Springer, 2006, pp. 298–310.

25. M. Zhanikeev. A Holistic Community-Based Architecture for Measuring End-to-End QoS at Data Centres. *Inderscience International Journal of Computational Science and Engineering (IJCSE)*, 2013.

26. C. Bhavanasi and S. Iyer. M2MC: Middleware for Many to Many Communication over Broadcast Networks. In *1st International Conference on Communication Systems Software and Middleware*, 2006, pp. 323–332.

27. D. Digby. A Search Memory for Many-to-Many Comparisons. *IEEE Transactions on Computers*, C22(8), 768–772, 1973.

28. Y. Keselman, A. Shokoufandeh, M. Demirci, and S. Dickinson. Many-to-Many Graph Matching via Metric Embedding. In *IEEE Conference on Computer Vision and Pattern Recognition (CVPR)*, 2003, pp. 850–857.

29. D. Lorenz, A. Orda, and D. Raz. Optimal Partition of QoS Requirements for Many-to-Many Connections. In *International Conference on Computers and Communications (ICC)*, 2003, pp. 1670–1680.

30. V. Dvorak, J. Jaros, and M. Ohlidal. Optimum Topology-Aware Scheduling of Many-to-Many Collective Communications, In *6th International Conference on Networking (ICN)*, 2007, p. 61.

31. M. Hattori and M. Hagiwara. Knowledge Processing System Using Multidirectional Associative Memory. In *IEEE International Conference on Neural Networks*, 1995, vol. 3, pp. 1304–1309.

32. A. Silberstein and J. Yang. Many-to-Many Aggregation for Sensor Networks. In *23rd International Conference on Data Engineering*, 2007, pp. 986–995.

33. M. Saleh and A. Kamal. Approximation Algorithms for Many-to-Many Traffic Grooming in WDM Mesh Networks. In *INFOCOM*, 2010, pp. 579–587.

34. E. Kohler, R. Morris, B. Chen, J. Jannotti, and M. Kaashoek. The Click Modular Router. *ACM Transactions on Computer Systems (TOCS)*, 18(3), 263–297, 2000.

35. M. Zec, L. Rizzo, and M. Mikuc. DXR: Towards a Billion Routing Lookups per Second in Software. *ACM SIGCOMM Computer Communication Review*, 42(5), 30–36, 2012.

36. M. Zhanikeev. Experiments with Practical On-Demand Multi-Core Packet Capture. Presented at 15th Asia-Pacific Network Operations and Management Symposium (APNOMS), 2013.

37. M. Zhanikeev and Y. Tanaka. Popularity-Based Modeling of Flash Events in Synthetic Packet Traces. *IEICE Technical Report on Communication Quality*, 112(288), 1–6, 2012.

38. M. Zhanikeev and Y. Tanaka. A Graphical Method for Detection of Flash Crowds in Traffic. *Springer Telecommunication Systems Journal*, 63(4), 2013.

39. J. Zhang, X. Niu, and J. Wu. A Space-Efficient Fair Packet Sampling Algorithm. In *Asia-Pacific Network Operation and Management Symposium (APNOMS)*, Springer LNCS5297, September 2008, pp. 246–255.

40. M. Aldinucci, M. Torquati, and M. Meneghin. *FastFlow: Efficient Parallel Streaming Applications on Multi-Core*. Technical Report TR-09-12. Universita di Pisa, September 2009.

41. P. Bodík, A. Fox, M. Franklin, M. Jordan, and D. Patterson. Characterizing, Modeling, and Generating Workload Spikes for Stateful Services. In *1st ACM Symposium on Cloud Computing (SoCC)*, 2010, pp. 241–252.

42. T. Benson, A. Akella, and D. Maltz. Network Traffic Characteristics of Data Centers in the Wild. In *Internet Measurement Conference (IMC)*, November 2010, pp. 202–208.

43. Source code for this chapter. Available at https://github.com/maratishe/fasthash4datastreams.

44. MCoreMemory project page. Available at https://github.com/maratishe/mcorememory.

45. Stringex Project Repository. Available at https://github.com/maratishe/stringex.

46. WAND Network Traffic Archive. Available at http://www.wand.net.nz/wits/waikato/5/.

47. MAWI Working Group Traffic Archive. Available at http://mawi.wide.ad.jp/mawi.

48. CAIDA homepage. Available at http://www.caida.org.

49. Rubis homepage. Available at http://rubis.ow2.org/.

50. Fullproof: Browser Side Indexing. Available at https://github.com/reyesr/fullproof.

Index

Note: Page numbers ending in "f" refer to figures. Page numbers ending in "t" refer to tables.